Seventeen Essays about how the God of the Hebrew Torah became the Christian Triune God—and then changed again into the God of Islam—and how this has become the cause of world conflict today.

Holy War

Holy War

♦

The Blood of Abraham

David Anderson

iUniverse, Inc.
New York Lincoln Shanghai

Holy War
The Blood of Abraham

All Rights Reserved © 2004 by David P Anderson

No part of this book may be reproduced or transmitted in any form or by any means, graphic, electronic, or mechanical, including photocopying, recording, taping, or by any information storage retrieval system, without the written permission of the publisher.

iUniverse, Inc.

For information address:
iUniverse, Inc.
2021 Pine Lake Road, Suite 100
Lincoln, NE 68512
www.iuniverse.com

InquiryAbraham.com

ISBN: 0-595-31456-2 (pbk)
ISBN: 0-595-66317-6 (cloth)

Printed in the United States of America

Contents

An Open Letter: To those of the three Religions of Abraham xiii

Author's Note xvii

Foreword xix

Introduction xxiii

I A New Way of Thinking about Our Existence 1
- 1. A World Ceaselessly Seeking GOD 5
- 2. My Soul 7
- 3. Understanding the Christian Experience/The Peace That Passes All Understanding 9
- 4. Entering Heaven/Entering into the Presence of GOD 10

II The Common Denominator on Which All Religions Must Judge Themselves What is happening in the Upper Room? 12
- 5. The Enlightenment of the Upper Room 14
- 6. The Temptations that Keep us Away From the Upper Room 16

III The Free Will to Make Our Own Choices 17
- 7. Opening the Barriers of our Self-imposed Limitations 20
- 8. Be Careful What You Wish For 21

IV From Each According to His Ability 23
- 9. Reaping Where He Has Not Sowed and Gathering Where He Has Not Strawed 26

V Breaking Through to the Other Side 28
- 10. Entering Into His Presence 32
- 11. Submission to the Power of GOD 33

- 12. From the Least to the Greatest 34
- 13. Seeing Beyond the Prophets 36

VI The Christian Evangelicals Pride and Judgment in the Bog 37
- 14. Jerry Falwell and His "Bog" of Believers 41
- 15. Croaking in Judgment of Those Outside the "Bog" 43
- 16. "Frogs" Bogged Down in the Muck of the "Bog" 44
- 17. The Gift of Redemption Outside the "Bog" 46

VII The Presence of the Light 48
- 18. The Meaning of the Light 51
- 19. The light Within Us 53
- 20. The Healing Power of the Light 55
- 21. Guided by the Light 57
- 22. My Face You Can Not See 59
- 23. Returning from the Light 61

VIII The Apostle Paul—Brilliancy and Turmoil 62
- 24. Misguided Minds 80
- 25. Judge Not 82
- 26. The Weight of the Law on All Religions 83
- 27. Through Jesus Christ? 85
- 28. Presenting Yourself to God 87
- 29. A GOD of Anger and Love or A GOD Only of Love 89
- 30. The Meaning of the Resurrection 91
- 31. Christ Within 93
- 32. Evil 94
- 33. Your Own Salvation 95
- 34. Pressing Forward 96
- 35. Have No Anxiety 98
- 36. The Higher Realm versus the Earthly Realm 100
- 37. Fragmented Through the Prophets 101

IX The God They Think They Know The Torah God The Triune God The God of Jesus Christ 102

- *38. The Eleventh Commandment* *119*

X The Uncertain Future of Islam 121

XI The Challenge to Rabbinical Judaism The Continuing Revelation of the Hebrew God 135

XII Three Different Approaches to Salvation 143

- *39. Three Monotheistic Beliefs* *145*

XIII Science, Evolution and the Hand of GOD 146

XIV Was Jesus of Nazareth the Messiah? Will He Come Again? 149

XV Not the God They Think They Know 174

XVI A Challenge for the Religions of Abraham in the 21st Century and Beyond 188

XVII The Origin of anti-Semitism The Story of Jacob and Esau 193

Concluding Statement The Legacy of Past Religious Belief for the 21st Century and Beyond 199

Sexuality and the Religions of Abraham 213

Comments on the Bibliography 217

Bibliography 223

How much power does the shared image of the God worshiped by Jews, Christians, and Muslims have over their thoughts and actions? Has this image from the very beginning been flawed? Declaring that we pattern our thoughts and actions after the God or Gods we worship, the author says that this is the underlying cause of world conflict today.

An Open Letter

♦

To those of the three Religions of Abraham,

The seventeen essays in this book were written for those of the Jewish, Christian, and Muslim faiths. They deal with a number of very important and urgent spiritual questions that, I believe, all must soon face.

These are questions about how all of us from the same Hebraic tradition, with our diverse historical backgrounds, can live in peaceful coexistence and with common purpose. They are of such importance that their answers may determine not only the quality of the lives of ourselves, our children, and the children of future generations, but possibly even the survival of the human species as we know it.

There is a far-reaching spiritual dimension to these questions that our generation is not addressing. Many think they are; however, they are living under an illusion. The reality is that those in all three of the religions of Abraham who hold an historical and orthodox view of their beliefs are embarked on a dangerous miscalculation. The beginning of its tragic outcome is already upon us.

As those of the next generation and the ones to come grow into adulthood and form their own thoughts about themselves and the world around them, they will have to face far-reaching and critical questions about the religious beliefs of their mothers, fathers, and mentors. The way each approaches these questions will make a difference in some way, large or small, for the entire world.

I have written this book in an attempt to help with some of the answers. They are answers that deal with our perception of the nature of the one GOD of our universe and our relationship to that one GOD.

You will see from what I have written that I believe He is not to be confined narrowly to the present belief systems of any particular religious institution that is today a part of Judaism, Christianity or Islam, or to the vision of any select group of clerics, or to any national or tribal identity. He is beyond that.

You will also see that I believe GOD has only one plan for our destiny as the human species, and it is conditioned on whether we, not as a chosen religious group, but individually, are able to elevate ourselves into a knowledge of His presence.

David Anderson
August 2004

"To this day these issues, Jewish, Christian, and Muslim, still simmer and fester. As they have in the past, they continue to be a major underlying cause of world conflict. Pointing to the inerrancy of their scriptures, as well as their own interpretations of these scriptures, fanatical factions within nations and in some cases the nations themselves brazenly justify their actions as the will of GOD."

from the Introduction
Holy War The Blood of Abraham

Author's Note

The following explanation is given to avoid any possible confusion on the reader's part with respect to capitalization of the word "God" and expressions referring to God, such as "Him" and "Word of God". The author has chosen to use the rules that existed before the advent of the modern word processor; as a great deal of religious writing remains in this form and, in the author's view, *The Chicago Manual of Style* which gives the modern rules does not allow for the subtle distinctions that are called for in this book. The rules used, therefore, are as follows:

- GOD—The God of all Creation

- God—a general definition of GOD, i.e., the God of the Jews, the God of Jesus, pagan Gods, etc.

- HE, HIM, HIS, CREATOR—used sparingly for author's emphasis to refer to the one true GOD

- He, Him, His, Creator—used generally

- WORD OF GOD—used to designate what any group of believers believe to be the inerrant word of the CREATOR

- Word of God—used generally

With respect to the use of the masculine form, the reader is directed to the author's comments in *Sexuality and the Religions of Abraham*.

Foreword

Holy War The Blood of Abraham is a book of seventeen essays about the image of the God of the Hebrew Bible, The Christian Old Testament and the Koran being the patterning, subconscious force driving present world conflict. It calls on its readers; Christians, Jews, and Muslims, to look within themselves in search for answers to two of the most important questions facing human civilization today:

- How dominant is the role of religious belief as a contributing factor in current world conflict?

- Should culpability extend broadly to all three of the religions of Abraham: Judaism, and Christianity and Islam?

September 11, by the enormity of its horror, was a marker in world religious history that said fundamentalist religious extremism grounded on archaic Hebraic texts has been forever left behind and has no place in an interdependent and enlightened 21st century world.

Since then, people have been looking for answers beyond those being given to them by their religious leaders, politicians, TV commentators, and the press. Whether in the Jewish, Christian, or Islamic world, they only find a confusion of extremist religious bias.

In the midst of this confusion, leaders and their advisors, who hold the levers of political power, secretly hold fast to deeply imbedded archaic religious images; images that often simplistically define choices as being between *good* and *evil*, and between *them* and *us*. As they make choices—that affect the lives of millions—they are convinced that their motives are justified as being the WILL OF GOD, without understanding that their motives are being driven internally by these misguided underlying religious images; images that have been firmly rooted since childhood in their subconscious, patterning their every thought and every action and overwhelming their adult sense of reason.

Diplomatic discussion and debate therefore has the appearance of superficiality. Underlying religious motives are never brought to the surface and examined openly. All strategies and moves appear to be taking place on the surface of a chessboard.

In the United States, there is a political correctness holding back any kind of open critical religious discussion—from the President on down. Under the guise of *Freedom of Religion* Americans are asked to pretend that the three religions that came from Abraham are all inherently *good* for society.

For this reason, Muslim suicide bombers are singled out and defined generically as *terrorists* while hateful Koranic reference to the beliefs of hundreds of millions of Muslims who silently support them is carefully muted. At the same time, fanatical Orthodox Jews are viewed as defending their right to occupy Holy Ground, land given to them by their Yahweh, land with a centuries old Palestinian claim, and only recently expropriated from them. And, Evangelicals like Jerry Falwell and Pat Robertson who see 9/11 as GOD'S (Yahweh's) punishment of a decadent, corrupted American society are viewed as harmless good Christian men only exercising their right to free speech, as they judgmentally lash out and attack those whom they themselves choose to define as corrupted instruments of the devil.

This unspoken political correctness has allowed powerful religious extremists to take center stage and, while drowning out moderate voices, place on Christianity, Judaism, and Islam their own fundamentalist stamp of approval. Only they are right. Everyone else is wrong. Only they have found the true religion.

It is a political correctness that has disguised reality. History has shown that those following the religions that grew out of the Hebrew Bible have repeatedly violated the sanctity of human life, inflicting pain and suffering on those not of their own kind who did not think as they do. As this was true in the past, it is true today.

The Blood of Abraham exposes the underlying flaws that are built into each of these three religious belief systems; and although it leaves it to the reader to decide, argues that culpability for world terrorism lies not only with the extremism of Islam, but also with the extremism of Judaism and Christianity.

It shows these flaws as having been present from their very beginning. It presents the argument that certain of these flaws are today so serious that they may over time even lead to the self-fulfillment of Biblical Apocalyptic prediction.

It explains how these flaws found in the Hebraic interpretation of the nature of the God found in the Torah, as they were incorporated by Muhammad into the Koran, are the underlying force behind the hatred of Muslims towards Jews and Christians worldwide. It explains why the Jewish and Christian response is inadequate now and will remain so.

The book begins with an examination of the ancient Hebraic image of GOD. It traces the early development of the concept of the nature of GOD through

Jewish biblical history into the radically different concept presented by Jesus Christ. It details with scriptural reference the disconnection between the Hebraic interpretation of the nature of GOD and the nature of the GOD presented by Jesus Christ. It also explores the reasons why Christianity never totally abandoned the Hebraic image.

It offers solutions to current world conflict based on a broad Christ centered interpretive view of scripture. It draws a connection between this as well as Buddhist and Platonic religious thought. It discusses the formation of the Christian Canon from an historical perspective and introduces new insights in light of the Gnostic Gospels and other writings found in 1945 at Nag Hammadi. It suggests that without this new view of the nature of GOD shown in this discovery, Christianity will remain incomplete in its understanding of who and what Jesus Christ was. It suggests that many of these newly discovered Gnostic images of Jesus Christ could be seen as erasing the last vestiges of the early Roman Catholic Hebraic and later Protestant ones.

It explains why, suddenly after years of stand off with the Soviet Union, the United Stated has become involved in Muslim countries such as Afghanistan, Saudi Arabia, Lebanon, Syria, Pakistan, and Indonesia. It explains why this list continues to grow. It answers the question of how long this will continue and more importantly what must take place in the religious beliefs of Jews, Christians, and Muslims before it ends.

The reader will find that criticisms of institutionalized orthodox Christianity and Judaism are as harsh as those of Islam. The central idea that the archaic religious beliefs in each tradition to one degree or another must bear much of the blame for present world conflict is the overriding theme. It is the rigidity of each belief system that goes to the core of the problem.

The book departs from a belief in the inerrancy of religious scripture and offers a view of the nature of GOD and our relationship to Him from a different perspective. It views religious scripture from all forms of belief, Jewish, Christian, Muslim as well as all others, as man's attempt through his eyes and ears and inner being to define the nature of GOD. It concludes that as man is fallible, so too can scripture be. It disputes the value of many parts of Jewish, Christian as well as Islamic scripture and the dogma that has followed it. It contends that man, ever since the beginning of his consciousness as a spiritual being, has been defining GOD from his own perspective, making GOD according to his own imagined man-made image, and that this may not necessarily be GOD'S.

It does look to certain mortal humans who have lived on this earth as being closer to a reflection of the image of GOD than others. This includes those from many different faiths, some of them well known and some not known at all. It looks to the life of Jesus Christ, not as it was defined by the Roman Church centuries after his death, but as we are now seeing it defined based on recent discoveries, as being as close to that reflection as any human being has ever shown the world. It sees the crucifixion, whether taken as fact or metaphor, as the most powerful symbolic message ever given by GOD to humanity, a message that revealed how HE looks upon each of us.

It views every life on the face of the earth as precious in GOD'S sight. No one is excluded. It sees GOD'S covenant not with any select group; Jews, Christians or Muslims, or any other religious belief group, but with each of us individually during our lives. It is a covenant that covers every human being. No one is predestined or pre-selected. It lasts only for the brief moment of each life. The relationship is direct. It is between each of us and GOD. Each must make the critical decision as to how to form his or her life in response to GOD'S purpose for that life.

We enter the world of our existence alone and we leave it alone. There are no religious institutional intermediaries. In the short amount of time HE gives us, we are charged by HIM with the awesome responsibility to search our lives for glimpses of His perfection and to live our lives for HIS purposes. We put at risk our eternal destiny if we do not find HIM. HE gives each of us the gift of life here on earth as a prelude to our eternal destiny. How we live our lives determines our eternal destiny.

Holy War The Blood of Abraham is a book that forces every Jew, Christian, and Muslim to ask: Why do we have world conflict? Is my own religious belief system at fault? Am I at fault? Am I part of the problem? How can I be part of the solution?

Introduction

The Beginning and the End of Religious Diversity

Sometime in the distant past, between 3500 and 4000 years ago, a small Semitic tribe of wandering *herdsmen* surrounded by highly sophisticated and literate ancient civilizations began to look inward to form their own theology. It would be a theology that would change the course of world history.

In forming this theology, the tribe redefined many of the myths and legends coming from the civilizations that had come before it. It also added many of its own. Out of this grew a new and radically different view of the nature of GOD and man's relationship to GOD.

This new view saw a monotheistic GOD, not only as the all-powerful creator of our Universe, but also as a GOD demanding a new kind of moral order from His people. This moral order extended far beyond the moral order demanded by the Gods of the other religions.

In setting out this new theology, the myths and legends from the past as they were redefined were no longer thought of as being from some other realm or dimension.

The Garden of Eden and the Great Flood were not events to be viewed in mythical terms as they had been in Sumerian literature, which dated back another 1000 years or more. They were events that happened on earth and they were real. The first man, Adam, was real. Abraham, their first patriarch, was real. The tablets brought down from Mount Sinai by Moses containing the Ten Commandments were real. Later in their history, King David was real. These stories as well as the laws that grew out of them that were subsequently spelled out in their Hebraic language were from their own tribal God, YAHWEH, and they were real. The idea of the inerrancy of religious scripture was born. Religious fundamentalism was born.

As they looked inward in their search for meaning, this small and unknown Semitic tribe began to see themselves as unique among all other tribes. They saw themselves as being *Chosen*. The idea of being separate from others in GOD'S eyes was born.

They told of this first in the stories they passed on from generation to generation, and then later in writing in their Torah. According to one story, their Nation of Israel represented a favored brother, named Jacob, whom GOD loved. The other brother, named Esau, representing all other nations, GOD hated.

With this Covenant came the call for obedience to their God. He told them what He expected from them and what they could expect from Him. He had chosen their nation to carry out HIS WORD. He had chosen them to fulfill a special role in His great plan. To do this, they must obey only HIM.

The idea of Monotheism was their idea alone to hold on to and to believe. He was their God alone. The Gods worshiped by the other nations were powerless and irrelevant. He told them:

Thou shall have no other Gods before me.

Over the course of many generations, with this belief in a direct line of authority from GOD, came the seeds of argument, debate, and ultimately conflict. The message was from GOD, but the interpretation of the message often had different meanings. The interpreter of the WORD was always human. Was the interpreter getting the message right? Was He to be trusted? What did GOD'S message really mean? Why were there ambiguities in interpretation?

These ambiguities became even greater when, 1500 years later, men began writing about the life and death of Jesus Christ, the long awaited Messiah, whose coming had been prophesied in the Hebrew Scriptures. Now, for many, both the Hebrew Bible and the canon of new scriptures depicting the life and death of Jesus Christ were the WORD of GOD. For the followers of Jesus Christ the cycle was now complete. The nature of GOD was fully revealed.

Most of the Jews did not accept Jesus and his teachings. The view of the nature of GOD had suddenly become very different. And their relationship to him had changed. He was not the same God. He was not a harsh judgmental God to be feared as He was shown to be in the Hebrew Bible. He was now a God of love and compassion. He was incapable of inflicting punishment on His people. In fact He was a God who showed sorrow over the pain and suffering of His people. He had offered His own son as a sacrifice to show the depth of His love. And His covenant was now with all of mankind—and with womankind—not just with the Nation of Israel.

In many other ways, this new concept of GOD clashed with the one that the Jews had accepted from the very beginning of their history. As a result, the argument over the interpretation of the WORD of GOD and HIS relationship to those interpreting HIS message became more complex and increased in intensity.

Then, six hundred and ten years after the birth of Jesus Christ, in the ancient Arabian city of Mecca, angels began to speak to a merchant named Muhammad and a third interpretation of the nature of the God of both the Hebrew and Christian Bibles was declared. A new religion was born. The Prophet Muhammad proclaimed that the Hebrew and the Christian view of GOD had been corrupted, and the only true view of GOD was the one given to him by the Angel Gabriel.

If the view of the nature of GOD had changed, then how could all that had been written about Him be true? These questions did not find solutions in scholarly disputes. They gave rise to deeper issues. For Islam there followed a series of great battles, resulting in an empire that expanded westward and eastward from Mecca, destroying all other religions in its path, and covering a land mass from the shores of Morocco to Afghanistan as well as parts of what is now Spain.

But Islam was not the end of the search for GOD. Fifteen hundred years after the death of Jesus Christ came another cataclysmic event that reshaped the view of the nature of GOD and how humans are meant to respond to Him. The Protestant Reformation had begun. The Christian Church itself was split in two, leading to generations of bloody warfare. Who is right and who is wrong? Who is *Chosen* and who is not? Who is saved and who is not? Who is predestined and who is not? These became the bloody contentious issues.

To this day, these issues, Jewish, Christian, and Muslim have not been resolved. They still simmer and fester. As they have in the past, they continue to be a major underlying cause of world conflict. Pointing to the inerrancy of their scriptures and their own interpretations of these scriptures, fanatical factions within nations and in some cases the nations themselves brazenly justify their actions as the will of GOD. They claim to be *Chosen* to carry out His will. This fanaticism has spilled over into social and political conflict of such proportion and potential danger that it may now threaten civilization itself.

This is the dangerous and unstable rocky path on which the religions of Abraham have left the human species as it enters the 21st century.

The time has come to question the inerrancy of all religious scripture and all religious thought, not with the mentality of ancient clerics, Catholic Bishops, Rabbinical scholars, Islamic Ayatollahs, American television Evangelists, or Apocalyptic *Pop* Christian evangelical authors, but as thinking men and women concerned about the human condition today in the 21st century and in the centuries beyond.

I
A New Way of Thinking about Our Existence

What you are looking for (heaven) has come, but you don't know it...It (heaven) will not come by watching for it. It will not be said, Look here look there! Rather, the father's kingdom is spread out upon the earth, and people don't see it.

The 5th Gospel of Thomas
Unearthed in the Egyptian desert in 1945
1st or 2nd Century Christian Coptic Gospel text excluded
from the New Testament by
the early Roman Church Fathers

The earliest evidence we have, going back into pre-human history, shows that from the very beginning of our awareness of a greater force outside of ourselves, there has been the question of whether that force exists somewhere in space and time away from of our naturally known and experienced world, or whether it exists here in the present as a part of our world. According to the 5th Gospel of Thomas, Jesus Christ said the force is here present with us in our world, but we just don't see it.

As the books of the New Testament were being brought together by the early Church Fathers, those who subscribed to the argument that the Kingdom of God is somewhere outside of us, above the earth, won out. After all, theirs was a flat earth surrounded by the mystery of the heavens above. What explanations there were had come over the ages from the astrologers. So GOD was said to be *up above* in the heavens. When the Holy Spirit came to man, it *came down*. When Christ was baptized, GOD came from *above* to say, *This is my son in whom I am well pleased*. When Christ left this earth, he *ascended into heaven*.

The early Hebrew Biblical idea of a *final judgment* fell into line with this concept of a duality between heaven and earth as two separate places. This gave logic to the early Christian idea that Jesus would return from heaven, at which time the earth would end and there would be a separation between those predestined for heaven, the elect, and those who would descend to hell. The early Christians believed that this would occur during their lifetimes. To this day, Christians continue to make this distinction using the words in the Lord's Prayer, *Thy Kingdom come, thy Will be done on earth as it is in heaven.*

Early Christian Fathers, such as St. Augustine, saw the Universe as divided into two Cities, *The City of God* (heaven) and the *Earthly City*. The Earthly City was defined as a city of corruption, conflict, wars, and violence. Earth, including man and his physical desires, was looked upon as corrupt, and the things of heaven above were looked upon as pure and good.

As the end of the world did not come, over the passing years Christians gradually accepted the idea that the end would come not in their lifetimes but at some future point in time, and then there would be a separation made by GOD. Some people would go up to heaven, and the rest would go down to Hell. A new concept, that of Predestination or Election brought forth by the Apostle Paul gave a vague sense of definition as to who would be among the *Elect* or *Chosen*. Only those who were *Chosen* would pass on to heaven in the *Final Judgment*.

As time passed, the words of 27 books considered the *New Testament* firmly establishing all of these concepts. They were believed by most Christians without question to be the inerrant and true account of the teaching of Jesus Christ. As Jesus was declared to be God Incarnate, they logically considered these approved writings to be sacred and to be the WORD of GOD. Most Evangelical Christians today believe this to be the fact.

It is not surprising that these concepts were so readily accepted by the early Church Fathers. The world was far different from what it is today. Christianity was in its infancy, and it was struggling not only against alien religious ideas but also against radical factions within the movement itself.

But what if the early Church Fathers had it wrong? What if Thomas was right? What if we are living in a dimension right now that is both heaven and earth at the same time? What if we are walking in judgment every moment of our lives and not on some final day? What if there is no such thing as predestination or election and each of us is free to live within the love of GOD or outside of it? What if this applies to each and every person on this earth and there are no favored so-called *Elect*? What if we pass in and out of the earthly and the heavenly dimension every moment of our lives, as by our thoughts and actions we move towards and away from GOD? What if the natural beauty of our world and all its

I A New Way of Thinking about Our Existence

forms of life are not corrupt as St. Augustine—as well as the Apostle Paul—would have had it, but are a miraculous expression of GOD'S presence.

The answers to the above questions may have come to us in 1945 when twelve books hidden in a sealed jar were discovered by two peasant brothers near Nag Hammadi, Egypt. They were written in Coptic, a late Egyptian language using Greek letters. They are now preserved in the Coptic Museum in Cairo, Egypt. One of the books is now referred to as the 5th Gospel of Thomas.

The four Gospels of the New Testament were brought together by the early Church Fathers long after the death of Jesus Christ. The first is dated approximately 70 A.D. Scholars have always known that many other Gospels existed. In the Gospel of Luke, we are told that there were many Gospels written. This is recorded in Luke 1:1-4 where he states: *Inasmuch as many have undertaken to put together an account of the events that have been fulfilled among us.*

The question may now be asked: Why did the early Church Fathers not include the 5th Gospel of Thomas in The New Testament? The content of the Gospel itself was very much in line with the accounts of the teachings of Jesus found in the other Gospels. There was, however, a fundamental difference of far reaching magnitude.

The answer may have been that the Thomas Gospel was a challenge to the institutional validity and continuity of the Roman Church as it had defined itself. The Thomas Gospel called not for *joining* a church but for *joining* GOD through an inner experience involving a thorough and penetrating inner search.

Was this the reason for rejection of the Thomas Gospel by the Roman Church? Some scholars have concluded that it was. They have suggested that the reason may have been that there would have been less of a need for an organized church to, so to speak, *control the Gate*. If man were asked to look within himself for GOD and look around himself for heaven, the authority of the Church could not hold.

The power of the early church came from the fact that it had the keys to the Gate. To enter heaven, you had to pass through that Gate. As the church and its Christian doctrines developed, the rules for entry to heaven—passing through the Gate—became more complex and more onerous. In time they became so onerous that they sparked the Protestant Reformation.

By the time of the Protestant Reformation, the main doctrines of the Roman Christian Church had been established. The definitions of heaven, hell, and judgment were fixed. With a flurry of new ideas, Protestantism set out to put down its own rules as to who would and who would not enter the Kingdom of heaven on the Final Day of Judgment.

The *Reflections* that follow are an attempt to explore GOD'S presence in our lives, not in a heaven at some future moment in time, but in the here and now on this earth. They reinterpret the descriptions of Judgment and the time dimension of heaven given in the books of the New Testament and Roman Catholic doctrine. While they do not disagree with the idea of our capacity for evil and ensuing Judgment, they look at the human species not as the early Christian Church Fathers did, as being corrupt, weak and degenerate, but as being GOD centered, loving, and powerful. They see a world moving forward directed by a redemptive GOD in the midst of all people, a GOD at work in each and every life, not just in the lives of those who have passed through the *gate* of the Christian Church. They do, however, look at the teachings of Jesus Christ given to us in the 5th Gospel of Thomas as the presence of GOD guiding the world in its search.

1.
A WORLD CEASELESSLY SEEKING GOD

> "and you all my soul where you stand,
> Surrounded, detached, in measureless oceans of space…
> Ceaselessly seeking…
> Till…the ductile anchor hold,
> Till the gossamer thread you fling catch somewhere,
> O my soul."
>
> *A Noiseless Patient Spider*
> Walt Whitman
> 1819–1891

For I am convinced that there is nothing in death or life, in the realm of spirits or superhuman powers, in the world as it is or the world as it shall be—nothing in all creation that can separate us from the love of God in Christ Jesus our Lord.

Paul's letter to the Romans 8:38-39

We sense the presence of GOD in the measureless oceans of space, but we cannot see Him. Where is He? How can we know that we have found Him? How can we know that He has found us? How can we be assured that even after we think we have found him, that the gossamer threads of hope we have cast out toward Him has taken hold? How can we know that the anchor that we have set will not drag and then suddenly break loose to cast us adrift into the vast reaches of darkness in outer space?

Like Walt Whitman's noiseless patient spider, we too spend our lives launching forth filament after filament into the measureless oceans of space, although our search is not the same. Ours is both within ourselves and without, into the endlessness of our souls.

Like a spider, we too can sense when a filament we cast out takes hold. We can feel that something out there is on the other end. But, we cannot be sure of what it is since we cannot see where our filaments have taken hold. As we extend them, sometimes in fear we ask ourselves: How can we be certain that we have found GOD? How are we to know we have found him?

Jesus Christ told us that those who search for GOD'S presence will find him. And he assured us that once we find him, the anchor will hold and we will not be cast adrift. He told us that as we reach out toward GOD, He will take hold of filament after filament and we will be drawn by him into His presence.

He warned us of what will happen to us if we do not search for Him. He said that when we die, we will exist as if we never were. He said GOD has given each of us a brief moment of time for our earthly existence and He wants us to use it to extend our filaments toward him. As He gave life and a gift of time to the spider to extend its filaments, He has given each of us life and a gift of time to extend ours. He said that the choice is ours. We can use His gifts in a life long process of extending our filaments toward Him, or we can turn our backs on Him.

Through Jesus Christ GOD gave us a new covenant, one that extends to all of humankind, to every human being born and to be born. He told us that for those who search the endless oceans of space within and without of themselves and find Him, the filaments once they are connected cannot be disconnected. Once the anchor is set, it cannot break loose. He told us that nothing in all of creation can break the hold. Nothing can separate those who find him from His love for them.

2.
MY SOUL

For what shall it profit a man, if he shall gain the whole world, and lose his own soul? Or, what shall a man give in exchange for his soul?

(Mark 8:36-37)
70 A.D.

"The soul is the junction point between my physical self and my virtual self."

How To Know God
Deepak Chopra
2000 A.D.

I (Mary Magdalene) said to him (Jesus), 'Lord, how does he who sees the vision see it, through the soul or through the spirit?' The savior answered and said, 'He does not see through the soul nor through the spirit, but the mind which is between the two.'

The Gospel Of Mary
Discovered at Nag Hammadi
1945 A.D.

Date of origin unknown

What is the soul? Where does it exist?

Is my soul here with me now or is it something that will only come into existence after my death? If my soul is present now, what form does it take? Is my soul inside my physical being or does it exist outside of my body in some other dimension of space and time? Did my soul exist before my biological birth? Why in Christianity is the saving of our souls so closely connected to escaping damnation? What happens to the soul in damnation?

The Hebrew Bible gave no exact definition of the soul. Most of the Christian definition has come to us from the early Church Fathers who were influenced by the Greek philosophers. As we examine all of this, we are left with an awareness of our souls in the here and now, an awareness of another *me* outside of my recognizable physical self. It is an awareness that has been common to many religions from the beginning of recorded religious history.

Today, modern quantum physics has taken this insight one step farther by showing us that our physical bodies are, in fact, no more than a soup of subatomic energy particles in motion separated 99.999% by space, and this energy is an interdependent part of an endless universal web of connectedness that exists throughout space and time in a dimension we can not comprehend.

Quantum physics deals with energy and matter, not with souls. It sets out equations that attempt to explain our universe and ourselves in mathematical terms. It does not deal with the question of what happens to the soul when it exists in alienation from GOD.

The message of the 5th Gospel of Thomas coming from Nag Hammadi is that each individual by his own free will must examine his life in its greatest depth to find the *light within* in order to *save his soul*. For those who refuse this union that GOD, Jesus Christ describes the soul's eternal existence as one of separation from GOD.

Modern Writers such as Deepak Chopra have gone so far as to suggest that our brains may be the junction point between physical reality and virtual reality, the later defined as that which exists outside and beyond our perception of space and time. The suggestion here is that the brain is more than just gray matter collecting and storing electrical impulses. It is the connecting link between GOD and us. This explanation follows that of Jesus Christ in his statement to Mary Magdalene.

Our souls are a real and recognizable part of us. We see and experience our souls as being at the same time both inside and outside of our bodies. We see our souls on the edge of GOD'S eternal dimension, but never in it. We sense that GOD is pulling us closer and closer to himself as we turn our lives over to him, but our souls remain within the confines of the comprehensible Universe of our imagination. We long to be brought into His eternal dimension and for the time when our souls will no longer be separated from it, but will be at one with it.

3.
UNDERSTANDING THE CHRISTIAN EXPERIENCE/ THE PEACE THAT PASSES ALL UNDERSTANDING

Be careful about nothing; but in everything by prayer and supplication with thanksgiving let your requests be made known to God. And the peace of God, which passeth all understanding, shall keep your hearts and minds through Christ Jesus.

(Philippians 4: 6,7)

Whatever things are honest...just...pure...lovely...of good report...virtuous...think on these things.

(Philippians 4: 8)

What is the connection between having pure thoughts and being careful about nothing? What is this *Peace* to which Paul refers?

From the beginning of human history, mankind in an effort to find spiritual union with GOD practiced various forms of ritual. With these often came a euphoria that transported the person into another dimension. Many people define religious experience in these terms today.

It was different with Jesus Christ.

With Jesus Christ, ritual played a minor role, as did euphoria. Rather, he emphasized a disciplined focus on pure thought. He said with this comes a total trust and reliance on GOD and a release from anxiety. What follows is not euphoria but a peace that passes all understanding.

4.
ENTERING HEAVEN/ENTERING INTO THE PRESENCE OF GOD

Make every effort (Strive) to enter through the narrow door, because many, I tell you, will try to enter and will not be able to....The lord will say; I don't know you or where you come from, Away from me.

(Luke 13:23-30)

Jesus said: 'Let him who seeks continue seeking until he finds. When he finds, he will become troubled. When he becomes troubled, he will be astonished and he will rule over all.'

(2)
The Gospel of Thomas

There is light within a man of light, and he lights up the whole world. If he does not shine, he is in darkness.

(24)
The Gospel of Thomas

Jesus Christ is telling us that the door is narrow, and not all who try will enter heaven. How can we be sure we will not be one of those excluded? Is it enough just to obey certain religious rules or to profess common creedal beliefs, or to go through certain rituals, or to say certain prayers? Or, is there more to it than that? Is something of even greater importance required of us?

We live in a desensitized world where we have lost our sensitivity to everything around us. We see this among both the religious and the irreligious. No one is excluded. We have lost our sensitivity to our inner selves. We know that GOD is diminished by this outer and inner insensitivity. How can we find him?

In the Gospel of Thomas, Jesus Christ says that we can find GOD, but only in one way. It is through a process that begins with our search for an understanding of who and what we really are. He says that before we can find GOD, we must embark on this search. He commands us to make every effort and warns us that it may be painful. He tells us that only through this search can we find GOD'S presence in our lives. He says that GOD will only acknowledge those who have made every effort in this search.

How can we know we have found him? How can we know He has found us? In the Gospel of Thomas, Jesus Christ tells us that GOD is already within each of us. He has been there all the time, and He is pleading with each of us to open ourselves to His presence.

Finding him takes more than going through the superficial motions of religious belief. First, we must know who we really are. We must dig deeply so that we can discover both the evil and the good within ourselves. We must search to the depths of our very being to uncover the pride and arrogance and hatefulness that is holding us back from knowledge of GOD. Only then will we find him. Only then will He find us.

We will know when we have found him. Everyone will know. We will no longer be insensitive. We will be different from what we were. We will become a light to the whole world.

II
The Common Denominator on Which All Religions Must Judge Themselves
What is happening in the Upper Room?

The number of names together were about a hundred and twenty…And when the day of the Pentecost was fully come, they were all with one accord in one place (The Upper Room of the Inn…and suddenly there came a sound from heaven as of a mighty rushing wind…And they were all filled with the Holy Ghost, and began to speak in other tongues, other language.

Act Of The Apostles
Chapters I and II

In the *Upper Room* of an Inn, by a sudden manifestation of His presence, GOD defined for the Disciples of Jesus Christ their purpose and their future.

A group of individuals—followers of the newly proclaimed Messiah—were gathered. Their Prophet and savior had been crucified. He had reappeared to a few, but for most he had not. It seemed that the end of a dream had come. Then, suddenly everything was changed. Their lives took on a new and powerful dimension. The message of salvation through self-sacrifice, humility, and love of one's fellow man filled them with a new kind of hope. They were free from fear. They left the Upper Room eager to preach the Gospel of their Savior. In the following years many of them suffered extreme hardship and some even lost their lives.

The idea of having no boundaries or having and *Oceanic Feeling*—a phrase used centuries later by Freud—has been common to other religions including the

II The Common Denominator on Which All Religions Must Judge Themselves
What is happening in the Upper Room?

eastern religions. In the pagan religions, going into euphoric trances is common, but there was far more to the experience of the Upper Room.

For the Disciples the experience was more than just a *feel good* or *euphoric* experience. It was the experience of the WORD of GOD entering their entire being. It was the WORD that had been defined for them by their Messiah, Jesus Christ, as they had observed him and listened to him. It was the WORD of universal love. It was the WORD of devoted service, not just to his or her own kind, but also to all of humankind. It was the WORD of humility. It was the WORD that said suffering is only temporary, and enlightenment is forever. It was the WORD of personal salvation.

This is the common denominator on which all religions claiming Freud's *Oceanic Feeling* must judge themselves. Any religious experience that does not meet the test of the Upper Room is not of GOD. It is of man.

5.
THE ENLIGHTENMENT OF THE UPPER ROOM

"The idea of two rooms is not new. For centuries spiritual directors in the church (like Augustine and Teresa of Alva) have been telling us of another place to be…the one the lord built for our souls where he waits ready to meet us."

The Safest Place on Earth
Larry Crabb
1999

"I can find nothing with which to compare the great beauty of the soul and its great capacity"

Teresa Of Avila

We have a Lower Room and an Upper Room.

In Our Lower Room

We are alone in our Lower Room. From birth we have poured into this room the daily experiences of our lives. Our Lower Room is filled with all of our past, the strife, anxiety, and anger as well as the joy and fulfillment from our successes. From this room we find our creative strength. The mental and physical energy we feel in this Lower Room at times can take hold of us, leaving us without control. Often this leads to poor judgment, which in turn leads to pain and suffering. Whenever this occurs, we attempt to fall back on discipline to bring our lives into balance. When we are not able to do this, we become frightened, depressed, and withdrawn. We lash out at others or even ourselves. This drains our energy and as we tire, often we reach out for help.

In Our Upper Room

In our Upper Room we receive a glimpse of the eternal. In this room we find ourselves facing GOD. We find that He is a God of love who accepts us as we are.

We find that the strains of the Lower Room disappear. We find an unlimited energy source, which quietly takes away the weariness of the Lower Room.

In our Upper Room we have:

- A new identity

- A knowledge and belief that in the eyes of GOD we have profound worth

- A passion to know His purpose in our lives

- An understanding of the love He has for us

- An eagerness to please Him and follow His word

- An understanding that each experience in the lower room, good as well as bad, is GOD'S gift to us for the purpose of bringing us closer to Him

- A peace that passes all understanding

Only saints spend all of their lives in the Upper Room. Many of us never visit the Upper Room. Others only visit the Upper Room when under the stress of the Lower Room.

The Upper Room is always there for us in good times and bad. Jesus said, *knock and the door will be opened, seek and you will find.* He calls each of us from the Upper Room saying, *come, spend more time where I am.*

6.
THE TEMPTATIONS THAT KEEP US AWAY FROM THE UPPER ROOM

For forty days and forty nights he fasted...the Tempter approached him...but Jesus said: "Begone Satin!"

(Matthew 4:1-10)

    GOD led Jesus Christ into the desert where he was tempted by the things of this world. Forty days later he left the desert not as man but as GOD MAN. Through self-denial he became one with GOD. Can we become the same? Can we too in the solitude of our souls rise out of the desert and walk the earth with the power of GOD in us? Can we look to this same experience as Jesus Christ to mold our own lives? Is the purity of GOD also available to us?

    Human beings of all religions from the beginning of humanity have always thought that they could have it both ways. They could attach themselves to the power, the influence, the position, and to the material things of this world while at the same time living in oneness with GOD. There has always been this duality of thought. But GOD is saying—as He said to Jesus—I want all of you, not just a part. I want every thought, every action. Half measures are not enough. There are no compromises. Like Jesus Christ in the desert wilderness, GOD is telling us that we too must detach ourselves from the things of this world. It is only then that we can enter the Upper Room and be in His presence.

III
The Free Will to Make Our Own Choices

> "Two roads diverged in a wood
> And sorry I could not travel both....
> Oh, I kept the first for another day!
> Yet knowing how way leads on to way,
> I doubted if I should ever come back".

The Road Not Taken
Robert Frost
1874–1963

Like the traveler in the poem facing a fork in the road, we too often must make choices that move us forward on new and uncharted roads, never to return where we started. Unlike the traveler in the poem, though, we often find that the choices are not always within our control. We find that we are on a road not by our own choice but by the choice of someone else, or by chance. The following Reflections explore these different kinds of choices. They explore the question of how much control we have over our future, and they explore what happens when we give up our attempts to control it.

Many of us have puzzled over the perplexing question: What if? We ask: What if I had done this instead of that? What if I had not done this or that? But, there is an even larger and more perplexing question. It is the question of whether I ever had any choice at all. At the split second of making choices, it is often hard to find the reason. Even those who think they have control over their futures know inside themselves that in the final analysis they made the choice because *they felt that it was the right thing to do.*

We do know that some choices are the wrong ones and some are the right ones. Some lead to bad outcomes and some lead to good outcomes. We know this from the outcomes of our choices, but then it becomes more complicated. There may be more than one choice involved, and some choices are prompted by past choices. If we make a choice, how far into the future will the choice take us? At what point will this call for other choices? And, when will it be too late to reverse our course? At what point will we be forced to make choices we would not otherwise want to make? What if Robert Frost's traveler doesn't want to take either road? What if he doesn't even want to be in the woods?

Should we be making our own choices? Can we create our own future? What are the risks in making our own choices? Will our choices bring destruction, pain, and suffering to ourselves as well as to others? We know from our own personal experience that choices, which seemed at the time to be well thought out, can be the wrong ones. There is no guarantee of success when we make our own choices.

We also know that human beings have the capacity to make choices in their self-interest that are evil in that their choices can lead to painful consequences. Examples are the two great wars in the twentieth century as well as the present world terrorist conflict. On a personal level we can make self-destructive choices. Alcohol and drugs are self-destructive in that they destroy the capability of individuals to think and act clearly, which prevents them from realizing their full human potential. This shows what can happen when the human mind is given total freedom to make its own choices.

How can I make the right choices, not only the singular *I* as an individual, but the interdependent universal *We* as the whole human race?

To answer this question, we must look at our lives as having the possibility of following one of two diametrically opposed paradigms:

- One is the paradigm we construct for ourselves moment-by-moment from the time we are born and begin to discover our consciousness. We formulate this paradigm into our consciousness piece-by-piece. In it we carefully store each experience as if it were the only reality of our existence. Based on these experiences, we make our decisions and chose the direction of our lives. In this paradigm we rely 100% on ourselves to make our choices. Each choice, or most of them, is made in our self-interest. This is the paradigm that most people in the world follow.

- The other paradigm is the one that GOD has constructed for us. When we follow this paradigm, we let GOD make our choices.

III The Free Will to Make Our Own Choices 19

The message of Jesus Christ was a call to turn our lives over to GOD and break out of our own earthly formulated paradigm. He told us that our earthly paradigm is not in fact reality. He said another higher and eternal reality exists beyond our earthly perceptions and constructions. This reality transcends our own. It exists in GOD'S dimension.

Jesus Christ said that each life on earth is precious in the sight of GOD. GOD loves each of us. But HE can only show HIS love for us if we turn ourselves over to HIS paradigm for our lives. GOD can only give to us if we give our lives to HIM. Jesus Christ said that when this happens, we are reborn into a new dimension where all of our earthly requests, material as well as spiritual, will be met. But we will not be making our choices. They will not come from us. They will come from GOD.

The following Reflections show that there is a way to make these GOD directed choices. They show there is a way we can open up our futures by choosing the right road. This is the road that GOD has chosen for us. The famous Prayer of Jabez (I Chronicles 4: 9-10) discussed in Reflection # 7 answers the question, "How do I know which road to take?" This prayer shows how we can break out of the earthly paradigm that is of our own making and expand our future into the paradigm that is of GOD'S making.

7.
OPENING THE BARRIERS OF OUR SELF-IMPOSED LIMITATIONS

Oh, that you would bless me indeed, and enlarge my territory, that your hand would be with me, and that you would keep me from evil, that I may not cause pain.

(I Chronicles 4:9-10)
"Live by your Bliss"
Joseph Campbell

Joseph Campbell tells us to "live by your Bliss." The Jabez Prayer tells us to ask GOD to *enlarge my territory*. The question is: As we move forward into the unknown, how can we be sure that the path we take will not lead to our destruction? If we break through our self-imposed limitations, will we lose control? What will happen if we cannot turn back? If, as we attain new territory, we hurt others, is there an eternal risk to our souls? As we move toward our expanded goals, do we risk being sucked into a vortex of evil drawing us into eternal damnation?

Expanding ourselves beyond ourselves—enlarging our territories—without asking for the power of GOD to guide us can lead us to our own destruction and the destruction of others. There is no discipline in simply *following our bliss*.

If we think that we can be in charge of the territory we open, we deceive ourselves. We will be opening it to our own self-centered view of its unlimited expansion and then, by the time we have moved into the new and unknown territory, it may be too late to turn back. We deceive ourselves if we think we can always return. We may not have the power to return. We may lose our way and not know how to return.

We need the power of GOD to guide us. We need His presence in our lives to *lead us not into temptation*. As we break through our self-imposed limitations, we need to follow our *Bliss* but only as we place ourselves in GOD'S hands. Only GOD can open our future for His purpose in our lives. Only GOD can protect us from our own self-destruction. We are powerless by ourselves.

8.
BE CAREFUL WHAT YOU WISH FOR

> Ask, and you will be given what you ask for…
> for everyone who asks receives.
> If a child asks his father for a loaf of bread,
> will he be given a stone?
> If you give only good gifts to your children,
> won't your father in heaven more certainly give good gifts to you?
>
> (Matthew 7: 7-11)

How do we *ask*? What should we be asking for and what should we not be asking for?

Are we expected to take action to get what we have asked for, or will it just come to us?

If we do not receive what we have asked for, does this mean that we have not asked for it in the right way? Does it mean that GOD is not looking with favor on us?

There is a human dynamic that psychologists now recognize which they call *intentionality*. Its study examines the question: At what point does our vision of the future become reality, and how does this happen? At what point does our subconscious play an active role, so that we physically and mentally carve out the future? At what point does conscious wishful thinking become subconscious all out drive? At what point do our powerful inner forces take over, and what are those inner forces?

In this process of subconscious desire becoming all out drive, a question of enormous importance arises. This question is: As we unleash these cybernetic forces, is there any ethical or moral restraint built within us as a part of our brain function that will serve to hold us back from causing pain and destruction to ourselves as well as to others? The history of man has shown that to get what he wants, that is to achieve his goals, man's potential for harm, to others as well as himself, is unlimited.

We know that what we ask for may in the end not be what we really wanted. As the saying goes: "Be careful what you wish for, you may receive it."

Jesus Christ is saying that GOD will not give us everything we ask for. He is qualifying the intentionality discussed by modern day psychologists. He is connecting GOD only with the *good gifts*. He is saying that to not be harmful to ourselves and others, our future must be in harmony with the future GOD has intended for us. The analogy of the parent and child is perfect. Out of love parents will only give their children what they think is in their best interests. GOD'S love for us is the same. He will only give us what is in our best interests.

As we open the territory in front of us and create the future out of our own self-interest, we must recognize that the landscape we are creating may not be of GOD'S design. He gives us the freedom to make the choices. He leaves it to us to exercise our own free will and to choose.

We must examine our dreams and desires with care and ask GOD to guide us. We must be aware of the powerful forces of intentionality within us and not mistake them for GOD'S voice. We must recognize that without His guidance we risk not only harming ourselves and others, but we risk our own eternal damnation.

IV
From Each According to His Ability

"Half of my life is gone, and I have let
The years slip from me and have not fulfilled
The aspiration of my youth...
Though, halfway up the hill, I see the Past
Lying beneath me with its sounds and sights,
And hear above me on the autumnal blast
The cataract of Death far thundering from the heights."

Mezzo Cammin
Henry Wadsworth Longefellow
1807–1882

"Give the world the best you have, and it may never be enough; Give the world the best you've got anyway."

Mother Teresa

The Henry Wadsworth Longfellow poem is about a life that has suddenly reached the halfway mark. Sadly, the writer looks back and says: What have I accomplished? Like the writer, we too ask the question: Is it too late to make my mark before I reach the top and face *The cataract of Death far thundering from the heights.*

The Longfellow poem is a sad poem. It is a poem about a person who has not yet made his mark. He has not yet found his niche. He has not discovered himself. He has not made his contribution. It is a poem about a life that is being wasted. It is a poem about a person in despair.

The words of Mother Teresa are not sad. They are the words of joy and of action. They are the words of a person in search for a way to make a positive and constructive influence on the world.

Each of us was born with the ability to make a contribution. Each person, no matter how strong or weak, how dumb or smart, how able or disabled was given gifts by the Creator. Each was given the potential to fulfill a purpose. Each was given the ability to make a mark, to change the world by some small—or large—amount.

Any religion or sub sect of a religion that does not encourage its followers to use their potential to its fullest to advance society, not just selectivity but in its broadest sense, is not a religion. It is no more than a mind controlling human activity. It is no more than an excuse to justify its own continued existence and to control its followers. This is true whether this is religion under the name of Christianity, Judaism, Islam, or any other.

The key word is *contribution*. The world today is the product of the contributions past and present of those from all backgrounds and religions who have realized their potential and made their contributions. It is not the product of those who have not. It is not the product of *False Prophets*. It is not the product of drug addicts, cheats, gangsters, terrorists and all others who are the parasites of society, who take as much as they can and contribute nothing. Nor is it the product of those, who because of material good fortune, choose not to contribute but to live in a somnolent state of luxury with their only purpose being to continue to maintain their level of opulence, and thereby satisfy their selfish desires.

The question comes down to what is and what is not a contribution. Jesus Christ answered this question clearly. He said it is anything that:

- Shows love towards all members of society

- Helps to elevate the human mind to the level of GOD'S presence

- Helps to develop the *talents* of others

- Makes a contribution to the welfare of society

- Protects good people from those evil people who would seek to destroy

This is the message of Jesus Christ for all people in our world. At least a part of it runs through every major religious tradition. It is a call for all persons on this earth, of all faiths and traditions, to look into their deepest parts. Any part of any religious tradition that runs contrary to this message is false.

It is the message found in the Parable of the Talents outlined in the following reflection, Reflection #9, a parable directed to all mankind. In the eyes of GOD, anyone who does not multiply his *talents* as best he can has wasted GOD'S gift of life.

9.
REAPING WHERE HE HAS NOT SOWED AND GATHERING WHERE HE HAS NOT STRAWED

The lord gave talents…(A currency of the time)…to every man according to his abilities…he that had received five talents…made another five talents…and he that had received two talents another two, but he that had received the one talent went and hid it…as he was afraid…and the lord said to him: Thou knowest that *I reap where I have not sown and gather where I have not strawed*…and the lord cast the unprofitable servant into outer darkness..

(Matthew 25:15-30)

By saying that GOD reaps where He has not sown and gathers where He has not strawed, is Jesus Christ saying that GOD'S purposes extend not only—as many religious beliefs hold—into the lives of those who have heard His word, but also into the lives of all people? Is he saying that every person, no matter what belief, who uses as best he can the abilities that GOD has given him will enter the Kingdom of Heaven? Is he saying that GOD'S presence and redemption is not exclusive?

Even today in the early spring to give new sprouts protection from the sun, rain, and wind, farmers will place straw over the newly planted seeds. This gives them an advantage, so they will be protected as they begin to grow.

What about the seeds that are not protected and nurtured? Do they too have a chance? Jesus Christ here says they do.

The servant has just told GOD that he feared him and did not want to take the chance of failure with his talent, so he buried it. GOD is telling the servant that only He—GOD—can be the judge and would not have given him the talent if it could not be multiplied. The servant's only choice was to overcome his fear and multiply his talent.

Jesus Christ is telling us in this parable that GOD'S presence extends to all of mankind. He is saying that every person on earth is a part of GOD'S plan. Each of us has abilities of which we are unaware. Only GOD is the judge of our inherent worth. Only He knows what we are capable of accomplishing. We are being asked to give up our fears and accept GOD'S judgment as to what we can accomplish.

V
Breaking Through to the Other Side

"Everything that we experience as material reality is born in an invisible realm beyond space and time, a realm revealed by science to consist of energy and information. This invisible source of all that exists is not an empty void but the womb of creation itself. Something creates and organizes this energy. It turns the chaos of quantum soup into stars, galaxies, rain forests, human beings, and our own thoughts, emotions, memories and desires."

How To Know GOD
Deepak Chopra
2000 A.D.

We live in the most tumultuous period in human history. The evolution of science is meeting the evolution of religion. As this is occurring, we are seeing evidence that the two are not contradictory, but are in fact in support of each other. We are discovering parallel meanings between our religious insights and our scientific discoveries. We are learning that there is a strong confluence of those ideas, which define both in religious and scientific terms, who and what we are in relation to our Universe and what lay beyond our perception of it. And, we are finding that the power of man to observe all of this extends far beyond the perceivable physicality of his senses. It extends outside of himself.

This is not so for everyone. As scientific inquiry began to take hold, for many it remained separate from religion. Today, for many, the two continue to remain separate, giving two separate and irreconcilable viewpoints to the questions of who and what we are.

Religion came first. It began its evolution at the very beginning of man's consciousness. It formed simultaneously among isolated groups of primitive man. In the beginning it took the form of man's primitive search for what lay beyond his

V Breaking Through to the Other Side

earthly perception. It also recognized that man was unique and not like other living things in that he could perceive what other forms of life could not.

Scientific knowledge is a more recent phenomenon. It has only been with us for a few hundred years, but it has progressed at a much faster pace so that now it is challenging much of traditional religious thought.

As these searches moved forward and converged, they did not always find a smooth path. The observations of Galileo were condemned by the Roman Catholic Church. Many of those who held to the inerrancy of the Hebrew and Christian scriptures refused to accept evolutionary scientific theory as it relates to life on the earth and the creation of the Universe itself.

For those who hold a metaphorical view of religious scripture, religious and scientific thought is seen as two codependent ways of looking at the same questions. They view the complexities of human metaphysical existence as extending far beyond past religious doctrinal understanding.

Our vision of reality, from the smallest (Quantum Mechanics), to the largest (Cosmology), to ourselves (Biochemistry), is broadening at an exponential rate and bringing religion along with it. As these developments are occurring, we are becoming more and more certain that there is such a thing as direction in our Universe and in the other dimensions beyond it. Godless theories of chaos and randomness are no longer a choice. Like in a symphony, the underlying directing presence of an orchestrator becomes evident.

In 1905, Albert Einstein made breakthroughs into our knowledge with his Special and General Theories of Relativity. This led to the Manhattan Project and the development of the Atomic Bomb. Further developments since then have led to a broader understanding of concepts relating to space and time. Since Einstein, we now have other theories that run from the String Theory describing the physical universe to Brane's law that says we ourselves are no more than the reflection of ourselves against the membrane of another dimension.

But we cannot see the things we are observing. Only our advanced instruments of measurement allow us to extend our vision. We are limited by the level of advancement of these instruments of measurement and the creative depths of our minds. It is only when we see in front of us the results of the creative depths of our minds, such as the explosion of an atomic bomb, or the heat of a microwave oven, or any of the other practical applications that we are convinced that our observations are real.

The combination of the advancement of scientific instruments and an understanding of the mathematical equations derived from their observations made possible most of the major discoveries of the 20th Century. This was aided by the development of the computer. The fact that computers since they were first developed have obeyed what is known as Moore's Law—their speed and complexity double every eighteen months—tells us that this may just be the beginning of our exploration.

These scientific breakthroughs are allowing us to describe in mathematical terms the language of GOD on this side of our perception of reality. As we develop and use this language, we are becoming aware of its limitations and the possibility that ours may be only one language, being used to describe even another, the language of GOD.

Scientific developments of the 20th Century presented entirely new kinds of challenges that would have shaken the very foundations of early Christianity. They not only challenged the inerrancy of biblical events such as the Creation Story in Genesis, but they challenged the inerrancy of biblical writings about the creation of man himself. In the past, organized Christianity only clashed with the scientific world when it was challenged in areas of scripture dealing with Cosmology. Galileo fought with the Roman Catholic Church over the relative positions in the heavens of the sun and the earth. But Galileo's science had not gone so far as to challenge the Creation Story itself.

As we begin to understand from these scientific developments more about the Universe and the evolution of man as a part of the Universe, we are seeing that much of the recorded message of Jesus Christ is not in conflict. In fact his teachings support the scientific findings. It is largely in the historical/mythological events of the Hebrew Bible—The Old Testament—that the conflict exists. Jesus Christ spoke in parables of the same dimension that science is speaking about today. He spoke at a time when science as we know it was unknown, but he was able to define this other dimension.

The evolution of science and religion will continue like two lines approaching each other but never meeting. The distance between them will continue to be reduced but will always be more than zero. This means that they will never meet nor cross over. They will just get closer and closer. As this occurs, they will present stronger and stronger proof of each other's validity. There will always be an area where the answers will have to come from both.

As this near convergence takes place, we should be testing the inerrancy of past religions beliefs against the new scientific information we are receiving. There is a harsh discipline to the forward motion of scientific ideas. They must be tested. This is not the case with religion. Proof is not necessary. Rather than retreat in fear, religions should look openly at undiscovered meanings in their scriptures that reveal ancient understandings of what is just now being proven.

V Breaking Through to the Other Side 31

The following Reflections examine what Jesus Christ said about this dimension beyond our perception, and they examine what he said about how we, even as mortals, can approach this dimension. The path that he described is not always a *feel good* path or an easy path on which we can with little effort stroll. It is not a path where a sudden flash of light will appear and lift us up to heaven. Nor is it a path where we can just stand and wait for GOD to comedown to us.

It is a path that calls for self-directed and disciplined concentration. It is an upward path that calls for strength and courage.

10.
ENTERING INTO HIS PRESENCE

Seek, and ye shall find; knock and it (the door) shall be opened to you...he that seeketh findeth; and to him that knocketh it shall be opened.

(Matthew 7:7-8)

What does Jesus Christ mean by saying that if we knock, the door will be opened for us? What happens then?

When we come to a door, we can just remain standing in front of it or we can knock on it. If it opens, we can remain standing and look to see what is inside or we can step through to the other side. There are three separate decisions on our part, the first, deciding to knock on the door, the second, knocking on it, and then the third, walking through.

For the first—deciding to knock on it—we have to want to find out who or what is on the other side. For the second—knocking on the door—we have to take action. For the third, and this is the greatest of the three decisions—walking through the door—we have to take a risk. We have to step through and enter the unknown.

Using this imagery, Jesus Christ is metaphorically describing for us our limited perception of our sense of reality in our earthly existence—outside of the door. He is reminding us that our minds can only comprehend the material world, and therefore we are unable to experience what lay beyond. But, he says if we take the initiative and move towards the door leading to what lay beyond and we knock, the door will be opened for us. This is the door to another dimension. It is the dimension where GOD is. Then, if we step through, we will find ourselves not in the material world of our earthly perception but in the heavenly dimension beyond it.

We will find ourselves in the presence of GOD.

11.
SUBMISSION TO THE POWER OF GOD

"Joy and happiness in this life come from remaining still and letting GOD speak to us. By turning our backs on the earthly things and their images that are pulling at us and taking over our minds, we can find this joy and happiness, and we can be nearer to GOD."

Meister Eckhart
1260–1327

How do we find GOD'S presence in our lives? Is it something that comes to us out of the blue? Or, do we have to work for it? Will it come to us from meditation and prayer? If so, how should we be praying? How do we meditate?

Jesus Christ called on us to seek out GOD. His teachings were very clear as to how we should go about this. He said we must turn our attention away from the things of this world and to GOD.

Great teachers of the Gospels such as Meister Eckhart, a famous Dominican Monk of the 14th century, said that searching for GOD takes more than meditation, words and prayers. He said it calls for a disciplined redirection of our minds. It calls for a turning away from the material and emotional things of this world that distract us and prevent us from seeing GOD. He said we must empty our minds of the things of this world. He said only then will GOD speak to us.

Jesus Christ told us that we must release the negative hold that the things of this world have on us. These are both emotional and material. We must turn our backs on emotions such as anger, hate, anxiety, and fear. We must also release the hold that our material desires have on us. We must turn from allowing the world to define our wants and desires and allow GOD to define our very being.

12.
FROM THE LEAST TO THE GREATEST

The Kingdom of Heaven is like a grain of mustard seed, which a man took, and sowed in his field...which indeed is the least of all seeds, but when it is grown, it is the greatest among herbs.

(Matthew 13: 31-32)

Why did Jesus Christ use the metaphor of a mustard seed to describe heaven? Why, when referring to our perception of the Kingdom of Heaven did he draw a distinction using the words *least* and *greatest*? Is it possible that there is a connecting linking between his words and our 21st century scientific understanding of the universe? Was Jesus Christ giving us a clue to help us understand our personal relationship to the physical and observable universe?

First Explanation

The standard model of cosmology postulates that before the Big Bang our entire galaxy existed in a state of singularity in a Black Hole with all energy and matter compressed inside an area of near infinite compression. Some 15 billion years ago, from this near infinite compression came a singular event—the Big Bang—and the expansion of matter (energy) into infinite space began, to become the universe as we observe it today. Just as life begins within the germ of a mustard seed, our universe began from the finite depths of a black hole. Both began as the least to become the greatest.

Second Explanation

We cannot see heaven around us. Like looking for a mustard seed, we have to make a strenuous effort and look very closely. When we do see it, we find that we have difficulty understanding its regenerative magnitude. We sense that the potential for life in a mustard seed is greater than anything we can perceive or understand.

Third Explanation

Just as life begins within the germ of a mustard seed and our universe began in the near infinite compression of a *black hole*, our lives began in near infinite smallness in the mind of GOD and, without nurturing, they will remain that way and at death pass on into nothingness; or, when we accept GOD in our lives, we will be born again into His presence. Then, our lives will take on another form. They will expand into the infinite dimension of heaven. Like a mustard seed, what began as the least will become the greatest.

Fourth Explanation

All three above.

13.
SEEING BEYOND THE PROPHETS

For now I see through a glass, darkly; but then face to face. Now I know in part; but then I shall know even as also I am known.

(I Corinthians 13:12)

Can we look to our scriptures to tell us what lies on the other side of the *glass, darkly*? Must we wait to see it? Is this other side the mind of GOD?

We are conceived and born into a universe that covers us like a dark glass preventing us from seeing what is beyond. We can only know and experience what is underneath. As we grow in knowledge and understanding, we become more aware of it as it presses upon us in its envelopment. It traps us in our earth bound understanding who and what we are. We strain to see the other side.

From the beginning of human history mankind has been in search of what lay beyond. From the words of the shamans and priests in the earliest years of human development, to the writings of the prophets of the Hebrew Bible, to the words of the New Testament, to the writings of the Eastern Religions, to the Arabic message of the Angel Gabriel in the Koran, we have searched for knowledge of the other side. Every piece of scripture ever written has been an attempt to penetrate the dark glass preventing us from seeing what lay beyond.

We must continue this search by studying the wisdom of all religious writings, but at the same time where they claim to be the word of GOD we must question their inerrancy. We must question what part came from GOD and what came from man. We must search these writings for GOD'S revelation, not man's. We must not blindly leave it to others in ages past to tell us how to see what is beyond the dark glass. We must search for it ourselves.

VI
The Christian Evangelicals Pride and Judgment in the Bog

"How dreary—to be somebody!
How public—like a frog
To tell one's name—the livelong June
To an admiring Bog!"

 # 288
EMILY DICKENSON
1830–1886

We see today two opposing branches of thought in each of the three religions of Abraham. There is what may be loosely defined as centrist thought and then to the extreme right there is fundamentalist thought. Fundamentalists in all cases rest their belief on the inerrancy of their scripture and the infallibility of the dogma that has grown out of it. They believe that it is the WORD OF GOD. At the extreme end of this fundamentalism we have individuals such as Muslim Ayatollas, Evangelical Christians Ministers, Orthodox Roman Catholic Bishops, and Orthodox Jewish Rabbis.

It is their extremist view of their scripture that controls their religious belief. The possibility of their scripture being flawed in any way is an impossibility. The scriptures they follow represent the truth frozen in time.

Even though their individual belief systems differ, religious Fundamentalists from the three religions of Abraham have many things in common. They all have a fear of the pervading values that come from the world outside of them. They look at these values as a threat to their own value system. They also believe that those people outside of their belief system, because they do not believe in what they believe, are doomed for all eternity.

Terrorism is an outcome of religious fundamentalist thought, although not all Fundamentalists can be defined as terrorists, in fact very few. This should not, however, take focus away from those Fundamentalists who do not actively engage in violent acts of terror. Fundamentalism can harm without the use of terror. It can harm if it isolates and denigrates those who are not in agreement. It can harm if it isolates and hurts other people. It can harm if it drives away from mainstream religious belief those who because of the high profile of religious fundamentalism can then only see religion as a form of extremism.

Fundamentalists rely on their literal scriptural interpretations as a way to fill themselves with a sense of self-importance. Like the frogs in Emily Dickinson's imaginary *bog*, they cluster together as a mutation from centrist mainstream religious thought. Like her frogs, with rhetorical gusto their spokesmen inflate their throats to croak the message. As the chorus among the followers of these spokesmen grows louder, the self-confidence of the group grows stronger. Theirs is the only true version of the message. They all shout: We in our *bog* are right and you outside of our *bog* are wrong. You outside our *bog* are doomed. We are the *Chosen* ones. If only you would hear us and believe what we have to say, then we would have a perfect world.

Religious Fundamentalists cannot understand that the power of GOD is at work in the lives of each and every human being and not exclusively in their lives and those of their fellow believers in their *bog*.

History has shown us that whenever those with extreme views have claimed a direct line to GOD'S power, human suffering has been the result. The word of GOD coming from man is always imperfect, because man is imperfect. The messengers who wrote the ancient scriptures were not gods, they were mortal. They recorded what they thought they heard or even imagined their prophets said, but it was in their own words using their own frame of reference. The message always came from the hand of man.

Many religious fundamentalists in order to legitimize their message make the claim that divine intervention brought their message. Moses met GOD. The Angel Gabriel met Muhammad. For Christianity, the Jesus Christ of Roman Catholicism through divine intervention did not meet GOD, He was GOD. The big question then always becomes: Who wrote down the message? Even with Jesus Christ as GOD Incarnate, he himself did not write his message down. The message has always come from the hand of mortal messengers.

There are common themes such as love and compassion that run through all of the religions of Abraham, but no matter how loving and compassionate the scriptural foundation, we always find self serving individuals growing out of them

VI The Christian Evangelicals Pride and Judgment in the Bog

intent only to preserve power within a particularly defined and fashioned institutional matrix created for themselves. Over history we have ample evidence that these individuals have conveniently fashioned religious scripture and dogma to fit their own specific human goals and objectives. Early on these were tribal objectives. Today they are National and geopolitical. These individuals have always managed to pull out what they want from the message and discard what does not suit them. Whether it is the Torah, the New Testament, or the Koran, this is now obvious.

Even after the scriptures and the dogma are cast in stone, they continue to slant them towards their own purposes. They pull out only what they need in order to give purpose to their belief. In doing so they leave out what does not fit their immediate needs.

Most religions hold to the belief that GOD is transcendent and represents what we call Higher Values, which are values such as the love of one's fellow man, and compassion. In the mainstream of Christianity there is, however, another idea. It also exists in some other religions, but not in all. It is the idea that GOD made man in His own image and that in doing so He gave man the ability to comprehend these Higher Values. These Christians believe that when GOD gave man a mind, He did not just give him gray matter, but He gave him an opening into HIS own presence. At the same time He obligated men—and women—to expand their knowledge in order to understand HIS purposes. These Christians believe that in order to do this, men and women must use their minds to explore the ultimate truths of both their own existence and GOD'S.

Those of some other religions also hold this view.

Man cannot do this if he confines his belief to the inerrancy of scripture. The reason is that the search for GOD is an ongoing process that demands exploration of the historical sources used for the construction of scripture, and it demands an understanding of the period conditions when the scripture was written. It also demands an understanding of the underlying mythological and legendary influence on scripture and the application of this to the revelation brought out in scripture. And finally, it demands a matching of underlying scriptural meanings to present day events, including the advances of science, and the current human sociological condition. It is only then that man can begin to understand the revelation of the nature of GOD and his relationship to GOD brought out in the scriptures.

All of this is impossible for the religious fundamentalist.

The world today is awash with religious controversy and flux—as well as dynamism—and religious change is, if anything, likely to intensify in the coming decades. In the secular pluralistic world of the 21st century we will always have people who live and think differently.

Fundamentalist Christians must not condemn ideas that are not their own. Other religious extremists must not condemn either.

To establish legitimacy, there are moral/ethical/religious questions that every religious spokesperson must ask of him or her self:

- Are my ideas hurting other people?

- Are my ideas helping other people?

This is where the examination of the inerrancy of scripture and those who rest their case on it should begin.

14.
JERRY FALWELL AND HIS "BOG" OF BELIEVERS

"I really believe that the pagans, and the abortionists, and the feminists, and the gays and lesbians who are actively trying to make that an alternative lifestyle, the A.C.L.U., People for the American Way—all of them who have tried to secularize America—I point the finger in their face and say; You helped this happen."

Jerry Falwell
September 2001

What does Jerry Falwell mean by his statement? Is he saying that GOD is angry with American society and therefore caused this to happen? Is he saying that GOD used the terrorists to act out His will? Does this then imply that in their desire to destroy our society the act of the terrorists was directed by GOD? What does this say about his view of GOD? Where is the merciful and redemptive Christian GOD of the New Testament?

Falwell's fundamentalist extremism provides him with a sense of meaning for the events of September 11. He views America as a disoriented and immoral society, except for those following his own inerrant belief in the words of the Christian Bible. As GOD punished the Nation of Israel when it went astray, GOD is now punishing America.

In his inerrant recourse to the punishing God of the Hebrew biblical texts, he turns a blind eye to the evolving revelation of the nature of GOD as recorded in the New Testament. Since he cannot support his reasoning with a dual definition of GOD'S nature, he only takes from scripture what he needs to prove his point. By avoiding the view of GOD illuminated by Jesus Christ, he has fallen into the same trap as so many Christians of the past. Throughout Christian history, from the Crusades to the Inquisition to the bloody religious wars of the 16th and 17th centuries, his kind of calcified thinking has led to far more blood spilled than that in recent years by Muslim terrorists.

Like the Muslim terrorists, the self-righteous thinking of Falwell and his followers leads them to an exhilarating sense of superiority over so called *non-believers*. This demeans those who choose reason and judgment to define their own view of the revelation of the nature of GOD.

Falwell and those who follow him are wrong in that theirs is a divisive message grounded on exclusiveness and pride. In a broad brush stroke he vilifies all people who do not subscribe to the inerrancy of both Old and New Testament scripture. He leaves no room for interpretation and exploration of deeper meanings. He casts aside into eternal damnation the vast numbers of people of all religious faiths who are making our world move in the direction of universal love and respect for the dignity of all human beings. His mindset is the opposite of the message of non judgment, humility, individual repentance and forgiveness defined by the life and death of Jesus Christ.

15.
CROAKING IN JUDGMENT OF THOSE OUTSIDE THE "BOG"

Judge not, that ye be not judged...And why beholdest thou the mote that is in thy brother's eye, but considerest not the beam that is in thine own eye?

(Matthew 7: 1-4)

Being judgmental of others—looking outward—shields us from looking inward, within ourselves. Why are we more comfortable being judgmental of others? Is it that we fear if we look into ourselves, we are afraid of what we will see? Is it because we are afraid that looking inward will be painful for us? Are we afraid that if we look deeply into our souls, we will see in its depths our own sinfulness?

Is it also possible that the fear we have of looking inward is based on a primitive and distorted view of a punishing GOD? What if the GOD who invites us to look inward is not a punishing GOD but a loving redemptive forgiving GOD? What if GOD is not the stern fearsome and punishing God of the Hebrew Bible?

Judging others is a self righteous excuse for not judging ourselves. We must look into the depths of our souls for our own failings. Jesus Christ is saying that we should look at others not with judgment but with unconditional love and compassion.

Jesus Christ is warning us not to think we can be GOD'S prosecuting attorney. He says only GOD can be our judge.

16.
"Frogs" Bogged Down in the Muck of the "Bog"

Q. What do you think of Americans?

A. I do not like them at all because they are not Muslims

I don't like non Muslims.

Q. How did you feel when you heard of the World Trade Center attacks?

A. It must be what GOD wanted.

Khashall Muhammad

Runs target practice in Quetta satelite town. Born 70 years ago in Kabul.

2001 A.D.

◆　◆　◆

If anyone comes to me and does not hate his father and mother, his wife and children, his brothers and sisters…yes, even his own life…he can not be my disciple.

(Luke 14:26)

    The statement of Khashall Muhammad has the appearance of being straight forward. He doesn't like Americans. But there is much more to it. There are deeper emotions at play. The statement of Jesus Christ gives us a clue.

    What is it about our father, mother, wife, and children, even ourselves that Jesus says we must hate in order to be born again into the presence of GOD?

VI The Christian Evangelicals Pride and Judgment in the Bog

What would Khasall Muhammad have to do to be *born again*? If he were, what then would happen to him? Would his tribe and family still accept him?

Khashall Muhammad has subsumed his identity into the tribal religion of the social unit to which he belongs. His statement most likely is the same as we would hear from any other of his family members as well as others in his community. The grounding for the ideas of his social/tribal unit is the Muslim religion. It is within this interaction of ideas that he has found his identity.

When Jesus Christ was confronting his fellow Jews with the idea of each individual being born into a new relationship with a GOD of all humanity, he was addressing a tribal people with deep religious roots extending back into the earliest history of the Jewish tribe. Their loyalty then, as to a great extent it is even today, was to the Jewish tribal unit and the Jewish GOD. The idea of an individual Jew relating directly to a GOD of non Jews unattached to Jewish tribal and religious identity was not understood any more than it would be for Khashall Muhammad. Hating your family and even yourself was a way for Jesus Christ to say that to accept the universal GOD of his teaching, every part of one's loyalty must be abandoned.

Loyalty to the tribal unit can be even stronger than religious ties. Even today in the 21st century it is common among Jews for a secular Jew or even a completely agnostic Jew to consider himself a Jew. This thinking applies today to almost all tribal groups. In parts of the Muslim world where loyalty to tribe and family goes back in time and calls for a total loyalty, even to the point of self sacrifice, as is currently occurring with Muslim terrorists, religion then just becomes a support for a tribal loyalty that rationalizes terrorism among extremists.

2000 years ago in a world dominated by tribal, family, and religious loyalty, Jesus Christ described how we must change in order to walk the path to GOD'S presence in our lives. He said we must reject all attachments that subsume us to all other loyalties. He pointed to the binding and exclusive traditions and beliefs of the Jewish people that separated them from finding GOD. As he spoke to the Jewish people 2000 years ago, he speaks to the world today. He said we can only have one loyalty. He said we can only have one identity. He said we must abandon all other loyalties and identities. We must become at one with the one GOD who extends His love not just to our own tribal, family, or religious group, but to all of humankind.

17.
THE GIFT OF REDEMPTION OUTSIDE THE "BOG"

(Some Galileans were killed by Pilate's soldiers while coming to the temple to offer sacrifice. Jesus was asked if God was punishing them for some great sin)

(Jesus replied)

Do you think that these Galileans were worse sinners than all the other Galileans because they suffered this way? I tell you, no! But unless you repent, you too will perish.

(Jesus then referred to other Galileans who had died previously when a building collapsed)

Or those eighteen who died when the tower of Siloam fell on them—do you think they were more guilty than the others living in Jerusalem? I tell you, no! But unless you repent, you too will perish.

(Luke 13: 1-5)

Does GOD punish here on earth those who are sinful? Does He rain retribution on whole nations that have gone astray and are living in sin? Did those who died in the World Trade Towers on September 11 die because GOD was displeased with our society? Did the Jews who died in the Holocaust die because GOD was displeased with the Jewish people?

What is the nature of the GOD defined in the Gospel of Luke by Jesus Christ? Is it different from the GOD as defined in the Hebrew Bible? What is Jesus Christ telling us about the nature of GOD?

For many Jews of the time and for a large part of the world's population today, Jesus Christ fulfilled a messianic hope. He brought to mankind a new understanding of GOD'S nature. Jewish writers of the Hebrew Bible wrote about a God of anger and retribution. Jesus Christ showed mankind a universal God of love and forgiveness. These were contradictions in the definition of the nature of this Jewish God. The Jews rejected Jesus for this, and he was crucified. Today, Jews and Christians may share a so called Judeo-Christian ethic based on the commandments given by Moses, but the Christian understanding of the nature of GOD is very different.

The Jewish God, Yahweh, was and is today the God of Israel under an exclusive covenantal relationship. From the very beginning of their tribal existence, GOD has been seen as their protector in every crisis. It is Yahweh alone who is invoked to give victory and deliverance. Earth, stars, and rivers come to His battle. The forces of nature bow to him. When Israel is good, He rewards and when Israel strays, He punishes. The God of Israel is a jealous God. He is subject to wrath and anger. He has the same emotions as humans. He calls for good works and insists that the Jewish people follow His law.

Jesus Christ revealed a universal GOD of unremitting love for every person, no matter how sinful or unworthy. He offered GOD'S forgiveness for transgression of the law. He elevated repentance as the central condition above all else, including good works, as the key to GOD'S acceptance.

His revelation of the redemptive nature of GOD powered the development of Christianity. It led to Paul's conversion and his burning desire to spread this message throughout the then known civilized world. When the Roman Catholic Church diverted its attention from this idea and emphasized good works and church doctrine, it found itself faced with the Protestant Reformation.

The exchange of ideas shown in Luke 13 illustrates this fundamental difference in the understanding of the nature of GOD. It is a fundamental difference that still exists today among people of all beliefs, including many Christians who confine their thought to the inerrancy of Old Testament Hebrew texts.

Those who questioned Jesus thought that GOD was punishing the Galileans. Hebrew scholars in the past would have interpreted it that way. Most Rabbis today would do the same. But, Jesus tells us that GOD does not cause buildings to fall or floods to occur as punishment for His people who have gone astray. Jesus turns us away from this kind of reasoning. Rather, he directs our attention to what is expected of each and every one of us by GOD. He says, *unless you repent, you too will all perish.*

His message penetrates our minds on a deep personal level. He tells us that tragic events of this world are not from GOD nor is pain in our lives. All that matters is individual repentance.

VII
The Presence of the Light

While he (Paul) was still on the road to Damascus, suddenly a light flashed from the sky all around him. He fell to the ground and heard a voice saying, 'Saul, Saul, why do you persecute me?'.... He got up from the ground, but when he opened his eyes he could not see...He was blind for three days.

(Acts 9: 3-9)

The story of Saul on the road to Damascus is a true story. It dates back to the earliest confirmed writings of Christianity. It was described in The New Testament in the Book of Acts and in Paul's letters. His life, which certainly can be proven, is in itself proof that it occurred.

This story tells us that our existence has a transcendental nature that goes beyond our perceived physical reality. It tells us that we can *break through* into something that is beyond our understanding.

What happened to Paul suddenly and dramatically altered the path in his life. On the Damascus road he was overcome by a power from a dimension beyond our understanding. After this transforming experience, he devoted the rest of his life to the spreading of the message of Jesus Christ throughout the then known world. It was a message that reflected a view of the Kingdom of GOD not only far different from, but in many respects opposed to the Hebraic one to which he had previously held fast and believed.

The story of Paul is not exclusive to Christianity. It has been repeated in many other forms of belief. For the religious person there is a sudden breakthrough to a heavenly dimension. This dimension is generally one where there is a bright light and a feeling of profound love. Then, there follows a change in the person's life.

As with Paul and for many others, there is a message that accompanies the experience. At the same time though, there is always confusion as to what really happened. The person generally finds it difficult to fully describe what he saw or felt except to describe it as a *bright light*. This is not so with the message which generally is clear and concise.

Only a few religions such as Islam claim that the messenger had a continuing and direct connection to GOD. But in Islam the message was given by Muhammad to individuals who recorded it. It was not written down by Muhammad himself. In Islam, it is claimed that the Angel Gabriel and other angels delivered the message.

In the case of Saul, he received a message from Jesus Christ saying: *Saul, Saul, why do you persecuting me?* and then he went out to preach the message of Jesus Christ.

For most Christians the light takes a more subtle form. It comes from a belief in GOD'S dimension joining theirs through an understanding of the life and death of Jesus Christ. This takes place through the indwelling of the Holy Spirit. But the Holy Spirit is not a *light*. The life of Jesus Christ, for Christians, is taken as the light. Jesus Christ is GOD in human form showing them the light.

We do not have to wait for another Saul to tell us about divine presence. In our world of today we hear stories of divine intercession repeated again and again. We have accounts of *after death* experiences where lives are changed. We have stories of healings where the people healed feel a bright light moving through their bodies from head to toe, and healing both mental and physical occurs. In almost all cases the experience is the same. There is a pure light that moves through the person. Then, afterwards there is a feeling of love for all of mankind, and there is joy over the possibility of new life.

Except in the story of Jesus Christ, the person is always overcome by the presence of the eternal, but remains a human being. In each case, like Paul himself, it is a human being who sees the light and then interprets it in the context of his own understanding of what it meant. He then lives the rest of his life and in time biologically dies. A life is changed, but not biologically and not completely. The person remains a living functioning biological human being.

For Paul the underlying behavioral patterns did not change completely. Paul before his vision was a man burning inside to punish those who defied the law of the Hebrew Bible. After his experience on the road to Damascus, he showed this same intensity as he interpreted the message of Jesus Christ. He did not leave his past completely behind. He relied on his own past knowledge of Jewish law and traditions to reinforce his new and altered vision of redemption. Inside, he was still Saul of Tarsus. The experience of being shown the eternal opened up another dimension for him, but did not take him into it and leave him there. The visit is always short. We must always return to earth and face ourselves.

The meaning of being in the light is being in the presence of GOD. Many never experience this and for those who do, being in HIS presence never lasts long. Many expect a sudden *flash* like Paul experienced and are sadly disappointed.

The following Reflections will discuss some of these *glimpses of GOD* taken from Biblical scriptures and comment on their possible meanings.

18.
THE MEANING OF THE LIGHT

The people that walked in darkness have seen a great light; they that dwell in the land of the shadow of death, upon them hath the light shined.

(Isaiah 9:2)

For God so loved the world that he gave his only begotten son, that whosoever believeth in him should not perish, but have everlasting life.

(John 3:16)

For GOD so loved all of His creation that He took the form of man in the person of Jesus of Nazareth, as prophesied by the Hebrew scriptures, to reveal Himslef, not only to the Jewish people, but to all of mankind his very nature, so that whoever would think and live his or her life by the example and meaning given in the life and death of Jesus Christ, would never be separated from GOD but would be reborn into the light of His presence here on earth and be in oneness with Him for all eternity.

An interpretation of *John 3:16*
by the author

Was Jesus Christ the revelation of the *light* referenced in Isaiah? What does it mean to *believe in Jesus Christ*?

The words of John 3:16 for many Christians amount to no more than a rhetorical belief in the reality of Jesus Christ. These Christians can then say that they are living in the *light*. But Jesus Christ asked for more than just rhetorical belief. He asked us to live our lives in oneness with GOD.

Acknowledging and even seeing the light does not assume accepting the light. The fact that a light shines on us does not mean that we are absorbing it. We can cover ourselves up.

John 3:16 has from the beginning of Christian history allowed many Christians to claim exclusivity in the matter of personal salvation based on a rhetorical belief in Jesus Christ. The message of Jesus went far deeper than that. It extends to whoever would think and live his or her life by the example given in the life and death of Jesus Christ. It is they who are reborn into the light of GOD'S presence to be in oneness with him for all eternity.

VII The Presence of the Light

19.
THE LIGHT WITHIN US

(The Apostle Paul was being questioned by the Jews about his belief in Jesus Christ.)

How well the Holy Spirit spoke to your fathers through the prophet Isaiah when he said: 'Go to this people and say you may hear and hear, but you will never understand; you may look and look, but you will never see. For this people's mind has become gross; their ears are dulled, and their eyes are closed. Otherwise their eyes might see, their ears hear, and their mind understand.'

(Acts 28: 26, 27)

What did Paul mean, to hear but not to understand, to look but not to see? What keeps us from hearing and seeing?

The Jews Paul was addressing had not accepted Jesus Christ as their Messiah. Paul was accusing them of hearing but not understanding, of looking but not seeing.

The words of Isaiah are words for all of mankind today. His message was pointed at a state of mind. Isaiah said that the minds of the people had become gross, their ears dulled, their eyes closed. It was a message that said you can not take cover. You cannot live in comfort and look the other way. The people had taken cover by directing all of their attention to the consuming activities of their lives.

We try to escape from the world around us by compartmentalizing our feelings, by living with each feeling isolated from the others. We are like a king in a castle surrounded by high walls. We try to maximize our pleasures and minimize our hurts, trying as best we can to protect ourselves from perils and dangers.

We think and act the same as those in Isaiah's time. We are no different. We compartmentalize our lives to the extent that we only see what we want to see and hear what we want to hear. Life is easier when we compartmentalize our feelings. We can have one personality in the work place, another with our families, another in our competitive activities, and another at our place of worship. For the sake of our reputations and our own peace of mind, we can then go through the motions and give the appearance to others, as well as to ourselves, that we are what GOD wants us to be.

Our institutions are also at fault. Our political parties compartmentalize their agendas, supporting the ones that attract the most votes, leaving other agendas behind regardless of the human impact. Our organized religions do the same, placing reputation and the comfort of tradition ahead of principle.

The problem with this way of thinking and acting is that it blocks out the presence of GOD. He is there waiting for us, but we do not hear him and see him because we have isolated ourselves in our compartments. We pretend to hear him, but we do not hear him. We pretend to see him, but we do not see him. We pretend to think we understand his presence, but we do not understand His presence.

Paul was telling the Jews of his time as he is telling the world today that unless the message of Jesus Christ becomes the framework for our total existence, our lives will be closed to GOD'S presence.

If His light does not shine within us, it cannot shine upon us.

20.
THE HEALING POWER OF THE LIGHT

"Dear Sigmund,
I admit that the techniques and insights that you and your followers have developed are vital to the treatment of troubled people. But there are questions of life, death, meaning and spirituality that you never touch.

Sincerely
Dr. Kenneth C Haugk"

(An imaginary letter to Dr. Sigmund Freud by the founder of the Stephen Ministry, A ministry using Christian healing methods)

"I firmly believe there is a divine light in every human being ever born or to be born"

> Malcom Muggeridge
> 1903–1990

Can the *light* heal? Does evil destroy?

A great mystery of our time is the question of why certain people become saints while others turn out to be evil. An example is the life of Mother Teresa in contrast to the lives of Adolph Hitler and Joseph Stalin. In our own daily lives we see the same contrast. We observe in those around us acts of love among some and acts of selfishness and hatred among others.

In some cases there are conditional factors that have made a very large impact at a young age. Often these are used by psychologists to show that the destructive behavior is irreparable. But even under extreme conditions there isn't always a correlation. There are those who overcome negative influences early on. Also, there are those who break out of the mold later on in their lives and undergo transformations. And then there are those who, coming from apparently normal backgrounds, turn out to be demonic.

The question then becomes: Can the power of the *light* take away even the demonic?

There is ample proof that it can. When it occurs, there is always something of great positive power that comes over the troubled person, and then there is a change. The negative presence disappears. The positive power enters. Proven examples can be found in prisons and in the transforming power of the Alcoholics Anonymous program.

We are not just physical/mechanical/chemical/electrical forms of life. We are spiritual human beings, and our mental and physical health is derived from the presence of the power of GOD within us. As we move toward GOD, we move away from the destructive forces, both biological and mental, that are working to destroy us.

21.
GUIDED BY THE LIGHT

"I rob myself of life's richest possibilities when I stop with the human situation and do not press on to the divine solution".

"GOD may be waiting to show us the next step to take because we have not yet taken the last one he showed us".

"GOD may be working on levels far beyond my comparative analysis of success and failure".

"When GOD gives, man must be willing to accept".

The Back of God Signs of His Presence
Bill Austin
1980 A.D.

What place does GOD have in our lives? Is He there all of the time or does He just show up once in a while? If He is giving us messages as to which direction to take, how can we know what they are?

We think we can control our lives when deep inside we know that this is not the case. When things go wrong, we are suddenly reminded of how little control we have. At death we come upon the final realization of this.

In the time period between our birth and our death, we can view our lives in two different ways:

- We can see ourselves facing the world alone with the control of our lives in our own hands.

- We can open ourselves to GOD'S presence and trust in Him as we allow Him to work in our lives guiding every decision we make.

GOD is ever present in all of His creation. He is everywhere. He is not confined to the space "above" in the Heavens. He is both inside of us and outside of us. We live either alienated from Him or as a part of Him. He only works in lives that open to Him and accept Him. When we open our lives to Him, they can then move far beyond our level of comprehension, in the direction of the divine, unfolding into the richest possibilities.

22.
MY FACE YOU CAN NOT SEE

(GOD is asking Moses to lead the people)

Moses said to the lord, 'thou bidst me lead this people up, but thou hast not told me whom thou wilt send with me....' The Lord answered, 'I will go with you in person and set your mind at rest'...and Moses prayed, 'show me thy glory.' The Lord answered, 'I will make all my goodness pass before you....' but he added, 'My face you cannot see, for no mortal man may see me and live...take your stand on the rock, and when my glory passes by, I will put you in a crevice of the rock and cover you with my hand until I have passed by. Then I will take away my hand, and you shall see my back, but my face shall not be seen.'

(Exodus 33:12-23)

Like Moses, we all long to see GOD, not just to feel His presence, but also to meet him face to face and to know Him. Why will He not let us see His face? Why does He remain a mystery to us? Why does He always step to the side of our perception of His reality?

If we could be face to face with GOD, we would not be mortal. We would not have to battle with the uncertainty of being human. We would be free from the stain of sin. We would be like GOD in His image, as we were in the original creation. We would be not in the image of mortal human beings but in the image of GOD. Our image would be His. We would be divine.

In Exodus we have this revelation not just to Moses, but also to all of mankind. GOD is saying that He is present in each of our lives; although, as we are mortals, we cannot see Him. He is telling us that He exists on the other side of our mortality.

But, GOD tells Moses that even though you cannot see Me, I will be with you. He tells Moses that Moses will see His presence, but only after GOD has passed through Moses' life. GOD'S message to Moses is His message to each of us. *I will make My goodness pass before you.*

Every moment of our lives GOD is watching us, waiting for us to take the next step. He wants us to take the next step, not by ourselves, but with Him. We never know what the direction will be. He asks us to trust the signs that He gives us. He asks us to listen and trust that He is working at levels we do not understand. Whichever direction our steps lead us, He asks us to accept what He gives us. All He demands is our faith in Him. It is a faith that says He will enable us to realize the full potential of what He has given us. This was His message to Moses.

As for Moses, for all of us, the real glory of GOD is not a momentary look at His face. It is an abiding relationship strengthening and preserving us all of our lives for eternity. It is our living with the belief that *Thy will be done* not only *in heaven* but also *on earth.*

23.
RETURNING FROM THE LIGHT

Jesus took Peter, James and John...up a mountain...and in their presence he was transfigured; his face shown like the sun, and his clothes became white as the light...and they saw Moses and Elijah appear.... Then Peter spoke: 'If you wish, I will make three shelters (Tabernacles) here....' While he was speaking, a bright light suddenly overshadowed them.... When they raised their eyes, they saw no one, but only Jesus. On the way down the mountain...when they returned to the crowd...a man...fell on his knees before him...and said, 'have pity on my son; he is an epileptic;' Jesus then spoke to the boy.... He was cured.

(Matthew 17:1-18)

Why did Jesus not encourage his disciples to build the three Tabernacles? Why did the light leave them as suddenly as it had appeared? Why was it that the first act of Jesus after he left the mountain was to cure an epileptic boy?

Peter, James, and John wanted the experience to last. They wanted to build three Tabernacles on the mountain. They wanted to remain in the presence of the light. But, Jesus did not want this. He knew that we could only be aware of GOD'S light for brief moments of time and then only when He has briefly entered and then passed through our lives. We must return to our mortality.

After the transfiguration, Jesus, Peter, James, and John went back down the mountain. Jesus had made it apparent to them that their place was not on the mountain; it was with the people. The first act of Jesus upon his return was to heal an epileptic.

The Christian experience is not one of lasting transcendence into the presence of GOD. It is an experience that takes place only temporarily. It is an experience that takes place in the here and now of this world. It takes place among and between people. Whenever a Christian is brought into GOD'S presence, he or she does not remain there, but is quickly returned to the real world with all of its pain and suffering. Christianity is a religion of people's presence among each other.

VIII
The Apostle Paul—Brilliancy and Turmoil

The Impact of Paul's Letters on Christian Thought

Fifty years after the death of Jesus Christ, it was a pharisaic Jew from Tarsus schooled in the law of the Torah who would set in motion a theology that would establish the pattern for all future Christian thought. Three hundred years later, his letters, which were written to the struggling Christian churches throughout the Roman Empire, by interpreting the meaning of the life and crucifixion of Jesus Christ, would form the theological foundation of Roman Catholicism. Another twelve hundred years later they would spark the Protestant Revolution.

The life and teachings of Paul were, from the moment of his conversion, surrounded by controversy. Not only the Romans, but also his fellow Jews and many of his fellow Christians were disturbed by much of what he wrote and said. As some of his statements are interpreted today in the light of 21st century secular values, the controversy continues.

Of one thing all Christians would agree. His life was suddenly transformed by the experience of the indwelling presence of Jesus Christ. All of his thoughts and all of his actions were in a moment of revelation one day, as he traveled on the road to Damascus, changed. His brilliant mind and all of his physical being from that moment on became focused on one thing and one thing only; revealing to mankind what, according to his belief, had happened in the world 30 years before.

Unlike almost all other great writers and thinkers whose central philosophical themes run in understandable patterns and coherent fashion, Paul's writings often appeared as just the opposite. They often showed what could be described as bursts of brilliance separated by mundane observations, some of them inconsistent with his central theme. It is these *bursts of brilliance*, as they have given insight into the real Jesus Christ and what his life and death meant for all of mankind, that have captivated Christian believers ever since.

Many of his statements show startling insights into the meaning of the Christian experience that are difficult to comprehend. This has not been helped as scholars and theologians over the years have attempted to interpret these meanings. The problem has been made the worse by inaccuracies in translation from the Greek language in which he wrote, as well as debate over which of his letters were actually by his hand.

His ideas not only reflected the impact of the every day Roman influences that surrounded him, but also his own temperament. Both physically and mentally he presents the picture of a driven human being. He worked under extreme pressure, some of it self-imposed and some not. Often he feared for his life. The strong influence of his Jewish educational and religious background is evident. At times he appeared to be boxed in by all of this: the Greco-Roman culture around him, the turbulent age in which he lived, his pharisaic religious upbringing, his fiery temperament.

Parts of his writings show insights of extreme depth and would appear clearly to be inspired not just by his knowledge of the teaching of Jesus Christ but even by the spiritual presence of GOD within his very being. Other parts read more like a list of rules and regulations drawn up by a Rabbi for a Jewish sect. It is for this reason that any study of Paul should be limited to those parts of his letters that clearly may give insights into the Mind of GOD as it was revealed by Jesus Christ.

His core belief, redemption of mankind through Jesus Christ, was not just a call for a rhetorical belief in the Prophet and his teachings; it was a call for a radical restructuring of human nature itself. It was a call for the turning over of one's life. And it was a call, not only to the Jews, but also to each and every individual on the face of the earth. It was a call for a faith in GOD like that of Jesus Christ. What this all truly means remains his message today. It is the reason that the writings of Paul continue to dominate Christian thought.

The Misplaced Emphasis on Paul as a Person

Because of the debate and controversy over Paul's writings, there has arisen in recent years a storm of criticism of him as a person. This has come from groups as divergent in outlook as liberal and middle of the road Christians critical of his views on sexuality, to Jews who see him as a traitor to his Hebraic religious traditions and biased by his Hellenistic Greek education and outlook.

Anything derogatory postulated about him as a person, now 2000 years after his death, can be no more than conjecture and therefore should be viewed with suspicion. What is most important about Paul and where the debate should be taking place is with the insightfulness of his ideas. Many of them offer Christianity's deepest and most far reaching understanding of the life and teaching of Jesus Christ. As such, they offer penetrating insights into the mind of GOD as given by Jesus Christ. Therefore, focusing on Paul the individual often turns out to be no more than a futile effort by those with other agendas designed to discredit the message that he gave mankind, as well as Christianity as a religion. This does not mean to say that we should not closely examine the life of Saul of Tarsus and the times in which he lived.

If he was in fact a messenger, by way of Jesus Christ, of the WORD, how much of what he wrote came from GOD and how much from Paul himself as a vulnerable human being? How much was the result of his pharisaic training and how much came from the inspiration of the teachings of Jesus Christ? How much was a wrong interpretation of the message of Jesus Christ? How much possibly came from his own inner turmoil?

The Early life of Paul

It was not a disciple of Jesus who was to be the distinctive and dominant voice in Christianity throughout the ages, but a Jew born far away from Jerusalem in the town of Tarsus on the coast of what is today Turkey. He was from an influential Jewish family, which we can assume from the fact that they were Roman citizens. They were members of a pharisaic Jewish sect that strictly followed the law of the Torah. In Tarsus, Saul would have grown up surrounded by other pharisaic families, separated from the Greco-Roman community. He would, however, have been exposed from an early age to the outside world. In addition to his pharisaic religious education, his family would have had him educated in Greco-Roman philosophy and rhetoric. He spoke and wrote both Latin and Greek. We can assume that he also understood Hebrew and Aramaic.

He became the key figure in the change of Christianity from a sect of Judaism to a religion independent of Judaism. His writings date from approximately 50–68 A.D., which predates the synoptic Gospels, which are thought to have been written 70–90 A.D. The Gospel of John was written even later. Therefore, his letters can be viewed as the first widely recognized written record of the Christian experience.

He was a figure of controversy from the very beginning. As has been stated, his writings ran from pure brilliance into the deepest reaches of the meanings of the teaching of Jesus Christ to statements on issues that clearly had very little to do with those teachings. He was a person of deep passion who often seemed unable to escape from his pharisaic legalistic thinking. His personality was so powerful that he dominated all of those around him. His Letters strongly influenced the theological foundation of the early Roman Catholic Church and the dogma that followed. The power of one of his insights into the teachings of Jesus Christ; namely his observation relating to justification by faith 1500 years after his death, was so powerful that it sparked the writings of Martin Luther and the Protestant Reformation.

In recent years many of his ideas have been challenged as being of questionable insight, especially those dealing with election, predestination, and the roles of husbands and wives. This has led many Christians to question whether they should accept all that he wrote. It has led to the view among some Christians that he should be considered less a Saint and more a brilliant but fallible human being.

The State of the Roman Empire in His Time

It is not possible to begin to understand Paul's writing without an understanding of the age in which he wrote. When he was writing to the small Christian churches scattered throughout the Roman Empire, Nero was Emperor and the Empire was at the zenith of its military power and intellectual influence. It extended from the Atlantic to the Euphrates and from the North Sea to the African Desert. It controlled 120,000,000 people.

Christianity was just another of the many religious movements in the Empire, but for Rome it immediately presented a problem. Roman society was built on defined class distinctions among its citizens. Society was stratified into those who were recognized as privileged—Roman Citizens—and those less privileged—non-citizens. And then there were the slaves. Christianity was classless. All were equal in the mind of the savior, Jesus Christ. This egalitarian thought belief of Christianity was in direct opposition to the prevailing Roman societal ideas.

There were other problems. A major one dealt with sexual behavior. Many pagan sexual religious practices prevailed in the Empire. Some involved both female and male prostitution. It is reported that there were over 1000 prostitutes at the temple in Corinth alone. There was no sacredness to sex, outside of the elevating experience derived from the pure pleasure of the act. This was its purpose in the pagan rituals. Fertility Gods and Goddesses were worshiped for procreation. Pedophilia and bestiality were accepted practices. Abortion and even the killing of unwanted newborns were common. There was little respect for human life. This view of sexual behavior was in direct contrast to the Christian idea of fornication as a sin and the belief in the sacredness of human life.

Paul's Writing as a Response to Roman Society

The Christian communities were small isolated islands in a vast Roman ocean. From every direction came rejection and persecution.

As a response to this, Paul's concept that only Christians are elected or predestined by GOD was taken on as a core belief. As GOD'S Covenant had once been with the Nation of Israel, it was now with those who believed in Jesus Christ as the Messiah. All society outside of the Christian belief system, including those in Jewish society who did not accept Jesus Christ, was to be viewed as corrupted. All, except for Christians, were destined for damnation.

The idea of being *Chosen* was essential for the survival of the Christian communities. It enabled them to face up to the harsh conditions under which they had to practice their new religion. It therefore became one of the most important concepts on which Paul would build his Church. The concept was not new. It was one that had grown out of the early Hebrew experience and essentially for the same reasons. It was introduced early on in the Torah going back as far as the story of Jacob and Esau. The messianic message from Jesus Christ, like the Torah message from Moses, was an exclusive message. It was available for everyone to hear, but offered no hope of salvation to those who did not accept it. For those who did not, there was only estrangement from the one true GOD. As with Esau, GOD would turn His back on them. In fact, he would *hate* them. It was an idea that continues to exist today with varying degrees of conviction in Judaism, Christianity, and Islam

Today, Christian evangelical fundamentalists view the outside world as Paul did. There is a parallel perception between Paul's view of Roman society and their view of 21st century society. The view of the depravity of all society outside of Christianity is much the same. Those outside the evangelical fundamentalist Christian communities are looked upon as being corrupted and therefore beyond salvation. All non-Christians are living in sin. There is no such thing as a *saved* person outside of the fundamentalist evangelical Christian community. Those outside are viewed as the enemy and a constant threat to the stability of those inside the community. Worshipers are told not to associate with those outside of the community. All of this is largely based on a literal belief in the letters of Paul as the word of GOD. It should be noted that this way of viewing the world is not only found in Christian evangelical fundamentalism. It is also found in the fundamentalism of Judaism and Islam.

The Special Place of Judaism in the Life of Paul

In Paul's letters we often see a certain schizophrenia that shows him trying, but not quite being able to break away from the strictures of the Jewish law. He had been a pharisaic Jew and then one day he was a Christian. Could he in fact totally give up his Jewish way of thinking and looking at the world around him?

The Torah and its interpretations presented a special problem for Paul. He was schooled in the law of the Torah. The Torah and its interpretive written arguments had a comment on every aspect of human behavior. Paul's inclination, based on his early life, was to outline for the early Christians every aspect of their behavior. As a pharisaic Jew schooled in the Torah this is what one would expect him to do, but he was now a Christian. He was a believer in the indwelling transforming power of Jesus Christ. Christianity was a religion that freed mankind from the weight of the law. A life of love, humility, truthfulness—the message of Jesus Christ—would miraculously free one from the weight of the law. This was the reasoning that Jesus Christ had used when he challenged the teachings of Judaism. He did not come like the writers of the Midrash to redefine the law in broad and penetrating legal arguments.

We see that Paul was not able to escape totally from his past. The Christian code of conduct set forth by Paul was in a mind set like the Midrashim commentaries that grew out of the Law of Moses. Paul gave a Christian interpretation of that law just as the Rabbis had used the Midrash to give it their own Hebraic interpretation. Paul's rules were to be the basis for human conduct under the command of a Christian view of GOD.

Paul's Clash with the Jews—Subjugation Under the Law

The clash between Paul and the Jewish community over the relevance of the Mosaic Law became an immediate source of friction. Over the years, the law had been extended further and further into the every day lives of the Jewish people. It went so far as to define every moment of daily existence for the individual Jew. What observant Jews could wear, the times of worship, with whom they could socialize, how they could eat, how they could marry, etc. became all important for a *Torah Life*. Disobeying the law was an act of disobedience that displeased GOD. Jews either obeyed their GOD or did not. It was that simple. It was a law that on the one hand clearly had certain practical benefits for tribal and religious continuity, but on the other was built on a fear of the wrath of GOD in the minds of those who transgressed it, even in the slightest detail. This fear gave tremendous power to the Temple Priests and Rabbis, a power that they would not relinquish.

It was this call to obedience through fear of displeasing GOD that had prompted Jesus to criticize the Jewish approach to the law and brand it as a pagan religious practice built on fear, a practice that demeaned Jewish worshipers in the sight of their GOD. He also criticized the Jewish authorities themselves, who held fast to the law and its interpretations. He criticized the authorities for the power they had assumed over the people through their insistence on adherence to all of the religious practices that had grown out of the law.

Paul ran up against the same form of resistance as Jesus did among the Jewish Rabbis and Temple Priests 30 years after the death of Jesus, even though he made it clear—as had Jesus—that his criticism was not against the Mosaic Law itself. In fact, Paul was in the process of building much of his argument on the moral and ethical foundation of the Mosaic Torah Law and the Bible prophecies. His criticism essentially took two forms, one dealing with the many rules that had grown around the law and the other with the obvious fact that human beings no matter how hard they try can never truly live up to the law.

This argument had far reaching implications. It tied directly into Paul's understanding of the cosmic meaning of the life and death of Jesus Christ. Paul believed that the crucifixion of Jesus was a message to humankind from GOD, a message that His love is absolute. This was demonstrated through the ultimate sacrifice, the sacrifice of His son, Jesus. From that moment on, the sins of mankind were forgiven. Mankind was released from the fear of GOD'S displeasure. The slate was wiped clean. He became as he was before the fall, a perfect creation made in the all-loving image of GOD.

For the Jews, since Adam, man had been in sin and he would remain that way until the coming of the Messiah. This would occur at the end of time. The Torah God was a judgmental and punishing God who would at that time decide Himself who would be forgiven and who would not. There was no forgiveness now. Forgiveness would have to wait. For them, Jesus of Nazareth was not the Messiah. With their Midrashim logic arguing against Jesus being the Messiah, the Jewish authorities turned their backs on Christianity.

The Polarity of His Thinking

The interpretation of the Mosaic Law by Jesus Christ extended it past how one acts to how one thinks. This presented a challenge to the Jews for whom adherence to the letter of the law was all-important. Also, it brought the Christian view of religion to the polar opposite of Roman understanding of the functionality of religious worship and belief.

Whether by actions or thoughts or both, Paul's letter to the Romans describes a Roman society existing in opposition to the Mosaic Law. In Romans 1:24-32 and 2:1-8 we can see from his word description how he viewed this society:

Vileness of their own desires
Degradation of their bodies
Shameful passions
Unnatural intercourse
Males behave indecently with males
Wickedness
Mischief
Rapacity
Malice
Murder
Envy
Rivalry
Treachery
Malevolence
Scandal-mongers
Hateful to God
Insolent
Arrogant
Boastful
No loyalty to parents
No conscience
No fidelity to pledged word
Without natural affection
Without pity

The Roman Empire had no need for Jewish-Christian values. It had developed a social-political system that had allowed it to become the most powerful political and military power on earth. It had done so without Judaism or Christianity. Its one objective, the expansion and the security of the empire overshadowed all else. Its success was evident everywhere, in its engineering, its military superiority, its law, its language, its arts and culture. The sanctity of the individual was defined only in terms of the practical use of the individual to the system and loyalty to the system. Allegiance to the state was given the highest value. The Roman society had prospered without the foreign values that Paul espoused. If the behaviors that Paul described in his letters were evil, it was of no matter. They were acceptable as long as they did not interfere with the objectives of the state.

When we look at the 21st century, we see, as do many evangelical fundamentalist Christians, many of the same behaviors, and this might lead us to the conclusion that they are not only correct in their observations, but that our future will be as bleak as that of the Roman Empire. Many Christians—as well as non-Christians—today hold to this point of view. Roman society was a secular society built on the pursuit of power. Ours is too. It worshiped Gods of its own choosing. We do the same. The Romans were often at the mercy of misguided minds. We often find ourselves at the mercy of the same. Its citizens exercised little or no control over their sexual passions. We have the same dilemma.

Even though we can see these many parallels, as we look more deeply, we know that our society and the Roman society are not the same. Too much history has passed with all of its pain and suffering as well as its creativity and enlightenment, and this has affected the way we think and the way we act. We know more about ourselves than they did 2000 years ago. We know more about why we as human beings think and act the way we do. We see the individual as a mix of Paul's good and bad.

Today, we face complex social challenges in our lives, which demand ethical choices that are far different from those in Roman times. It is true that the words Paul used are an accurate description of a part of human behavior, but the words do not take into consideration the fact that we are a combination of all of them to varying degrees at any moment in time. As absolutes they are an imperfect measure of our responses to life.

We see that Paul's categories of evil are too narrowly defined. Some have the potential to cause far-reaching harm, while others only cause harm to the self, if at all. Certainly murder cannot be equal to arrogance and boastfulness. Some are far too broad in scope. Shameful passions cover far too wide a range of human activity.

Paul was living and writing in a different age and at his own level of consciousness. As brilliant as he was, his knowledge of the world would be considered shal-

VIII The Apostle Paul—Brilliancy and Turmoil

low today. He had no idea as to what makes up matter or what lay beyond the earth and the Sun. Sensitivities to the feelings and emotions of others that we take for granted today were unknown in his time. He used the word *love* as defined by Jesus Christ, but a reading of his letters shows that he did not extend it beyond his flock, and often not even that far. He comes across as a man in battle against all who would not conform to his rules and his point of view. There is no love left for those outside of his point of view. Words and concepts familiar to us today would have drawn a confused blank stare. He never heard Stravinsky's *Rite of Spring* nor would he have understood it; and if he did, he would have considered it an expression of evil primordial sexual desire, not a work of high art examining in musical form the regeneration of life. Likewise, Mahler's expressionistic *Sixth Symphony*, if he had been able to understand it, would have been equally disturbing to him. He was incapable of understanding that the dark inner passions of human nature are not all evil but can be the wellspring from which powerful inner forces can be summoned to bring forth human energy moving us towards creativity.

We have found that few if any can reach the utopian purity that lay on the other side of all of the character faults that Paul describes. At the same time, we have found that some individuals have a purity within themselves that is close to GOD. And, we have found to our surprise that some of those who seem to be close to perfect turn out to be far from perfect.

We have found that many of those who have reached Paul's level of *goodness* have not in fact been Christians, nor had they any more than a passing familiarity with Paul's dictums. We see people throughout the world of all religions who have witnessed by their lives and are witnessing every day GOD'S love for others as seen in the life and death of Jesus Christ.

Today we know more about the GOD revealed by Jesus Christ. We have had time to look deeply into Paul's and other writings about the life of Jesus Christ and to debate what the writings really mean. We have been able to sort out Paul's ideas and to draw the line between those that were his own and those that were from Jesus Christ. We have found new material from archaeological discoveries such as the *5th Gospel of Thomas* that places the teachings of Jesus Christ in a new light. So, today we do not have to take Paul's word for it. We can study Jesus Christ uncolored by Paul's pharisaic bias. We can look beyond the vision that was Paul's. When we do, we find a combination of the pure brilliance of Paul's insights into the teachings of Jesus Christ and the sometimes-extreme biases and emotional turmoil of Paul as a human being.

Another criticism is that Paul does not choose to see the *good* people in Roman Society. No doubt, there were individuals who performed heroic acts of love and mercy. Their actions were grounded on the sophisticated philosophical thought that had come from Greek culture. Some of this thought was in fact borrowed by later Christianity. For Paul, those who were not part of his community were the enemy regardless of how they thought. This is understandable given the way he was treated personally, but it shows he had fallen into the same trap that many Christians today—as well as Jews and Muslims—fall into when they are up against those who oppose them. They look at everyone else as unspiritual and evil. This is especially true of modern day Christians and Muslims who think this way and have the view that those who do not believe exactly as they do are overcome by evil. All non-believers for them are doomed to eternal damnation.

The fact is people pass through various stages in their lives. GOD'S work in the lives of people is always a work in progress. It is through the experiences of our lives that we move closer to or farther away from GOD. So, the line between good and evil is not static and cannot be so easily drawn as Paul—and many modern day Christians, Muslims and Jews—would like it to be.

When we acknowledge this, we see GOD as powerful and redemptive, working every moment in the life of every human being on the face of the earth. We see him as a GOD ready to forgive each of us for any and all of those sins that Paul writes about in his letter to the Romans.

The Theory of His Possible Homosexuality

Paul was single all of his life. His letters showed him wrestling with powerful inner emotions and bodily desires. Under the Jewish law homosexuality was punished by ostracism and even death by stoning. Therefore, it has been suggested that his conversion to Christianity may have been prompted by the sudden realization that under Jesus Christ there was no separation from GOD'S love. All are accepted, including homosexuals. GOD'S love is so strong that there is nothing that can separate us from it. This was not the message of the Torah. There is no hope for the homosexuals in Torah.

This narrow Torah interpretation today has led to a form of homophobia on the part of many Evangelical Christians who believe in the inerrancy of the Christian Old Testament, the inerrancy of the New Testament and the statements on both relating to homosexuality. These Christians join the words homosexuality and fornication as being one and the same. A closer look, however, at the Letters of Paul shows that the issue can not be so narrowly defined.

The interpretation of the word *fornication* taken from the original Greek language used by Paul refers to any kind of impure thought towards either the same or the opposite sex. It is not, therefore, confined narrowly to homosexual relations. It covers any and all impure thought.

The question then becomes: What is an *impure thought*. By definition it is any thought that does not project pure love towards another. The next question then to ask is a rhetorical one: Does this mean that this love can only be expressed male to female and female to male?

An even more accurate interpretation of the word *fornication* from Greek in the way that Paul used it relates in a broad sense to what may be called *spiritual fornication*, that is thinking in any impure way outside of the purity of Jesus Christ. During Roman times when Paul was writing, this would have applied to all of the impure thoughts and actions that were a part of the life style in the pagan society.

This whole issue raises serious questions about accepted sexual behavior of human beings in 21st century society. The biggest question for Christians is whether they should blindly accept the premise of Paul relating to sexual behavior—as well as the very limited and confusing references in the Torah—in its most narrow sense or look outside of it for a broader definition based on the broader message of Jesus Christ. We know that Paul was strongly influenced both by the teachings of the Torah, the social behavior of the Pagan society around him, and even possibly his own sexuality. Therefore, this is an issue that calls for a thorough examination separated from the presumed inerrancy of ancient scripture and the homophobic response of many Christians.

A view of acceptable sexual behavior in the eyes of GOD among many Christians would define it in far broader terms than Paul did; as any relationship that is *pure* between any two people regardless of their biological sex. Purity of thought then would not be measured by the laws of the Torah dealing with sexual behavior or even linguistic interpretations of the Greek meaning of the English word *fornication* in the New Testament, but by the overriding message of Jesus Christ telling us how we should think and act towards each other. These are qualities that Jesus Christ instructed us to apply such as love, devotion, fidelity, respect, honor, and understanding. This message is a far cry from the vitriolic rhetoric that one hears today from parts of the Christian community. It is far from the accepted norms of Orthodox Judaism, Christianity, and Islam. At some point all three of these religions will have to reexamine what Jesus Christ said about how we should love each other and face this issue.

GOD'S Final Revelation of HIMSELF in Jesus Christ

Paul believed that Jesus Christ was GOD'S final revelation of HIMSELF to all of mankind. The act of the crucifixion was an expression of the depth of His love for all of humanity. It was an act that the Jews of the time would know well from their scriptures, a father's sacrifice of His son, the ultimate act of sacrifice. GOD chose the crucifixion because it was the worst and according to Hebrew and Roman tradition the most debasing way a human being could be put to death. It was the ultimate form of societal rejection. Therefore, according to Paul, for GOD it was the ultimate sacrifice of GOD HIMSELF. In the crucifixion, GOD metaphorically showed both the depth of His sorrow for the transgressions of each of us and the extent of His love toward each of us. HIS was a love beyond the dimensions of our understanding.

The Jews of the time could not comprehend this idea. Their God was a God in some distant place who stood in judgment of them. He was a God of harsh judgment. He had given them laws; even telling them how to live their daily lives down to the last detail. Who should be rewarded except the most religious? Why should He care about a person who could not live up to all of His laws? Why have the laws at all if HE is a GOD who loves even those who do not obey them?

Most human beings in the world then, as well as many today, could not fathom the idea that GOD is all loving. For them, GOD had to be both loving and punishing. He had to be a God of judgment and a retributive God of justice. For the Jews, their Hebraic scriptures as well as their life experience pointed to this description of GOD. Punishment and reward had been a part of their history and their individual life experience. This was not Paul's understanding. He, as well as many of the early Christians, understood the new idea about the nature of GOD revealed in the life and death of Jesus Christ.

With his conversion on the road to Damascus, it was this total understanding that drove Paul afterwards every moment of his life. Paul saw the crucifixion of Jesus Christ as the ultimate expression of GOD'S love for all of humankind and the final act of reconciliation that the Jewish people had waited for over their history. And it was for Paul an act of reconciliation offered to everyone, not only to the Jews. It included every person on the earth, even himself, a former persecutor of Christians and a man who had wanted to live by the Torah Law, but was unable to do so.

A New Interpretation of Pauline Theology—The Faith Experience

The question then becomes: Is the *act of reconciliation* free. Is it dispensed to everyone regardless of whether they have followed the law? The answer is *No*. According to Paul, GOD only recognizes those whose lives are changed. The next question then becomes: How is one's life changed?

In 1983, Richard B. Hays, a doctoral student, wrote a thesis entitled *The Faith of Jesus Christ*. It concentrated on several verses from Paul's Letter to the Galatians. His book quickly drew national attention among scholars because it reinterpreted several words from the ancient Greek in which Paul wrote. The new interpretation challenged the accepted belief among many Christians today that one's belief in Jesus Christ as his or her personal savior is all that is necessary for personal salvation.

Quoting from the introductory remarks by Luke Timothy Johnson in the Introduction to the second edition as well as from Hayes himself:

"Hayes invites us to read Galatians (and perhaps Paul's other letters) as a discourse that clarifies and corrects.... Paul does believe that humans are put into a right relationship with GOD through faith. It is not through their own faith, however, but through the faith of Jesus."

And

"...faith is clearly a quality or power by the human person Jesus, not something directed to Jesus by others."

(Introduction)

And to quote directly from Hayes:

"I have grown increasingly convinced that the struggles of the church in our time are a result of its losing touch with its own gospel story. We have gotten 'off message' and therefore lost our way in a culture that tells us many other stories about who we are and where our hope lies. In both the evangelical and liberal wings of Protestantism, there is too much emphasis on individual faith-experience and not enough grounding of our theological discourse in the story of Jesus Christ."

(Introduction)

The value of scholarly religious works such as the one written by Hayes is in its formal academic process. It is a process that allows the author to zero in on a single issue taken from scripture. As with the work of Hayes, the same can be said for the works of Hebrew and Muslim scholars. The shortcoming is that this forces the scholars to tie their conclusions into the past. They are restricted to an interpretation of what was. The questions we must ask in the 21st century are: Can we go beyond this? Can we take from the past and add to it? Are there things we must change?

The brilliance of many of Paul's words is that they reveal a message that cannot be explained solely through scholarship. It is a universal message that takes us beyond scripture. It is a message not only for Christians, but also for Jews, Muslims, and those of all other religious beliefs. It is a message given by GOD to all of humanity. This message is contained in the metaphorical meaning of the life and death of Jesus. It says that all of us are being called on to accept the same power directing and controlling our lives that Jesus had accepted for his own life, even to the point of our own physical deaths. We are being asked to bring into our own lives the same faith in GOD that Jesus had. In doing so, we are to let GOD shape our very existence—as Jesus allowed GOD to shape his. Faith, therefore, is not to be in Jesus—a point that Hayes makes very clear—but is to be in GOD. It is a faith that calls for the same absolute connection to GOD that Jesus had.

Connecting With GOD Through Jesus Christ

The God of the Hebrew Bible was not one connected to the individual. He was elsewhere beyond the individual, looking down, judging and only occasionally intervening. The God of Islam, as He was described in the Koran six hundred years after Jesus, was the same kind of God. He was modeled after the Torah God. This is the God of Judaism and Islam today. This was not Paul's God of Christianity. The God of Paul's Christianity was an active indwelling God working in the lives of Christians every moment of their lives.

Over the course of history we have seen that this *working in the lives* has not come about that easily. This is the important point Hayes makes in his interpretation of Paul's Letter to the Galatians. According to Hayes, many Christians today have gotten *off message*. Although he does not discuss it in his book, we can see that over history many never got the message. They did not understand then

VIII The Apostle Paul—Brilliancy and Turmoil

and they do not understand now that it is not their belief in Jesus Christ that matters but the example of the faith of Jesus Christ in GOD that matters. This is what gave Jesus Christ another dimension. It gave him a oneness with GOD. The Hayes interpretation says that during his life on this earth, Jesus was at one with GOD through his faith.

Many Christians are quick to argue that their faith in Jesus Christ is what connects them to GOD. We can see that, according to Hayes, it is not that simple a formula. It is more than faith as a rhetorical statement in the literary sense of the word. It is a connection with Jesus Christ that can only be made by being like him.

How can we be like him? Paul says by grounding our lives on the life of Jesus Christ as his life was presented to us. In other words, we must think as Jesus Christ thought. Paul tells us we must radically change our very being.

Paul believed that only by living and thinking about our lives like Jesus Christ lived and thought about his can we be connected to GOD. A way of looking at this is to picture a two-way electrical wire connecting each of us to GOD. The wire is made of a material with a high resistance, so that very little current can pass through. For the resistance to be lowered and the current to flow, it must be connected through Jesus Christ. But, that in itself as a rhetorical statement of belief, will not make it flow, as the resistance caused by our preoccupation with all of the things of this world—our worship of other Gods—prevents the current from flowing freely. Its conductivity is dependent on our living our lives as Jesus lived his, so that we can become like him. To the extent we become like him, the resistance is lowered and a stronger current will then flow back and forth through the wire. As we live closer to the life of Jesus Christ, the current will flow more freely both ways between GOD and ourselves. As this takes place, we will find GOD'S presence in our lives.

Unfortunately, most of us live lives swallowed up by the secular society in which we live. Many of us worship false Gods. The society and the false Gods we worship define who and what we are. We don't define ourselves in the model of Jesus Christ. We let other influences define us. This keeps us from being like Jesus. We can make shallow statements about believing, and we can go through the motions by giving the appearance that we believe, but this in itself will not connect us to GOD. It will not free up the resistance in the wire just described. We will not have GOD within.

With a broad-brush stroke, Paul marked for exclusion all those who were not Christians. To him it was a *You're either with us or against us* issue. For him, nonbelievers in Jesus Christ could not be connected to GOD. It was a technical impossibility. Two centuries later, when the image of Jesus Christ and the meaning of belief in him was finally and irrevocably defined for all time by the early Roman Church bishops, a preordained description of Jesus of Nazareth became the institutional belief of all Roman Catholic Christendom. This was carried over into Protestantism in the 16th century, and so exists today throughout all of orthodox Christianity.

For 21st century geopolitical and georeligious society the issues are three:

- For Christians, is simply professing a belief in Jesus Christ all that is necessary, or is there more to it than that?

- Is the description of Jesus proclaimed by Roman Catholic Christendom the real Jesus?

- If a Jew, Muslim, Hindu, Buddhist, or a person of any other faith intellectually rejects the person of Jesus Christ as the reflection of GOD within, will that person then be rejected by GOD? Will salvation then be denied? Will salvation be given only to those who rhetorically profess a belief in Jesus Christ?

- Can a person reflect GOD within in some other way? In our enlightened 21st century secular society, is it possible that there are many individuals, not believing in Jesus as the Christ—and even atheists and agnostics—who are nevertheless living out their lives as Jesus of Nazareth did?

The revelation given by the life and death of Jesus Christ, according to Paul, was a redefinition of the Hebraic nature of GOD and our relationship to Him. Any disagreement with Paul must therefore begin—and discussion of the above questions—not with disagreement over history, Hellenistic influence, Roman Catholic doctrines, dogmas or creeds, but with a refutation of Paul's premise. It must center on a discussion of the nature of the God within and without.

These issues raised by Paul are as contentious today as they were during his time. They are where the debate should be. They are not being debated. They should.

Paul's Insights into the Mind of GOD Absent the Torah

When Paul started writing his letters to the churches, the death of Jesus Christ was still a recent memory in the minds of those who knew him. Paul personally knew many of those who had followed Jesus Christ. Through them he had an intimate knowledge of the teaching of Jesus Christ. In many ways some of his insights penetrate deeper into the life of Jesus Christ than the later purported eyewitness writings in the Gospels.

As with all ancient Christian texts, when reading Paul's letters, it is necessary to separate what was most likely authentically from Jesus Christ from the ideas that were from Paul, the fallible human being. And we must take into account the age in which he wrote. Certainly, Paul's writings about wives being subject to their husbands and man being the head of the woman (Ephesians 5:22), as well as slaves obeying their masters with fear and trembling (Ephesians 6:5) in today's world are rules of conduct that are out of place. They show a lack of understanding of the complexity of the dynamics of human relationships, as we now observe them in the 21st century. It is hard to imagine that these and many other similar ideas that came from Paul are truly from Jesus Christ and will have any applicability at all in future centuries. It is only by an utmost stretch of the imagination that ideas such as these can be taken as the inerrant WORD of GOD.

Critics would argue that it is these inconsistencies that brand the Apostle Paul as an imperfect messenger of the WORD of GOD. They are wrong. His main message has little to do with Pauline codes of conduct such as those just mentioned. His is a message that overall speaks to the truth of the teaching of Jesus Christ. Therefore, in Paul's letters it is always necessary to separate the ideas that were from Paul from those that were from Jesus Christ.

The following Reflections discuss a number of the major insights, which in the author's view, Paul made into the teachings of Jesus Christ. They show how we can open our lives to the presence of GOD. They are meant to reveal to everyone, Christians, Jews, Buddhists, Muslims, Hindus, to all people of the world, the nature of GOD. They reveal HIM as a God who looks upon each of us as a part of HIS perfect creation. They say that no human being should be separated from GOD. They show the road to HIS presence in the life of anyone who lives and thinks his life according, not to any particular religious laws or customs, but to HIS will as it was reflected and later recorded by human beings, not always with perfection, in the life and death of Jesus of Nazareth.

They show a different side of Paul from that held by orthodox Christianity. They challenge all Jews, Muslims, as well as Christians, by warning:

*You must work out you own salvation in fear and trembling; for it is GOD who works in you, inspiring both the **will and the deed**, for his own chosen purpose.*

(Philippians 2:12-13)

24.
MISGUIDED MINDS

In their wickedness they are stifling truth...For all that may be known about God...lies plain before our eyes...they have refused to honor him as God...hence all their thinking has ended in futility, and their misguided minds are plunged into darkness.

(Romans 1:19-22)

If the truth about GOD lies plain before our eyes, why do so few see it? Many choose to live anyway they want. Why do they ignore him? What happens to those who do not honor him?

When we look for GOD, we see him both by the consequences of His presence and by the consequences of His absence.

We do not need religious scriptures to tell us about the consequences of ignoring Him. If we look at the history of mankind, we can see the consequences everywhere. From the rise and fall of ancient Greece, to the rise and fall of Rome, to the rise and fall of Nazi Germany, to the rise and fall of the Soviet Union, everywhere in history we see the consequences for mankind when he has defied GOD.

GOD is not present where evil is. He turns His back on our evil actions. He is not with us when we defy Him. We can see this not only in history, but also in our own lives by observing the self-destructiveness of those who defy GOD.

We can see His presence in the lives of those who are a testament to His love for us. We see Him in the lives of powerful and influential people from all societies and all religions. We see Him in the lives of many who are not well known. We see Him in the inventiveness of scientists whose discoveries improve the lives of people. We see Him in the artists who let us reach into the depths of our human imagination. We see Him in the unnoticed everyday actions of people who help other people.

We also see Him in our physical world, in the beauty of nature and all forms of life. We see Him in the mathematical precision mixed with chaos that forms our universe. We see Him in the complexity of the creation of the human mind and its intelligence to understand His creation.

Paul's message taken in the context of today's 21st century world is telling us that all we need to know of GOD lies plain before our eyes. We only need to open our eyes to see Him. He is telling us that GOD'S revelation of both His nature as well as the consequences of our defiance of Him is evident all around us, and only those who live in darkness with minds misguided do not see Him.

25.
JUDGE NOT

For in judging your fellow man you condemn yourself.
(Romans 2:1)

Why did Paul raise this point with his fellow Christians? Why did they need his advice? Why suddenly, after accepting Jesus Christ, did they turn to judgment of those around them? Why did Paul use the strong word *condemn*?

The early Roman Christians as they were looking at the evils of the Roman society around them were passing judgment on its people. It made them feel good about themselves. It made them feel superior. They felt that they had made the right choice by following the teachings of Jesus Christ and therefore they had a right to pass judgment on the corruption of those around them.

Paul was telling them that it is not for them to judge others. He was echoing the message of Jesus Christ not to judge others but to look inward at one's own sinfulness.

Jesus Christ said that only GOD knows our inner thoughts. Only He knows the desires that drive us. Only He knows who and what we are. Nothing is hidden from Him. Even we ourselves can only see our inner selves dimly.

Paul's is a message that turns us inward and demands our searching to the depths of our souls for our weaknesses. Jesus Christ said it is only after we have done this that we will find the path to our own personal redemption and to GOD.

Judging ourselves opens us to the presence of GOD. Judging others closes off His presence. Looking outward prevents us from looking inward. It is easy to look for faults in others. It is a way to disguise our own faults. It takes courage to judge oneself. It takes no courage to judge others. Judging others closes off having to face ourselves and GOD. It is the coward's way.

26.
THE WEIGHT OF THE LAW ON ALL RELIGIONS

No human being can be justified in the sight of God for having kept the law; law brings only the consciousness of sin...for all alike have sinned,...all are justified by GOD'S free grace alone,...man is justified by faith quite apart from success in keeping the law.

(Romans 3:20-28)

Does GOD judge us by our adherence to religious law, or are we judged by some other means?

Whether it is the Hebrew Bible, the Koran or any other written religious set of rules, the belief is always the same. Our laws are from GOD. They must be followed. The words are inerrant. Disobeying means estrangement from GOD. Our laws are the only true ones. Yours are incomplete and untrue.

Why does religion need laws? Would religion be the same if the laws were eliminated? Would there be a need for priests, rabbis, mullahs, and shamans? Would there be a need for structured institutional religion as we know it? Religious institutions and their leaders would lose their relevance. No longer would they have control over their people. These spiritual leaders have always held tightly to their laws. They have enlarged them, adding their own interpretations. It has always been in their interest to hold fast to the law. It is their justification for what they do. It gives them power and makes them feel important and necessary. It gives them control over their people.

Jesus centered his teaching on a way of thinking that transcended the Mosaic Law. He revealed a new and revolutionary paradigm, one based on a loving and redemptive relationship between GOD and man. In defining this relationship he did not eliminate the law but rather he dismissed the need for adherence to it as a way for man to justify himself before GOD. He dismissed the need to obey it as a precondition for salvation. He said that man was created with an imperfect nature and can never live up to the law. He said that GOD is looking at man in another way.

The very core of ancient Hebrew belief was being challenged. Jesus Christ had redrawn the lines between GOD, Man, and the Mosaic Law. He was challenging the Jews then as he is challenging all of mankind today as to how we are to view religious law in relation to individual salvation.

27.
THROUGH JESUS CHRIST?

If God be for us, who can be against us?...neither death, nor life, nor angels, nor principalities, nor powers, nor things present, nor things to come, nor height, nor depth, nor any other creature, shall be able to separate us from the love of God, which is in Christ Jesus our Lord.

(Romans 8:31-39)

Likewise recon ye also yourselves to be dead...unto sin, but alive unto GOD through Jesus Christ our Lord.

(Romans 6:11)

When Paul uses the words *through Jesus Christ our Lord*, does he mean that the *love of GOD* is reserved only for *us* Christians? Is he saying that all others in the world who are not Christians are separated from *the love of GOD*?

Paul's message was that one must believe in Jesus Christ to be saved. It was a message that gave hope to the small and isolated Christian communities that were being besieged on all sides by both Roman society and traditional Judaism. The Jews and the Romans were actively persecuting Christians. Paul was therefore able to make a clear distinction between Christianity and all else. For Paul, those who rejected Jesus as their Messiah and their Savior were doomed.

For Paul, it was a black or white issue. There are those with Christ dwelling within and those without Christ. Only those with Christ dwelling within can be saved.

This is the belief among many Christians today, and in particular Evangelical Christians, who look at themselves as the early Christians did. They see themselves living in a wicked and corrupt world besieged by non-believers. They take Paul's words as inerrant fact. They look upon themselves as being separated from the rest, as having been elected and predestined by GOD for eternal grace.

But, was this what Jesus meant?

The unique conditions of the time had a profound influence on Paul's theology. As we view the world in the 21st century, we must recognize this and break away from a literal interpretation of Paul's words. We must center our thoughts on the broader message of Jesus Christ, who often spoke in other terms.

To have *the love of GOD, which is in Christ Jesus our Lord,* as understood by many Christians today, is to live life thinking and acting in the same way that Jesus himself thought and acted. It is walking his path. It is having his faith.

Paul was wrong when he confined this exclusively to his Christian community. *The love of GOD* extends to anyone who walks His path, Christians and non-Christians alike. For Christians, as well as all others, nothing can separate the love of GOD from those who direct their lives along His path. But, they must walk His path!

The path is the one Jesus Christ showed the world. This is the message of Jesus Christ for the 21st century. It is the real meaning in a 21st century context of Paul's words, *through Jesus Christ our Lord* and *shall be able to separate us from the love of GOD.*

It is the message of Jesus Christ to those of all religions and those with none at all.

28.
PRESENTING YOURSELF TO GOD

Offer your very selves to him...a living sacrifice.... Adapt yourselves no longer to the pattern of this present world, but let your minds be remade and your whole nature thus be transformed.

(Romans 12:1, 2)

When Paul refers to our *whole* nature does he mean both our physical nature as well as our spiritual nature? How do we remake our physical nature?

Yes, he also means our physical nature. We are to turn over our physical bodies as well as our spiritual being.

To understand the significance of this statement we must look to the beginning of the Hebrew Bible and examine the early Jewish concept of purity and impurity. It was this concept that Jesus Christ challenged.

A detailed account of the pure and the impure is found in the book of Leviticus where there is a description of impure animals and physically diseased persons. The impure is described in terms of those afflicted by diseases such as ulcers, sores, and leprosy that are any sort of disorder, *either loathsome or infectious.*

The distinctions between the pure and the impure were further developed throughout Jewish history and expanded to include foods for consumption. The reason was always a practical one that even today we can understand. The objective was to preserve the health and well being of the Jewish tribal unit.

When Jesus Christ appeared—more than 1000 years after the book of Leviticus—He refuted the mindset of the Jews regarding their interpretations of the Mosaic Law and the rules of conduct that had grown around it. At the same time, He challenged their definition of purity by giving the physical body a spiritual dimension that saw both the physical and the spiritual as having equally high value in the eyes of GOD, regardless of visible outward flaws. He demonstrated this when he healed the sick. He touched and healed impure untouchables such as lepers. He befriended impure unclean individuals such as prostitutes.

The Apostle Paul did not look upon this definition of purity of the body in the same way as Jesus Christ. He looked upon mankind as being burdened by earthly unclean physical/spiritual desires. He looked at the body as weak and sinful. He took on the Jewish view. He only saw it as a vessel to contain the soul.

Paul departed from the teaching of Jesus Christ and reached back into the ancient Hebrew texts using the concept of diseased persons with physically unclean bodies as a metaphor for the physical/spiritual condition of mankind. In his letters he even related this to the weaknesses of his own body.

Paul and Jesus Christ looked at the human condition through two different lenses. Paul was an imperfect human being as well as a product of his own pharisaic religious training. This was his lens.

Paul's reasoning was correct in that the transformation of one's nature cannot take place without the abandonment of all physical attachment to the profanity of this world. The whole person; the physical body with its weaknesses, as well as the soul, *our whole nature*, must be transformed.

Jesus Christ did not see the body as unclean but along with the spirit as the perfect unflawed metaphysical creation of GOD. He saw in both the body and the spirit the possibility of perfection. The idea of one's *whole nature* being transformed both physically and spiritually by turning one's life over to GOD was at the center of his teachings.

29.
A GOD OF ANGER AND LOVE
OR
A GOD ONLY OF LOVE

Love your neighbor as yourself;...the whole law is summed up in love.

(Romans 12:10)

Love is patient; love is kind and envies no one. Love is never boastful; nor conceited, nor rude; never selfish, not quick to take offence. Love keeps no score of wrongs; does not gloat over another man's sins, but delights in the truth.

(I Corinthians 13:4-7)

Must we love all others, even those who hurt us, who reject us? Will GOD be angry with us, withhold His love from us if we don't? Or, will He continue to love us? Does GOD Love everyone?

Throughout human history, in the early stages of all religious thought, it was common for man to personify the nature of GOD in terms of his own human emotions. The interpretation of the nature of GOD in the Hebrew Bible was no exception. The God of the Hebrew Bible was not always a God of love. He was a God of both anger and love. He acted like we act. He rewarded for obedience and He punished for disobedience. This is still the belief of Judaism today. Events such as the Holocaust are studied by Hebrew scholars with the question: Was it just another historical event in the long history of Jewish persecution or was GOD angry with the Jewish people, and if so, why?

The Apostle Paul takes us one step beyond the Hebrew Bible and its characterization of the duality of GOD, but not as far as he should.

In his letters he writes about GOD'S love, but unlike Jesus Christ he directs his observations to those within the Christian communities. He does not extend the idea of GOD'S love to all people in the then Roman world, both Christian and non-Christian. He paints those outside of the Christian communities with a broad-brush stroke as sinful people without love, respect, fidelity, trust, and honor. He does not affirm that the love of GOD extends to them.

Jesus Christ affirmed that GOD'S love is a love that extends towards all of mankind: Christians, Jews, pagans. It is not, as Paul would have it, limited to any special predestined or elected group of people.

By the death of Jesus Christ GOD showed the world that He is not a God of anger as was portrayed in the Hebrew Bible but a God of unconditional love. He is not a God who chooses to punish and to reward.

In the crucifixion, GOD revealed to mankind His meaning of what it means to *love*. He pulled us through the limits of our self centered earthly barrier into His own heavenly dimension and revealed His love for all of us by sacrificing, for our redemption, the life of His earthly son, a sacrifice He knew, we in our human way of understanding things, could comprehend as the ultimate sacrifice. He told us we are to respond to each other with this same depth of love. He said we must not limit our love only to those we favor. He said you must *love your neighbor as yourself*. Then, to make sure we understood, He defined the word *neighbor* in the parable of the Good Samaritan.

Finally, to make sure again that we understood the universality of His love, He said in the dying words of Jesus Christ; *forgive them for they know not what they do.*

30.
THE MEANING OF THE RESURRECTION

He appeared to Cephas, and afterwards to the twelve. Then he appeared to over five hundred of our brothers at once, most of whom are still alive, though some have died. Then, he appeared to James, and afterwards to all the apostles. In the end he even appeared to me.

(I Corinthians 15:5-9)

What is the importance of the resurrection? How much proof do we have that it happened? Would Christianity be the same had it not happened?

Unlike many other phenomena recorded in the Torah; the Creation of the Garden of Eden, Moses receiving the Ten Commandments, the Exodus from Egypt, the resurrection of Jesus Christ is a claim that was recorded at the time by eye witnesses with historical credibility. When The Apostle Paul wrote his letters, many of those who were followers of Jesus Christ were still alive to tell the story. Paul himself had witnessed the presence of Jesus Christ on the road to Damascus.

Beyond this there is an observation that gives strong credence to the argument. The Christian movement had been crushed by the crucifixion. Their Messiah had been brutally executed. Both the Jewish and the Roman authorities had turned against the followers of Jesus. Suddenly, their leader no longer existed. Dispirited and doubtful, they must have been left to wonder whether their Messiah had been just another of the many spiritual leaders who were suddenly to appear and then disappear to be forgotten in time.

But just as suddenly they were elevated and energized and took on a resolve that for many led to total ostracism within their families and communities. The risks in fact were so great that some ultimately lost their lives. Clearly, something unexplainable in human terms occurred shortly after the death of Jesus Christ.

2000 years later, the resurrection story as told in scripture is debated as to historical fact, and there is ample evidence to suggest that it can be disputed as to the details of how it happened.

Was Jesus physically real or did he just exist within the minds of those who saw him? Was his body laid in a tomb? Did the entrance stone roll away? One thing is certain. The arguments that he was not crucified are very thin. The first writing about his death and resurrection came from those who had witnessed this event. After his crucifixion these writings state that as many as 500 witnessed his presence. Several years later, although he did not appear in person, he spoke to the Apostle Paul, totally transforming Paul's life.

The meaning of the message, metaphor or other, coming from the crucifixion of Jesus Christ is authentic. It was 2000 years ago and is today a direct challenge to the definition of the nature of GOD as found in Judaism and Islam.

GOD came to men and women incarnate in the person of Jesus Christ. He told them to be like I am in him. His message in the resurrection was that if we live our lives by the example of the resurrected Jesus Christ, we too, like Jesus Christ, will be resurrected into GOD'S eternal dimension.

31.
CHRIST WITHIN

We too have put our faith in Jesus Christ in order that we might be justified through this faith, and not through deeds dictated by law;... The life I now live is not my life, but the life that Christ lives in me.

(Galatians 2:15-20)

How does Jesus Christ come to live in a person? When he does, what happens to the person? Why is the law of the Torah—and the Koran—then unnecessary?

Unlike Judaism and Islam, Christianity is a religion that calls not only for a belief in GOD but for a belief that GOD enters and then is present within the person. The Eucharist (Last Supper) is a material expression of this. The body and blood—in the form of wine and bread—of Jesus Christ is taken into the supplicant, and as this occurs, miraculously GOD in the form of Jesus Christ, comes into the person. Paul is explaining that when this happens, the law—the rules for conduct laid out in the Torah—are no longer relevant, since GOD himself becomes the underlying determinant of the person's behavior.

Belief in this calls for an act of supreme faith. We must not only believe in the existence of GOD but also that GOD is within our very being in the here and now. Our thoughts and actions then cannot be conditional. There must be a willingness to risk everything, even our lives. We have seen this kind of faith and its results in many holy individuals as well as ordinary Christians—and others—throughout history. Human self centered and earthly desires are overcome by GOD'S presence within.

Paul is saying that GOD in the form of Jesus Christ lives in him and that this is the controlling force behind his behavior, not his obedience to the man made law of the Torah. Paul is elevating GOD above the Torah as both the motivator/determiner and the judge and jury of his—Paul's—life.

32.
EVIL

For the fight is not against human foes, but against cosmic powers, against the superhuman forces of evil…

(Ephesians 6:12)

Is there such a thing as evil? If so, exactly what is it? Does it have power over our lives? On a broader scale, is it the cause of man's inhumanity to man? Using man as its surrogate, has it set out to destroy our world? Will it succeed?

Evil can be defined as a destructive dehumanizing force that denigrates and destroys the very act of human existence.

History can be interpreted in these terms. It can be seen as a war between the positive forces of good and the destructive dehumanizing forces of evil. The tendency of man to be driven by the forces of evil can be seen as the causal factor behind much of the past as well as present human degradation and suffering in our world. From the wars of the Middle Ages, to the German Holocaust, to the tribal genocide in Africa, to the jihad inspired terrorist suicidal acts in the Middle East, there is ample proof that the primary causal factor is man's willingness to be taken over by the forces of evil.

Evil may be taking a new form unknown in the Apostle Paul's time, as man denigrates his environment and opens to question whether the planet earth can continue to support him. We see that our human species in recent years has become a determinant part of the denigration of our interdependent ecosystem. The extent of the impact of humans on this ecosystem may determine the continued existence of the human species.

We have ample evidence that the superhuman forces of evil to which Paul refers are real and that they exist both inside and outside of each of us. We fool ourselves if we brush this all off as an archaic religious idea. We should take heed of Paul's warnings about the power of evil. Its power is truly cosmic.

33.
YOUR OWN SALVATION

You must work out your own salvation in fear and trembling; for it is God who works in you, inspiring both the will and the deed, for his own chosen purpose.

(Philippians 2:12, 13)

How hard is it to be saved? How does GOD work in us? What must be our role?

Most religions work under a simple formula. GOD is up there. We are down here. If we follow a certain set of rules, GOD up there will favor us. Then we will be saved.

Christianity does not work that way. It is different. The GOD of Jesus Christ is not in some far distant place. He is in the here and now. He is in the life of each of us. He is a universal GOD who works in the lives of everyone, not only Christians.

As GOD works in our lives, individual salvation takes the form not of compliance to law or ritual but as an inner struggle to find GOD'S purpose for our lives. It is a struggle that takes place between negative forces such as hatred and jealousy and envy and the positive force of love.

As this struggle takes place, GOD is always present. He is there to work in the lives of those who invite him in. But He is not there to take over the struggle. He is only there to help in the struggle. It is up to each of us alone to enter into the struggle and fight against the negative forces that pull us away from GOD.

The Christianity of Jesus Christ is a religion that challenges every person. It calls every person to work out his own salvation, as Paul writes, *with fear and trembling*. There are no worldly intermediaries. There are no rituals, pilgrimages, daily prayers, sacred rites, or holy shrines that can guarantee salvation. What happens must come from within. What takes place must take place from within, in the depths of one's soul.

It is in these depths that GOD waits to be called.

34.
PRESSING FORWARD

Forgetting what is behind me, and reaching out for what lies ahead, I press towards the goal to win the prize, which is GOD'S call to the life above, in Christ Jesus.

(Philippians 3:13, 14)

How can we forget our past and reach out for what lies ahead?

Many of the experiences from our past hold us back, drag us down, and sap the energy from us. These experiences work against us mentally as well as physically and keep us from moving forward with new energy, enthusiasm and ideas. In the extreme, these experiences can lead to severe depression and even suicide.

To move forward with creative energy, we know that we must remove many past experiences from the control that they have over us. But how do we? The experiences are inside of us, influencing every thought, every move. Some have been so traumatic that they seem to be etched in the granite of our minds. We move throughout life carrying the weight of them.

Is it possible to wipe the slate clean? The Christian experience says that it is. Christianity is a religion not just of atonement for past sins, it is a religion that removes human failure and removes it forever. It is a religion of renewal.

Through the mystical experience of rebirth, Christians are reborn into the presence of GOD. With this rebirth, Christians give their lives to GOD, and by doing so accept His purpose for their lives. Then they can no longer be held back by their past. All that is left is the possibility to move forward into the future that GOD has prepared.

How do Christians become what they become, and into what are they reborn? They are reborn into the presence of GOD by accepting the life of Jesus Christ as the one determining how they are to think and act. They are then reborn into a person like Jesus Christ. This is the mystical experience Christians seek to have.

In this mystical experience the board is wiped clean and they become new people. They are recreated in a new form. They become a person at the same time living here in this world and in the other dimension, a person in union with GOD.

35.
HAVE NO ANXIETY

Have no anxiety, but in everything make your requests known to God in prayer.... Then the peace of God, which is beyond our utmost understanding, will keep guard over your hearts and thoughts.

(Philippians 4: 6, 7)

Why must we block out all feelings of anxiety about the future in order to have the peace that passes all understanding? Does faith overcome anxiety? If so, faith in what?

To have anxiety is to fear for the future. To fear for the future is to sense that at any moment we may lose control over the future.

Just before an earthquake, animals become nervous and hide wherever they can to find shelter. They feel a sense of loss of control over their environment.

Like animals, humans experience the same nervousness whenever conditions around them change. One reason is that in the past we have all experienced unexpected outcomes. These unexpected outcomes have come suddenly at unexpected moments in time and from unexpected directions.

At birth there is no fear of the unexpected. In youth there is little of this sense. That is why the young will take risks that older people won't; however, as the years wear on, with the first negative experience and then more as time passes, fear of the unexpected becomes stronger. Ultimately it takes the form of anxiety towards the expected outcome of impending death.

Unlike animals, humans use self-confidence as pretence to hide the fear of the unexpected that lies underneath in the subconscious. Behind the surface of our self-confidence, though, is always the underlying thought that the unexpected may be just around the corner.

Jesus Christ said that we must remove from our subconscious every vestige of fear for the future. He said we must have faith that GOD will take over our future. He said that this faith cannot be conditional. It must be total. It must have the same depth and conviction that he referred to when he used the expression, *If you have faith....* And it must even include fear of death.

It is only after we have taken this final leap of faith that we can experience the peace to which Paul refers, and it is only then that we can truly be ready to *make our requests known to GOD in prayer.*

36.
THE HIGHER REALM VERSUS THE EARTHLY REALM

Were you not raised to life with Christ?...Then...Let your thoughts dwell on the higher realm, not on this earthly life.

(Colossians 3: 2, 3)

What is the higher realm to which Paul refers? What is the difference between the higher and the lower realm? How do we connect to the higher realm?

All religion from the beginning of human consciousness has been an attempt to connect to the higher realm. Priests, shamans, healers have always staked their authority on being able to make this connection.

Jesus Christ, in the 5th Gospel of Thomas found at Nag Hammadi, defined the higher realm in terms of a parallel reality, a reality that coexists on earth and in heaven. He spoke of a heaven that is *all around you*. He introduced the idea that man in his physical, earthly form can live at the same time in this higher realm. By his life, death, and resurrection he showed mankind that the higher realm transcends the earthly one.

The *Higher Realm* for Judaism had over its religious history been defined in terms of a separation between the material world and the mystery of GOD above. The same understanding was presented by Mohammad in the Koran.

Jesus Christ introduced the idea to the Jewish people that by being like him, they could live in the earthly realm and in the higher realm—heaven—at the same time. He told them they are offered this possibility by a GOD who exists in space and time in all dimensions at the same time.

37.
FRAGMENTED THROUGH THE PROPHETS

When in former times God spoke to our forefathers, He spoke in fragmentary and varied fashion through the prophets. But in this final age He has spoken to us in the son... The stamp of GOD'S very being.

(Hebrews 1: 1-3)

If as Paul states, the messages of the prophets were fragmented and varied, how much of them can we believe? Are there dangers in looking at every word of the Hebrew scripture as the inerrant word of GOD? Will we be misled?

Paul is attempting to explain away the contradictions between the teachings of Jesus Christ and the words of Hebrew scripture.

During Jesus' ministry he questioned Judaism on two fronts; one the Hebraic law that had grown out of the Hebrew Bible over the centuries, and the other the inerrancy of parts of the Hebrew Bible itself.

The teaching of Jesus Christ relating to the nature of GOD was in many respects a contradiction of the definition of nature of the God of the Hebrew Bible. He changed the definition of the absolute nature of GOD that had been accepted by Judaism.

The Hebrew Bible set out the foundation for Christian theology but only, as Paul states, in fragmented and varied form. Much of it has no place in Christian theology. It cannot be taken as the final word as to the nature of GOD. Only GOD as expressed in the life of Jesus Christ can.

We must look to the life of Jesus Christ for the complete and final word as to the nature of GOD. All else from before him came to us *in fragmented and varied fashion*. We must critically examine every word of the Hebrew Bible and cast aside those portions of it that are not of Jesus Christ. The word of Jesus Christ, not the word of the Hebrew Bible, is the word of GOD.

IX
The God They Think They Know

The Torah God
The Triune God
The God of Jesus Christ

The God of the Torah began as more than just the Creator of the Universe and giver of the law. He had human emotions. And these human emotions were the same as those of His human creation, man. Like man, He had a dark and fearful side. But, He was not like any man. He was like a father. He was perceived in the eyes of His people as a small child looks with fear and respect at a powerful and protective father. Like a father, He could be loving, merciful, and kind, but then just as quickly He could be manipulative and punishing.

In the very beginning of man's appearance on the earth this God of the Torah would cast Adam out of the Garden of Eden for his disobedience, to live by the sweat of his brow. He would do the same with his mate, Eve. Years later, as a punishment for the disobedience of their offspring, He would bring a great flood upon the earth when all but His *Chosen* would perish. Years after the Flood, as a test of faith, He would call the first Jewish patriarch, Abraham, to kill his son Isaac.

He was the exclusive God of the Jewish people as well as their protector. In their Egyptian captivity 1000 years after Abraham had died, He would stand by as Pharaoh killed every first born child. He would allow Moses to survive, so that in later years Moses could lead the Children of Israel in their Exodus out of Egypt.

When He gave His law to the Nation of Israel, He made a covenant with its people. He said that as long as you obey Me, I will protect you. He said He would only punish them if they disobeyed Him. Later, when they did disobey, His anger was to be feared. His judgment could be severe. Then, He showed no mercy to the Nation of Israel.

He was also a warrior God who would bring victory in battle to the Nation of Israel. He was by David's side when David's army slew the Philistines, the Moabites, the Syrians, the Edomites, the Ammonites, and the Amalekites. Their destruction was part of His plan. They were a threat to the reign of David and the future kings after his reign. The cause was always His cause. It was not to be questioned. The outcome was always connected to the continuity of the history of the Nation of Israel and the lessons learned from their obedience or disobedience. Their history was always about the God of Israel favoring His *Chosen* people. It was always about their special destiny as His *Chosen* people. Whatever happened, it was always assumed to be woven into His Covenant with His *Chosen* people.

None of the Kings of Israel were punished by their God for going to war and slaughtering their enemies. It was enemy blood, not Israelite blood. There was no mercy shown towards the vanquished. In the mind of the people of Israel, the victories in battle were always a part of His plan. They were of His will. He was their protector. Battles won against great odds were His miracles and they were rewarded as a part of His Covenant with their nation.

At times He performed miraculous acts. He separated the sea to allow the Jews to escape from Egypt. Joshua could not have brought down the walls of Jericho with a blast of a ram's horn if the God of Israel had not been there to aid him.

He was also a personal God who could give comfort to those overcome by pain and suffering. He brought them relief. He could be called upon to protect them against their enemies. He could strike down and plunge into a fiery furnace the enemies of those who believed in Him. He could give them vengeance. He could shield those who obeyed Him from their enemies. He could bless the righteous. He was their shelter and refuge. For those who believed in him, He could be the light of their salvation. There was nothing they needed to fear.

As time passed, He became a God of the law. It began as His law written in His hand. It defined the actions forbidden by the people of Israel. It passed out judgment on those who disobeyed it. The law started with just a few commandments, but as time passed and the Hebrew society became more complex, it became a law of many words and many interpretations. Even the interpretations remained His law, although they were now coming not from Him but from those who were interpreting what they thought He meant. Then it became necessary to devise subsets to the original law. These were rules and regulations related to every area of the lives of the people, such as how to eat, how to pray, how to worship, how to dress, how to marry, and how to bury the dead. They became necessary, not so much to please their God, but to assure that the people of Israel would continue to exist as a unified tribe and nation.

This was the Jewish peoples' understanding of the nature of their God and their law when Jesus Christ, 2000 years after the death of Abraham, lived among them preaching about a new and radically different vision of God and the Hebrew scriptures. His was a vision that contradicted the Jewish view of the nature of God, as well as the body of laws and rules of behavior that had been woven around the original commandments. He did not dismiss the Hebrew Bible or the Mosaic Law. On the contrary, he rested his new theology on the prophecies of the Hebrew Bible and its law. But, the overall view of the nature of GOD and how humankind is to respond to him was different.

It was a message that was to bring an end to Jewish History. Israel would no longer be a nation. Jews would no longer have an exclusive relationship with their God. There would be a new kind of covenantal relationship, this one between GOD and all of mankind. It would be a covenantal relationship that redefined the relationship between man and GOD and in doing so redefined the very nature of GOD Himself.

The God of Jesus Christ was not an exclusive God, as the God of the Nation of Israel was. He was a God not of a nation but of the world. The God of Jesus Christ was a God for everyone, no matter who they were. He valued every human being. In His eyes everyone was His child; the rich, the poor, those with hope, those who had lost hope. He was a God ready to show His love towards anyone who asked and even those who didn't.

He was not a God of divine retribution. Nor did He lead armies into battle. He gave those who followed him not victory over other people or nations; He gave them victory over evil. He was a God who rejected the temptations of worldly power. He worked not with outward signs such as seas dividing or walls tumbling, but quietly in the hearts of people.

He did not punish those who did not obey Him. He did not cause pain and suffering to His people. He defined pain and suffering as a condition of life and then said He would help them to live with pain and suffering. He brought to those who followed him a peace that passed all understanding, a peace that would overcome all pain and suffering. It was a peace that showed those who followed him the path to His presence in eternity. It was a path that promised eternal life.

The coming of the Messiah had been prophesied in the Hebrew Bible. The fulfillment of this prophecy, for the Jews, was to reveal the Kingdom of GOD here on earth, at the end of time. Also, it was to reveal the true nature of GOD.

The Jews at the time of Jesus assumed that this would incorporate the fulfillment of their idea of Israel as a powerful and influential nation. This is how they interpreted the prophetic messianic vision in their Torah. But Jesus Christ had more to say about their nationhood. He said that fulfillment is to come from the inside of Jewish men and women, not come from the outside in terms of worldly power and influence. He invited Jewish men and women to enter GOD'S grace in the here and now and to leave all other ambition aside, including the ambition of nationhood.

Jesus Christ presented a redefinition of the way Jews were to respond to GOD. The God of Jesus Christ was a God who asked every person to turn his life over to Him so that His purpose in that life can be fulfilled. The Torah God did not require this. The Torah God was a God who required every Jew to engage in a life long study of the Torah so that he could live a Torah life in obedience to GOD.

There were other differences. The Torah God was a retributive God to be feared. The God of Jesus Christ was a God who could not be feared, as He was a God of love incapable of retribution. The Torah God was a God who punished those who did not obey him. The God of Jesus Christ was a God who defined punishment as estrangement from GOD.

How did the Jews come upon their definition of the nature of their God? On what grounds was it challenged by Jesus Christ? Can it be challenged using Genesis itself, using the very words that appeared there? The Jews believed that each word of the Torah was sacred and therefore could never be changed except by GOD Himself. Man could only interpret the Torah, not change it. Is it possible that Jesus went back to the very beginning and saw an error? We must go back to the very beginning of the Torah and try to find the answer.

As we examine a single line in the Book of Genesis, we find the source of two opposing interpretations of the nature of GOD, one the Jewish interpretation and the other the interpretation that was given by Jesus Christ. Genesis describes GOD'S creation of man as follows:

Let us make man in our image and likeness.

(Genesis 1:26)

The key words are *our image*. If man was originally made—before the fall—in GOD'S image, what was, and is, GOD'S image? The view of Jesus Christ was that it is an image of love, perfection, and harmony. It is an image of enlightenment. It is a heavenly image.

The Jewish interpretation of the nature of GOD was not the same. The Torah makes that unquestionably clear. It is based on a statement made later on by the serpent to Eve just before the temptation:

*Then your eyes shall be opened, and ye shall be **like Gods, knowing good and evil**.*

(Genesis 3:5)
(Author's bold)

The Tempter is telling Eve after she eats from the tree of *knowledge of good and evil*, she will become like a God. The Tempter then goes on to describe **the definition of the nature of GOD** as a deity **with knowledge of both good and evil**.

The nature of GOD not previously defined in Genesis was now for the first time being defined. The serpent is in effect giving GOD the same nature as that of man as we know him to be, a living thing having knowledge of both good and evil. The serpent (tempter) is making Him an anthropomorphic God! But, we must ask the questions: Who was defining His nature? Was it GOD Himself? No, the definition of His nature was coming from the serpent, a liar and a deceiver. GOD is, according to the serpent, a creator with knowledge of both good and evil, and God is like the man He has created.

This was the definition that would be accepted by the Jews. Their God would be like man. He would be anthropomorphic.

Then comes the question: What kind of man? Would He be like any man? No, He would be like a father. He would be a powerful stern and protective man with a paternal love towards His children. Like a father; He could be angry, He could be vindictive, He could punish, He could be jealous, He could reward, and He could take away. He could even be a murderer of enemies. This was to be the nature of the monotheistic God who would dominate the Torah. This would be the scriptural reference point for the thoughts and actions of the Jewish people. This was the nature of the God on which the Hebrew Bible would build its theology.

The question must be asked today, as Jesus Christ asked two thousand years ago: Is this definition true? Is it what GOD is? Can this Hebrew vision of the nature of GOD that became the core definition from the beginning of its history be trusted?

This was not the picture of the God of Jesus Christ. He tells the Pharisees in the Gospel of John:

IX The God They Think They Know The Torah God The Triune God The God of Jesus Christ

Your father is the devil, and you chose to carry out your father's desires. He was a murderer from the beginning, and he is not rooted in the truth; there is no truth in him. When he tells a lie, he is speaking his own language, for he is a liar and the father of lies.

(John 8:44)

The difference between the God of Jesus Christ and the God of the Jews becomes clear. We can see in the Book of Genesis that when GOD made man in His image, man had not yet sinned. He had not yet eaten of the tree of good and evil. He was not like we are. He was a different living being. As he had no sin, he was pure and good. He was incapable of anything but love. Original man existed as a living human being in the image of a God of pure love. This was the picture of the God illuminated by the life and death of Jesus Christ. It was not the picture of the Hebraic image of the nature of GOD.

Unlike the Torah and its commentaries, where the nature of the Jewish God was defined over the millennia by means of the oral and then written word, the nature of the God revealed by Jesus Christ was beyond being revealed orally or in words. His was a God revealed by his life and death as a person. His followers, based on first and second hand knowledge, wrote down, within the first 90 years after his death, stories that described that life and death. In their own imperfect way, these stories present Jesus Christ as a reflection of the mind of a God of love and love only. They show his life opening a path to GOD not made possible by the Torah. It is a path leading to a perfect union with a perfect GOD, the same union that had first existed between GOD and man in the Garden of Eden before the fall of man. The life of Jesus Christ revealed a way of thinking and living that would bring men and women into an eternal and perfect union, not with the God as defined in the Torah, but with the God as defined by Jesus Christ, a God of pure love.

This was a picture not only at variance with the Hebraic description of the nature GOD, but also at variance with the Hebraic understanding of GOD'S will for our relationship to Him. The God of Jesus Christ was a God who values every person on this earth, so much so that in an act that Jews could understand from their own biblical history—a father's sacrifice of his son—He sacrificed His own son as an symbol of His love. He revealed Himself as a God of forgiveness who does not require us to meet the demand for perfection that the God of the Hebrew Bible requires. By His mercy He offers forgiveness to those who make every effort to think and live as Jesus Christ did. This is His only requirement.

Does this mean that the Hebrew image of GOD held throughout all of Jewish history, and also accepted by Islam, is not true? If so, from the beginning the theologies of Judaism as well as Islam have been flawed.

Why did the Jewish authorities 2000 years ago resist the message of Jesus Christ so strongly? Why have the Jewish people over the following 2000 years resisted it so strongly? The answer is that Jesus Christ challenged the vision of the God that had been the Torah vision from the beginning of Jewish history. This is the reason they rejected him.

Where did this new vision of GOD come from? Was it just from a reinterpretation of a few lines from Genesis? How do we know it was authentic? Out of nowhere there appeared a young Nazarene preaching about a different kind of God. He spoke as if he were speaking the very WORD of GOD itself. How did he know what he knew? On what authority did he say what he was saying? Most importantly for the Jews: Where could what he was saying be found in the Torah, the WORD of GOD? It was a vision of GOD and man's relationship to GOD in very many ways contrary to the vision encompassed in the Torah and the scholarly interpretations that had grown out of it over the course of Jewish history.

If Jesus had been a prominent temple priest who had taken on a new and radically different view of the nature of GOD and the relationship of all Jews to that GOD, no doubt he would, after a period of vigorous debate, have been rejected. These views would have been considered by the ruling orthodoxy a blasphemy against the WORD of GOD. But the family of Jesus was not a member of the priestly hierarchy. Nor was his father an intellectual. Joseph was only a carpenter. Jesus too was most likely a carpenter. His ministry, therefore, did not introduce these ideas at a high intellectual level. Jesus went directly to the people.

He was first heard from at the age of 12 on what is thought to be his first trip to Jerusalem. He wandered off among the crowds and was separated from his parents, Joseph and Mary, for 3 days. When they finally found him, he was in a Temple discussing the Torah with the Temple Priests. It is noted in scripture that his knowledge of the Torah astounded the Priests at the Temple. There is no mention of any radical ideas, only of his superior knowledge.

Then his life becomes a blank for the next 18 years. There is no record of where he lived or what he did. All that is known is that his father, Joseph, was a carpenter, probably a scaffold builder, and there were other children. In fact, he may have had a twin brother. We are also told in the scriptures written long after his birth—and in some part disputed today—of his miraculous Virgin birth, of which he may or may not have been aware. Suddenly, at the age of 30 he reappeared on the scene.

The question of how this young Nazarene became what he became has been debated over the centuries, and not without a considerable amount of bias. For many Jews the influence was Hellenistic—the spread of Greek philosophy throughout the area following the conquests of Alexander—and for many others the influence was from the eastern religions such as Buddhism. Jesus lived 500 years after Buddha. Buddhist, as well as Hellenistic thought, was well known in Jesus' day throughout the Roman Empire. For many Christians the very idea of any outside influence other than from GOD would be considered an anathema. Therefore, there has been only limited Christian scholarship in this area. We can assume that with his brilliant mind, by the age of 30 he may have mastered Latin and Greek, if in fact he were exposed to these languages. He could have been exposed to the Hellenistic ideas associated with these languages.

Jesus may very well have spent many of those 18 years working as a carpenter apprentice with his father. In one or more of the towns in the local area, he could have come into contact with Romans who had knowledge of Greek as well as Buddhist ideas. In fact, the Romans were, at that time, reconstructing a Roman city town very near to the home of Jesus. Highly skilled Roman engineers and architects were, no doubt, brought in. If Jesus did have contact, the conversations between this brilliant young Nazarene and these people, had they been recorded, would give us valuable insights today. These discussions in themselves may have changed history.

At the age of 30, Jesus began his ministry. To say it was a ministry that was built upon the philosophical streams of thought coming from the Roman Empire, as has been suggested, may be partially true, but this would be a very serious understatement. It was built on an altogether different foundation.

It was in part built on the foundation of Judaism. This was the understanding of man as a living creature with two natures, one good and the other evil. On the one hand, he was like GOD, on the other, he was the opposite of GOD. No religion in the history of the human race had ever before defined man in such terms. The religions of the Egyptians and Sumerians did not. Greek and Buddhist thought which developed in the same general time period did not address it. Buddhism does not address it today. Judaism did. It represented a change from the way that man had looked at himself. For the first time in all religious thought, the true nature of man was being revealed in very specific terms as a struggle between good and evil.

Jesus Christ would reveal a new theology that would define the relationship of man in his imperfection to a God of perfection.

It can be concluded that as the answers to the most basic of questions about the nature of GOD and man's relationship to GOD were revealed to Jesus Christ, many influences may have been present. However, his message taken in total was without parallel. It gave mankind a breakthrough into his predicament that no prior religion or philosophical discipline had ever done.

There are two questions that every monotheistic religion must address. Both the Nation of Israel and Jesus Christ addressed these questions. They came up with different answers.

- What is the nature of the one GOD of the Universe?

- What must be the response of every human to that GOD?

We have already seen how Jews and Christians differ in the answer to the first question. They also differ with respect to the second. How GOD expects us to respond to Him differs between the God of Judaism and the God of Christianity.

Jews believe that the study of the Torah and its commentaries is the way to achieve the happiest and most fulfilling and observant way of life. Engaging one's intellect in the study of the Torah as the core of one's life is the highest attainable human activity. This is not just a matter of study. Life is to be lived in a process of trying to reach the perfection of the Torah. For Christians, studying the Hebrew Bible—Old Testament—is important for its insights into the teaching of Jesus Christ, but not as important as being *born again* into a union with GOD. This calls for a conversion experience that in a sense serves to bring the person into the presence of GOD. This God is not the angry, fearful, yet merciful God of Judaism. The God of Christianity, as has been stated, is a God of pure love. This *born again* experience in and of itself is an experience that changes the person forever so that he or she can then be able to live life in the presence of GOD.

It is universally accepted that Christianity over the millennia adopted this Christ centered view of GOD and the relationship of Christians to him and rejected the Jewish one. This was not always the case.

To understand why, we must address the following question:

Did the early Christian Church completely accept the vision of GOD defined by the life and death of Jesus Christ? Did they abandon the God image of the Torah? Or, did they combine the two so that today they are responding to and worshiping the God of both Jesus Christ and the God of the Torah?

Many early Christians combined the two. After all, they had been practicing Jews all of their lives. Most Christians today are under the impression that early on the choice between Jesus Christ and Judaism was cut and dry. You were a Jew one day—or a pagan—and then suddenly you were born again into a new life in Jesus Christ. This may have been the case for many early Christians, but not all. The influence of the Torah and Jewish customs was always present. The message of Jesus Christ was not always completely understood. During the first 300 years of the early Christian Church, the message of a radically different view of the nature of GOD as Jesus presented it was never allowed to stand completely on its own. The influence of the Hebraic vision of God was always present.

There were many serious doctrinal debates towards the end of this 300-year period. The council of Nicaea, which established the Nicene Creed, a creed that firmly put in place Christian Church doctrine, did not take place until the year 325 A.D. By then, the Roman Empire was in support of Christianity. The first Christian Roman Emperor, Constantine, lived from A.D. 306 to A.D. 337.

Was the message of Jesus Christ so diffused from the very beginning that it never really had a chance of being fully understood as Jesus Christ would have wanted it to be understood. If this was the case, then what was the original message?

There is very little information available relating to the state of Christian Church doctrine from the time of the crucifixion up to the time when the Apostle Paul wrote his Epistles—from 50 A.D. to 68 A.D. Then, for the following years from 80 A.D. to 150 A.D. there are only fragments of information. What there is, however, tells us enough about the early church to say that it was in search of a common identity. An identity that would separate it from the Judaic influence of the Torah and Jewish customs, and that it was not always able to make this separation. The early domination of those with a Jewish background and bias shifted only slowly to those with little or no Jewish biblical and life experience.

The movement away from reliance on the Hebrew Bible and Jewish customs and toward autonomous reliance on the Gospel writings was a slow one. Often the leaders in the Christian Churches were Jews who were not about to give up all of their Jewish traditions and Jewish practices. So, there was from the very beginning a tension among Christians as to whether to follow the dictates of the Old Testament as well as Jewish Law and tradition or the varied sources of information they had about Jesus Christ. This was not just a matter, as many church historians—until recent years—would have had everyone believe, of practices such as circumcision and dietary laws. The scriptural definitions of the nature of the God of the Old Testament and the way mankind is expected to respond to him were often in conflict. There is evidence that this caused considerable strain and led to major disagreements within the early Church.

Jesus did not challenge all of the Torah. What parts did he leave unchallenged? Early on in the letter of the Apostle Paul to the Hebrews we see seeds of doubt as to the validity of areas of the Hebrew Bible itself. Paul says:

When in former times God spoke to our forefathers, he spoke in fragmentary and varied fashion through the prophets. But in this final age he has spoken to us in the Son..., the stamp of GOD'S very being.

(Hebrews 1:1-3)

We must remember that the Jews at that time, as do many today, considered every word of the Hebrew Bible to be literally from the hand of GOD. Paul before his conversion was one of them. Orthodox Jews today believe this. The stories themselves and the meanings of the Hebrew words can within reason be interpreted, but they can not be changed. The fact that Paul was talking about the Hebrew Bible using the words *fragmentary* and *varied fashion* would for the Jewish authorities have been considered blasphemy.

Jesus Christ set the stage for the clash between the Hebrew Bible and the New Testament. He would make statements such as *You have learned that they were told...But what I tell you is this....*

He was not just clarifying Hebrew scripture and its Jewish interpretation; he was saying that it was incomplete and even wrong. Often he used the personal pronoun "I" when making statements to correct Hebrew scripture. This infuriated the Jewish authorities, as they believed that the words of the Hebrew Bible were from GOD and that only GOD could correct them by use of the personal pronoun "I". They saw Jesus Christ as taking on the role of GOD himself, and they considered this to be blasphemy.

Two cases where Jesus Christ corrected scripture are worth mentioning as they point out the difference in interpretation of the Mosaic Law. They Follow:

You have learned that our forefathers were told, 'Do not commit murder; anyone who commits murder must be brought to judgment.' But what I tell you is this: Anyone who nurses anger against his brother must be brought to judgment.

(Matthew 5:21, 22)

You have learned that they were told, 'Do not commit adultery.' But what I tell you is this: If a man looks at a woman with a lustful eye, he has already committed adultery with her in his heart.

(Matthew 5:27, 28)

By taking the issue of obeying the commandments beyond the Mosaic Law and extending it generally into the way one thinks, Jesus Christ was challenging the superficiality of the written Torah. He was casting aside all of the Jewish religious customs and practices and saying they are superficial and meaningless without the element of what would be called today in modern psychological terms "intention".

After the death of Jesus Christ, is clear that there was a tension in the early Church that arose from a debate as to what to consider and not to consider from the Hebrew Bible as the Word of GOD and what to consider as the word of Jesus. Noteworthy in the early period are two records, one the letters of a Bishop named Ignatius and the other writings relating to the Gnostic movement.

The most recognizable evidence of this tension within the early church comes from the Letters of Bishop Ignatius who was one of the earliest Apostolic Fathers. He was the Bishop of Antioch in Syria and was arrested and sent to Rome around 110 A.D. where he was martyred. During the trip, like Paul only a few years before him, he wrote letters to various churches. These letters in large part addressed a problem in these churches, which was that some individuals in them were placing the authority of the Old Testament above that of the Gospels. These letters are important because they point out the problem many in the early Christian community had with their perception of the God of the Old Testament and the God as redefined by Jesus Christ. Excerpts from some of his letters follow:

It is monstrous to talk of Jesus Christ and to practice Judaism. For Christianity did not base its faith on Judaism, but Judaism on Christianity, and every tongue believing in God was brought together in it.

(To the Magnesians 10.3)

Be not led astray by strange doctrines or old fables, which are profitless. For if we are living now according to Judaism, we confess that we have not received grace. For the divine prophets lived according to Jesus Christ. Therefore they were also persecuted, being inspired by his grace, to convince the obedient that there is one God, who manifested himself through Jesus Christ his son, who is his word.

(To the Magnesians 8.12)

Ignatius viewed the Old Testament only in terms of those areas that prophesied the coming of Jesus Christ and otherwise supported his teaching as the messenger—son—of GOD. He condemned those areas of scripture as well as Jewish law and tradition that did not, or detracted from His message. He left open the

Old Testament as a valid document, but declared that only those parts that derived their authority directly by way of a connective link to the Gospel of Jesus Christ were true. For Ignatius there was no contradiction between the Old and New Testaments as long as this was the understanding. This is the view today of many Christians who view the Old Testament as a source of knowledge as opposed to an authority for knowledge.

This challenge to the Old Testament was most pronounced in a religions movement called Gnosticism which flourished in the second and third centuries. Many of the Gnostics seem to have been full-fledged Gentiles who had little contact with real-life Judaism.

Although many Gnostic beliefs—it should not be defined as a single form of thought, but as many interconnected forms—were considered by the early Christians to be heretical, and would be considered so today, some that permeated early Christianity are accepted today. Gnosticism emphasized the importance the teachings of Jesus in opposition to the word of the Torah. It looked upon man in a way that would today be termed metaphysical. The idea of a final judgment day when souls will be separated was not a part of Gnostic theology. Rather, it was a theology that looked at heaven as being all around us, with our essence passing at death into a present heavenly dimension. Given the fact that the early Christian church had thrown its lot in the direction of the concept of heaven being "up there" and a future and final apocalyptic judgment when Jesus Christ would reappear, these Gnostic ideas were considered to be heretical by the early Roman Christian church, and they were fought tooth and nail.

The following passage gives an idea of the bitter feelings that existed against Gnosticism:

I made it clear to you that those who are Christian in name, but in reality are Godless and impious heretics, teach in all respects what is blasphemous and godless and foolish.... If you yourselves have ever met with some so-called Christians, who...dare to blaspheme the God of Abraham, and the God of Isaac, and the God of Jacob, and who say that there is no resurrection of the dead, but that their souls ascend to heaven at the very moment of their death—do not suppose that they are Christians.... But, all other entirely orthodox Christians, and I know that there will be a resurrection of the flesh, and also in a thousand years a Jerusalem built up and adorned and enlarged, as the prophets Ezekiel and Isaiah, and all the rest, acknowledged.

Justin Martyr, Dialogue with Trypho (circ. 80 A.D.—160 A.D.)

IX The God They Think They Know The Torah God The Triune God The God of Jesus Christ

This statement by a Christian not far removed in time from Bishop Ignatius illustrates the dissention that existed in early Christianity and the influence of the Hebrew Bible on early Christian thought. It is worth noting—as an example of overall Jewish influence—that it sounds very much the same as a Jewish judgmental quotation from the Mishnah:

These are they that have no share in the world to come: He that says that there is no resurrection of the dead prescribed in the law, and he that says the Law is not from heaven....

(Sanhedrin 10:1)

Many of the leaders of the early Christian communities believed that every word of their Old Testament (Hebrew Bible) was the Word of GOD. They did not give up the Hebrew image of the God described in the Hebrew Bible. For them He remained the same fearful, angry, judgmental and only sometime merciful God that the Jews believed in. They also accepted the God defined by the life and death of Jesus Christ. He was a different kind of God. He was God of love. Can GOD be both? This is a question that has perplexed the Church ever since.

To quote from the eminent Biblical scholar Oskar Skarsaune in his book, *In The Shadow Of The Temple*:

"It is quite clear that for the early Christians the distinction between orthodoxy and heresy amounted to something very simple and basic: Do you confess faith in the God of the Old Testament as the one and only God, Creator of heaven and earth, or do you not?"

By the end of the 3rd century the stage was set for a theology that would emerge under the name of Christianity. It would be a theology that would embrace writings about the God of the Old Testament and the God of the New Testament. The words of both would be without flaw. Every word of both was the WORD of GOD. The fact that the very nature of the God illuminated by Jesus Christ was clearly different was of no importance. GOD would be looked upon as being inscrutable. Any argument that challenged this duality and the challenges it imposed on a coherent theology would be considered heretical. The stage was set for the next two millennia of Christianity.

How could the God be the same? There were enormous differences between the two Bibles. The God of the Hebrew Bible was not in all respects the same as the God of Jesus Christ. As has been stated, the God of the Hebrew Bible could be vengeful, he could be capricious, he could be angry, and he could only sometimes be merciful. This was not the same God as that described by Jesus Christ.

After lengthy and considerable debate, an answer finally came. There would be in the Christian Church a Trinitarian God, a God with three faces or characters—described as three *persons*. There would be a Father, a Son and a Holy Spirit. The part of that Trinitarian God who would be the Father would be in non-specific terms the biblical reference Father God of the Old Testament. Jesus Christ himself had often referred to "My Father." It would be assumed that Jesus was referring to this God of the Old Testament.

The God illuminated by Jesus Christ as recorded in the New Testament would be a loving and forgiving God. He would be called the *Son*. There would be a separation of the natures of the two; the Father Hebrew God as presented in the Old Testament and the God of Jesus Christ as presented in the New Testament.

When punishment was required for Heretics who did not agree with church doctrine, the judgmental angry punishing Father God would be called upon and these Heretics would be put down or if need be burned at the stake. This would be the God who empowered the Roman Church to have the Inquisition and to embark on the Crusades. He would be a God of judgment and of punishment. The God of the Old Testament would not tolerate blasphemy. He would show His wrath on those who disobeyed as He had done with the Nation of Israel whenever it disobeyed. Christianity could have it both ways.

There is no reference to a *Trinitarian God*—one God in three—in the Hebrew Bible. The Christian Church has for 2000 years been searching for a reference to this three part God in the Old Testament and not found a trace of scripture to support it. The nearest they can come is a reference to a plural God in Genesis where it says *Let us make man in our own image* (Genesis 1:26) and some other areas where GOD is referred to in plural form.

The Gospels do make a distinction between the Father, the Son, and the Holy Spirit, but do not speak of a Trinitarian God. The Apostle Paul in his letters written shortly after the death of Jesus Christ did not refer to a Trinitarian God. He did, however, speak of each of the three in separate but synonymous terms. More important here is the question: Was Paul referring to the image of the Father as the term was used in the Hebrew Bible or to the God as defined by the life and death of Jesus Christ? The tone of his letters reveals both the personalities of the ancient Hebrew God and the personality of the God revealed by Jesus Christ.

By the year A.D. 300 the debate among Christians had moved away from the influence of Judaism on Christianity to an acceptance of the definition of the nature of the *Father God* presented in the Hebrew Bible. The Old Testament in its literal form was accepted as the WORD of GOD. The debate was now moving in the direction not of the meaning of each of the three Triune elements, but in their relative hierarchical positioning.

The problem for the early Christian Church, as to how to position the three elements of the Trinity, was subjected to intensive debate and finally settled at the Council of Nicaea in 325 A.D. The creed that resulted is today a part of almost all Christian services. It makes the statement of belief in the Father, the Son, and the Holy Spirit, but it does not define what they are, how they differ, how they relate or with their differences how they connect to each other.

Christians know what the Jesus Christ person or part of the Godhead is. They are told that He sits on the right hand of GOD. They also, from their own life experiences, know what the Holy Spirit is. But do they have a clear definition in their minds of what the *GOD* part is? He is only referred to as the *Father*. Is it the Hebrew definition the *Father God* of the Hebrew Bible or is it the God revealed by the life and death of the *Incarnate* Jesus Christ?

We pattern our behavior after the God or Gods we worship. The persona of the God or Gods we worship underlies our thought processes and makes us think the way we do. It follows that it also governs the way we act. In the early Christian Church, as well as in the Christian Church of today, most Christians patterned their behavior after the God revealed by the life and death of Jesus Christ. But, this was not always the case. Since the Trinitarian issue of definition was avoided from the very beginning and continues to be avoided, the God of the Old Testament often has taken the lead, and then behavior is patterned after the judgmental and punishing God of the Old Testament. As a result, looking back on the last 2000 years of Church history, we do not always see in the actions of Christians the God image of Jesus Christ. Nor do we always see it in the Christian Church today.

This archaic God of anger and retribution has not yet disappeared. He still rules corners of the world and controls the actions of many extremist Jews and Christians. He also rules the religion of Islam. The God of Islam, which was constructed out of the archaic Hebraic vision of God, rules Muslims thought. The God of the Koran remains calcified in the ancient God image of the Hebrew Bible. The Hebrew Bible God of judgment, anger, fear, retribution, and only occasional mercy remains in control of the consciousness of Muslims and governs their actions.

It is clear that much of Christianity still remains in the grips of a frightful schizophrenic God, one with two often-contradictory natures. Because the early Christian church would not face the fact that in the Trinity the image of the Father is not that presented in the Hebrew Bible but a God of love and love only,

Christians are left with an inscrutable Hebrew Bible God of the Trinity who, like a father, deals out mercy one time and then punishment the next.

As has been stated, this is not a description of the God Incarnate revealed in the person of Jesus Christ. The God illuminated by Jesus Christ is a God of love and love only. He is GOD in Genesis before the fall of man. He is not the God defined by the deceiver and accepted by the Jews.

To show the depth of HIS love for every person on this earth, in a final revelation of HIMSELF, HE made the ultimate sacrifice, using a symbolic act that all human beings of every belief could understand, the sacrifice by a father of his son. This message of GOD'S unconditional and unrelenting love did not reach all of Christianity, in fact only a small part of it. However, it continues slowly to penetrate thought and belief.

38.
THE ELEVENTH COMMANDMENT

For I the Lord thy God am a jealous God, visiting the iniquity of the fathers upon the children into the third and fourth generation of them that hate me.

(Exodus 20:5)

The Author's interpretation of the message of GOD from Jesus Christ follows:

I have sent the Messiah to give you the eleventh Commandment.

I want you to know that the Ten Commandments that I gave to Moses and the laws you derived from them did not truly reveal MY WORD

I am not a jealous God nor am I an exclusive God of the Jewish people. I am God of all people. I am a God of love. My love extends to every person on the earth. Nothing can separate anyone from my love. The words of Moses, that I will punish the sins of third and fourth generations of those who hate me, are wrong. I am not a God who hates nor do I punish. Those who do not follow me punish themselves by their separation from me. Those who enter into my presence by following the path of love that I showed to all of mankind by the life and death of Jesus Christ will be with me in eternity without punishment.

My eleventh commandment to you is this:

Honor all that I have given you. Love the earth that I have given you. Show your love and respect for everything that is a part of it. Love yourselves. Love your neighbor. Love all of man and woman kind. Do not confine or segregate your love. It must be unconditional.

As you have shown unconditional love to everyone, not just to those of your own tribe, nation or religion, you show your love for me.

Those who do not show this unconditional love exist separately from me.

Why do we need an eleventh commandment? Why weren't the ten enough?

The God of the Hebrew Bible is not the same God as the God of the New Testament. The definition of His nature and man's relationship to Him is different. This is the central fact that marks the difference between Judaism and Christianity and Islam. It was the principal reason that Jesus Christ and his followers were rejected by the Jewish authorities. It is the principle reason that Jews today cannot accept Christianity. Since Islam grew from the Hebraic roots of Judaism, this also marks the difference between Islam and Christianity.

It is this eleventh commandment that separates Christianity from Judaism and Islam.

X
The Uncertain Future of Islam

"There is no Deity worthy of worship except Allah, and Muhammad is his messenger."

Welcome to the Islam Page
Internet Site

If anyone desires a religion other than Islam (Submission to Allah), never will it be accepted of him; and in the Hereafter he will be in the ranks of those who have lost (their selves in the Hell fire).

(Sura 3:85)

Six hundred and ten years after the birth of Jesus Christ, in the ancient Arabian Cities of Medinah and Mecca, angels began to speak to a merchant named Muhammad and a new religion was born. Within 100 years, converted Muslim Arabs in a series of great battles swept out of the Arabian Peninsula and conquered most of the hard lands of Eastern Mediterranean civilization. The Muslim Empire then expanded further to the west and to the east from the shores of Morocco to Afghanistan. It had become, in a very short period of time, the greatest empire of its day.

Today, more than a billion people in the world claim the religion, and it continues to find new converts. Fewer than 25 per cent are now a part of the original Arab population from which it sprang.

Unlike Christianity and Judaism which originated as purely religious movements, Islam originated as a military and political force as well as a religious one. Through military/political dominance those who were conquered were converted. If they did not convert, the consequences were extreme even to the point of death.

This was not the case with the other two religions. The Jews for over two thousand years had only gone into battle to protect and preserve their tribal religious identity or to gain land for their own tribe. They had no intention of bringing others into their special relationship with their God. Christianity on the other hand was a religion that told its followers to convert all non-believers, but not through military conquest. It was a religion of peaceful conquest of the mind. Christians were asked to show their love toward all people by the way they lived and thought. From this came conversion—called rebirth—into a personal relationship with Jesus Christ. Christians were told to spread their theology, making disciples of all nations, not by war, but by demonstrating to others the meaning of the life, death, and resurrection of Jesus Christ in their own lives.

As Islam rapidly spread, a need arose to bring its beliefs into a unified body of thought leading to a common code of conduct. Scholars, called *Ulama*, were appointed to do this. What they wrote was based on the Holy Book, the Koran (*Qur'an*), and on the life of the Prophet Muhammad; which had been recorded in the *Sunna*. This combination of the Verses of the Koran and the life of Muhammad, the *Sunna*, was then brought together in what became known as the *Shari'a*. It was, in a sense, a codification of the Koran and the *Sunna*. This exercise was completed in the 11th Century

This has led to major divisions within Islam. Known examples today are the Sunnis of Iraq, the Shiites of Iran and Iraq, and the Wahhabis of Saudi Arabia. Their core beliefs, however, remain very similar. All believe that the Koran given to their prophet Muhammad by the angel Gabriel, as well as other unnamed angels, is the true and only word of GOD.

The Koran as well as the Islamic commentary about Muhammad himself, the *Sunna*, rested its proclamations on many of the tenets of Judaism and Christianity. Muhammad had close contact with the Jewish settlements in and around Mecca and Medinah, and Christianity was already over six hundred years old. The Koran was to a large extent built upon the scriptures of the Hebrew Bible and the New Testament. It recognized most of the Hebrew prophets including the patriarch, Abraham. It repeated, at least in part, many of the events recorded in the Hebrew Bible such as the Creation Story. It even borrowed from the Jewish commentary, the Midrash. It looked to Jesus Christ as a great prophet second only to Muhammad himself.

According to Muhammad, all of Judeo/Christian scripture was considered to have been corrupted by man. God had spoken to Muhammad to reveal the culmination of Judeo/Christian tradition. Only the Koran represented the true and inerrant word of GOD and it was everything anyone would ever want to know. It was to be the final word of GOD never to be altered until the final judgment day. Muhammad proclaimed that the Koran existed outside of history.

X The Uncertain Future of Islam

Even though Islam relied on the Christian canon of the New Testament, it was nevertheless a religion that remained basically a derivative of Hebraic, not Christian thought. It was a legalistic religion. Allah was still the same fearful and punishing monotheistic God identified in the Hebrew Bible by the Jews more than 2000 years before, a God who had laid down a set of very specific laws. And like the Jewish God, he was an exclusive God who said that the Jews alone—now the Muslims—are the *Chosen* ones and all others are misguided and less than you are in my sight.

The God of the Koran was a God who placed a heavy burden on its followers and then expected them to please him by living with that burden. It was the task of Muslims to spend their lives in an attempt to please their God. The emphasis remained on a God who set out the rules of human conduct down to the smallest detail. Allah had given the law to Muhammad and said that this is what I expect of your followers. There was room for some compassion though. He was a God who looked upon human beings as weak and therefore unable to come to absolute perfection in the law. Like the Christian God, He required each and every person to try as best he could. But, at the end of time He would be the one to hold back the final judgment until He determined whether an individual had lived according to the Sharia law of Islam and was deserving of salvation.

For the Jews over their long history and for the Christians under their short history, the search had been to know the mind of GOD. Muhammad wanted to end that search. He would do this by first proclaiming that we can never know the mind of GOD, but then by defining in the most precise terms how all of mankind can please Him.

At the time Muhammad was receiving his messages from the angel Gabriel, Jesus Christ had already been proclaimed GOD incarnate by the early Christian Church. His life and teaching was for Christians a window into of the mind of GOD. But, there was a conflict with the God that Muhammad, although claiming Muslims cannot know Him, nevertheless envisaged. Jesus Christ had presented a view of God that was different in many respects from the Hebraic view of God that Muhammad had used for his template. This Christian God was a God who valued each and every human being regardless of who or what they were and how they were able to live according to the Mosaic Law. He was also a universal God who said that as you show your love towards everyone, not just those of your own tribe or religion or family, you show your love for Me. He even had gone so far as to say we must turn the other cheek towards our worst enemies.

For Muhammad, there was an even greater problem with Christianity. It had already been in existence for over six hundred years when Muhammad appeared on the scene to proclaim his new religion. Christian creeds and doctrines were already formed and set in stone. The New Testament Canon of authorized scriptures was decided. Other Christian movements, such as the Gnostic and Marcionite and Ebionite and been crushed, leaving in their place a unified Roman Catholic Church. Muhammad strongly objected to one part of this Christian doctrine. It was the doctrine of the Trinity, the idea of three Gods in one. This concept ran totally counter to the view of GOD given to Muhammad by the angel Gabriel.

This Christian Trinitarian God was not the kind of God that the angels had described to Muhammad. The God described to Muhammad was a monotheistic God with one, not three natures. He was a God who agreed with some of the philosophical statements of Jesus Christ, but rejected the idea of Jesus Christ as being GOD incarnate. He rejected the idea of the transcendence of Jesus Christ by way of his resurrection. There was no place for the idea of the Holy Spirit. Muslims were to have no direct line to God through Jesus Christ or the Holy Spirit. Allah wanted them to look to Muhammad himself who would tell them how to approach Him.

The Christian idea of a Trinitarian God presumed the divinity of Jesus Christ. How could Muhammad accept this and remain the greatest Prophet? The answer was to refute the idea of a Trinitarian God, insisting on the Hebrew monotheistic God and leave Jesus Christ as the second greatest Prophet after Muhammad himself. To make sure this was all completely understood, the angels spoke to Muhammad in the Koran saying that *there is no GOD but ALLAH and Muhammad is the Messenger of ALLAH.*

If not the God of Jesus Christ, then who was the God of the Muslim religion? The Koran and the Islamic writings described a God who demanded a heavy burden of compliance to a far greater extreme than that of the Hebrew Bible and Midrash. There was little room for individual choice. The *sharia* dictated the way followers of Muhammad must live from dawn to dusk. Muslims were told not only to pray five times a day but also how to pray and in which direction to pray. The rules even dictated the specific movements and prostrations. And for those who did not comply or did not try hard enough to comply, eternal bliss would be withheld. At the time of final judgment ALLAH would examine every part of one's life even as to the way he had prayed. Then there would be the final judgment. Everything was being recorded and placed in the *Book of Records.* Every last detail during life was being taken into account.

X The Uncertain Future of Islam

Islam was built upon fear of an almighty powerful and distant God, existent in some other place and time. It disallowed the Christian idea of any kind of direct forgiving and redemptive relationship between man and GOD through transcendent oneness with HIM, a central part of the message of Jesus Christ. This was a message that was at the core of the belief system of the followers of Jesus Christ.

Muhammad would not acknowledge the Christian message that we cannot be separated from GOD'S redemptive love and that this love transcends all human weakness in the face of all rules of conduct and religious laws of the Hebrew Bible and the Midrash. Like the Jews who had rejected Jesus Christ, acknowledging this for Muhammad would have meant seeing GOD in an entirely different light. It would have prevented him from laying down his own new set of rules based on the rules of the Hebrew Bible. Islam therefore kept the Hebrew vision of GOD. Essentially, the God of Islam remained a Hebrew *eye for and eye and a tooth for a tooth* God, not *a turn the other cheek* Christian God. He was a God who crushed the enemies of Islam. He was the Hebrew Bible God of harsh judgment and retribution.

For Muhammad the idea was to bring together all the prophets, Jesus Christ included, at least his own understanding of them, into one final and true revelation and then to banish all those who did not believe in his revelation to eternal damnation. He did, however, make an exception for Jews and Christians, who would have a special place on the Day of Judgment.

Muhammad knew that this revelation could not be delivered to humanity by a mere mortal such as himself. There was the problem of credibility. He was just a common man and a mere merchant in Mecca. It could only be done by an angel speaking through Muhammad. There are only two angels mentioned by name in the Hebrew Bible. One is the angel Gabriel. He appeared and spoke to Zechariah in the Hebrew Bible and to Mary in the Christian New Testament when he gave the good news to the Virgin Mary. This was the principal angel who would speak to Muhammad.

Today, all worshiping Muslims believe that this is what happened and the writings of the Koran given by the angel Gabriel, as well as others without names, were from the mind of GOD. They believe that the Koran as the final and inerrant WORD can never be altered until the final Day of Judgment, the very end of the world. Muslims believe that, except for Christians and Jews who will have a special place, any who are not Muslims are infidels who will be banished from GOD for eternity.

Muhammad expected that the Jewish and Christian communities in and around Mecca and Medinah would convert to Islam. Only under conditions of extreme coercion did this happen.

To a casual observer, Islam can be looked upon as a variation of Judaism, and the Koran as no more than a derivative of the Hebrew Bible. The religious practices of the Muslims and Orthodox Jews can be looked upon as being similar. It appears that this is what Muhammad thought.

He fully expected that all of Judaism would convert to Islam. What he did not understand was the stubbornness of the Jews. Over 3000 years of Jewish history would make them stand fast. The Jewish people had been searching throughout this history, which for them began with the very beginning of creation, to find the deep and hidden meanings of their scriptures. It was an endless search that continues to this day. Suddenly in the year 610 a merchant from the city of Mecca claimed that he was receiving messages from angels telling him that these ancient Hebrew scriptures were corrupted in the process of transmission, and that their interpretations of them were also corrupted, and he alone was being given the ultimate truths about them. At the same time he was telling the Jews that they should convert to his new religion, Islam. The Jews showed no interest.

Muhammad was saying the same to the Christians. Christianity was just over 600 years in the making when Muhammad appeared on the scene. The doctrines of the Christian Church had been firmly established, including that of the Triune God. As stated, Muhammad had decided to borrow just the pieces of the Gospels, the ones that suited him best, but leave ALLAH as a God with essentially the same nature as the Hebraic God. For Christians being pressured to convert, this presented a problem. The nature of the God revealed by the life and death of Jesus Christ was entirely different from the nature of the God presented in the Hebrew Bible, and now in the Koran. The God of Islam was more like the Jewish God that Jesus had redefined. This would have been the same as going back to Judaism. Therefore, Christians showed no interest either.

The way Christians were asked to respond to the presence of GOD in their lives was entirely different. Islam did not recognize the possibility of the transcendence of man in all of his weakness to be at one during his biological life with a loving redemptive God. Muslims would have to wait for a final judgment day. This Christian *presence* came through the indwelling of the Holy Spirit—the presence of Jesus Christ—in the lives of Christians, demonstrated in worship by the sacrament of the Eucharist.

Islam, except for some fringe elements of mysticism (Sufism), rejected the possibility of any kind of union here and now in this life. Even with Sufism the

X The Uncertain Future of Islam

objective was to connect more closely to GOD'S will, not to be at one with Him. The Koran, like the Hebrew Bible, said that we must wait for a Judgment Day when all who are living and all who have died will be judged taking into account everything they have done or left undone in their lives. Only then will there be a possibility of being in GOD'S presence for eternity.

With the passing of years, the differences between Christianity and Islam became even greater. Christianity is a religion of revelation and change. Although its core beliefs remain inflexible, the search for the meaning of the life and death of Jesus Christ has continued.

As an example, for many modern day Christians the idea of a final Day of Judgment has lost its meaning, as has the parallel idea of a Second Coming of Jesus Christ on that judgment day. These Christians question the biblical concept of time which is so much a part of the idea of a future *Judgment Day*. They look at time in modern relativistic terms as a construct of our perception of this earthly dimension, non-existent in the dimension of space and time that is GOD'S. They believe that Jesus Christ is with us in the presence of the Holy Spirit and that heaven is all around us at every moment of our lives. They believe that we are moving in the here and now by how we think and live either towards or away from a loving and non-judgmental God in a heavenly dimension that is both inside of us as well as outside of us.

Unlike in Christianity, there is in Islam very little room for change. A large percentage of Muslims today can be considered *Fundamentalist* in the sense of the understanding that Christians and Jews have of the word, which is Muslims view the Koran in its entirety as the inerrant word of GOD. Viewing it in this way is, in fact, a precondition for being a Muslim. All Muslims must believe that every word of the Koran was from ALLAH and therefore cannot be changed. This is not the case for Christianity and Judaism where only certain groups hold to the inerrancy of their scriptures. There are elements of the Koran that clearly show hatred towards non-believers. This has given rise to the terrorism we see in the world today

If Muslims today existed in isolation from those of other religions living in other parts of the world, as they existed over past millennia, there would be no problem. But this is not the case. The world has become an interdependent society of people who must live together in some form of harmony.

An Islamic concept that has grown out of its theology is the concept of *Jihad,* which literally means to struggle to meet GOD'S challenge and to do what He expects. To the extent that this is interpreted to mean destroying a Western World perceived as being secular and corrupt, many Muslims take this as a God given license to a never ending pursuit to destroy the West. As seen in the conflict between India and Pakistan, this conflict has extended beyond the Western World to those of other faiths in other areas.

The hatred toward the Western World that has been manifest through *Jihad* has in recent years reached such intensity as to lead to the question of whether there can be any kind of future co-existence between Muslims and non-Muslims. *Jihad* is based on a visceral hatred towards all people of other beliefs. The World Trade Center bombing showed just the tip of the iceberg. It is not only the major recognized groups such as al-Quaida that hold these beliefs. There are many smaller ones just as active. The Muslim world silently harbors and supports them. These non combative Muslims may not be on the front lines, but they are as much responsible

The question of complicity on the part of the Muslim community cannot be addressed without reference to the biblical concept of evil. Both the Hebrew Bible and the Christian New Testament clearly state that evil is an active force present in our world. The very first book of the Hebrew Bible, Genesis, defines man as a creature with two natures, one good and the other evil. Evil is described by Christians as a force of darkness that blinds the eyes and takes over the minds of human beings. It is a force that destroys the human creative spirit. It separates us from GOD. Hatred is described as being overcome by the forces of evil. Jesus Christ made it very clear that any one who harbors feelings of hatred toward others cannot enter GOD'S presence.

Christianity does not make a separation between *thinking* and *doing*. Those who hold to a desire to harm or kill will be as if they had actually harmed or killed. They have been overcome by an evil desire. It is therefore the Christian view that those in the Muslim world who harbor feelings of hatred have been consumed by the forces of evil. Muslims should make no mistake about the underlying motive of the Western World to defend itself against these forces of evil. For those in the West it is a battle against darkness in the souls of all Muslim men and women who hate. It is a battle against evil.

If this underlying force behind the hatred of Muslims towards Jews and Christians worldwide has been with us for over 1400 years, why then did it only recently explode onto the world scene? What was the catalyst? No doubt the recognition of the State of Israel in 1948 by the United States was a reason, but was this the primary reason? The answer is that it was not. The primary reason is that the world around Islam had changed while Islam remained the same.

The seeds of Islamic hatred towards western society were firmly planted in the Koran from the very beginning. All it would take was their nurturing. This is what happened when the intellectual hero of all Islamic terrorists, Sayyid Qutb (pronounced KUH-tahb) from the agony and horror of an Egyptian prison wrote his vast, many-volume commentary on the Koran, *In the Shade of the Qur'an*. This was a work that would inspire future generations of Muslim terrorists. Cast under its spell, many thousands of young Muslims would chose martyrdom and death. Qutb was executed by the Egyptian government in 1966, but by that time it was too late to stop the contagion that was to follow.

The idea of a utopian society coming about by way of the righteous destroying the unrighteous was not a new one. It had existed throughout the Hebrew Bible and with Muhammad it became an important part of the Koran. An example of the Hebrew roots is found in a comment by the author John J. Collins in his book, *The Scepter and the Star: The Messiahs of the Dead Sea Scrolls and Other Ancient Literature*. He writes about the expectations in the Qumran community (140's B.C.–68 A.D.) of the coming Messiah:

He is the scepter who will smite the nations, slay the wicked with the breath of his lips, and restore the Davidic dynasty.... He is also the Messiah of righteousness, who will usher in an era of peace and justice.

The members of the Qumran community believed in a God who can be righteous on the one hand and a destroyer of the wicked on the other. This was both the Hebraic and Koranic interpretation of the nature of their God. Qutb believed in this kind of God. ALLAH would be the destroyer of the infidels.

Qutb saw a world corrupted by Christianity and by Zionism. He would brush off Judaism as "a system of rigid and lifeless ritual." He saw Christianity as a two faced religion that had lost its direction. One part of it was secular and the other religious. Its biggest mistake according to Qutb lay in the words of Jesus Christ when he said:

Render unto Caesar the things that are Caesars' and to God the things that are Gods

For Qutb, everything was to be rendered to ALLAH.

How could Qutb achieve this perfect world? The answer was clear. It would not be by way of Christianity. The Christian idea of a direct connection with a loving redemptive God made no sense. There was no way to discipline people living under a God who allowed them to make their own choices between good and evil. Besides, according to Qutb, Christianity had been polluted by Greek philosophy. Like Muhammad, he would choose the Koranic distant and fearful God. In order to please that God, Muslims must live according to a system of mandated laws set down by the ancient *Qur'an* and *Shari'a*.

Like the Apostle Paul many generations before him, Qutb saw a world overtaken by wonton sexual expression and undisciplined excess. He blamed this on the Christians and Zionists who had turned their backs on GOD for the pleasures of this world. He considered western man to be consumed by his passions and therefore fallen. For Qutb the world had become a den of moral degeneration.

To bring about his New World, the Christian/Zionist world would be destroyed and replaced with the world described by the prophet Muhammad, the messenger of GOD. It would be a world where every human being would live a Sharia life under Islamic law. The entire world would become a utopian Islamic clerical state.

What Qutb could not understand is that Christianity has an enduring strength built upon the knowledge of every Christian that he is valued by GOD for his strengths and forgiven for his weaknesses. This Christian God loves every individual for who he or she is. He is a God who extends His love beyond the inability of man to please him. By connecting man in all of his weakness with a loving and redemptive God, as opposed the fearful punishing God of the Hebrew Bible, Jesus Christ redefined both the nature of GOD and man's relationship to Him. Man was released from the fear of a Hebrew punishing God. Islam in its Koran gave man no such assurance either. Its God was taken from the ancient Hebraic scriptures. The Koran was built upon a retributive God of fear. Man, no matter how hard he tried, could never totally and completely please ALLAH; unless according to Qtub's interpretation of the Koran, he were, for the cause of ALLAH, to die as a suicidal bomber!

Qutb's was a philosophy of death; the philosophy of Jesus Christ was a philosophy of life. Qutb's was a philosophy of fear of the unknown. Jesus Christ's was a philosophy of liberation of the mind into the unknown.

This Christian view of GOD and mans' relationship to him over a period of 2000 years laid the foundation for the strength of western civilization. It allowed its advances to occur on every level. Christianity chose to place its faith in a loving redemptive God who did not restrain mankind but instead gave him the freedom to expand his vision into the unknown. It is understandable that for Qutb Jesus Christ and the world he produced would be an anathema. Given the freedom to think beyond the earth bound constraints set in place by an oppressive and fearful God, the potential of men and women becomes unlimited.

Over the past 1400 years, the fruits of this potential have been far more than economic. They have also been spiritual. They have become manifest throughout the entire society in everything from music to law to the sciences. For Qutb, as well as for his many terrorist followers today, this has been the cause of enormous resentment. The enemies of ALLAH are the Christians and the Jews and all they stand for. They are also the secularized Muslims who have been polluted by non Islamic values. These terrorists see only two pictures, one black and the other (Islam) white.

Time is running out on Islam. It has been betrayed by extremists like Qtub. It has been betrayed by ignorant, illiterate, medieval-minded village clerics with a simplistic reductionist view of the world and anger toward a modernized democratic westernized way of life. In most of the Middle Eastern countries, the mullahs who spew out the message of hatred are today protected as a cover by a powerful and elite wealthy class determined to continue its own privileged position. These monarchs, sheikhs, tribal elites, political leaders, business tycoons, and their followers live off the fat of the land, bullying, harassing, humiliating and trampling on their subjects who are forced to live in shantytowns, in starving villages, in depraved slums and in the homelessness of refugee camps. It is time for Muslims to realize that the seeds of its torment lie not with the West but within its own distorted socio/political/economic Islamic belief.

If we were living during the Christian Crusades of the 12th century or the European Imperialism of the 19th and early 20th or the Cold War of the mid and late 20th, the mullahs might have an argument saying Muslims are being oppressed by infidel outsiders. This argument does not hold in today's world. The world economy and its political systems have rapidly moved past the last thousand years of its history.

Oil revenues have for the last 50 years provided many of the nations in the Middle East with a tremendous bounty. Today these nations form the cradle of Muslim hatred towards the West. They have had ample time to enter the world economy and take on democratic reforms. They have had ample time to assist their less fortunate Muslim neighbors. It is no surprise that the frustration of the masses with a failure to progress economically and socially has curdled into a simmering hatred towards the West and in particular America. Where else could scapegoats be found?

Not just the West but the whole world; Christians, Jews, Hindu, Sikh, Buddhists, Taoists, and all others of all beliefs are today asking the question: Is this all that Islam is?

Recent events have shown Islam to be:

- *A religion of*—crazed terrorists with box cutters slitting the throats of defenseless airline stewardesses.

- *A religion of*—bodies falling from the World Trade Towers in New York City which make sounds thumping as they hit the ground.

- *A religion of*—young people running from a horrific explosion in Bali that an Indonesia described in the following way: "It was sometimes hard to know whether the man who appeared to be running toward him through the flames was alive or already dead…Like you look at their face and you can't make anything out; there's nothing left…People were missing ears, people were missing limbs, their skin was peeling off. There were blind people with glass in their eyes running around screaming that they couldn't see."

- *A religion of*—teen-age Palestinians with explosives strapped to their bodies blowing themselves up in crowded disco clubs and pizza parlors and shopping centers, sending pieces of steel in all directions, killing and maiming innocent people nearby.

- *A religion of*—parents who rejoice at the martyrdom of their children as suicide bombers.

- *A religion of*—silence among its leaders; who, if they were to criticize their Mullahs, would fear for their own safety.

- *A religion of*—hatred towards all Jews and Americans because of a festering jealously over what these people holding to faiths other than their own have made of their lives.

Is it only a religion of evil mind control leading to darkness and death? Is it only a religion of hate? Is it a failed religion? The constant stream of graphic pictures of carnage worldwide is leading the non Muslim world to this conclusion.

Moderate open minded secular Muslims need to respond by asking four questions of themselves, one aimed at current perceptions, one at their clerics who tightly hold Islam under their control and who are directly responsible for the current state of Islam, one about the inerrancy of their scriptures, and the last about how they can contribute to the future of the world. They are:

- Does Islam have a distorted perception of the Western World?

- Have the minds of Islam's Clerics been overtaken by the forces of hate?

- Was or was not the Koran the inerrant Word of ALLAH?

- Does Islam have contributions to be made to the thought of the world?

X The Uncertain Future of Islam

Central to the answers to any of the these questions is the question of whether Muhammad was just another spiritually gifted and even prophetic human being who interpreted the existing body of theological knowledge in his part of the world 1400 years ago in a way that would form a deeply spiritual and at the same time economic, social and politically binding religion in the context of conditions at that time and in that place. And if this was the case, how much of it then has application in the 21st century? How much impedes the free flow of political expression and ideas that serve to elevate human potential? How much is harmful in today's world? What parts of Islam are causing its followers to hate? These questions from the West are not new. Muslims for many years have rejected such inferences and termed them the *Orientalist fallacy*.

For a Muslim even to ask these questions is a sacrilege punishable by death. It is a defiance of acknowledgement that Muhammad is the prophet of God. It is a repudiation of the Koran as the word of God. It promises eternal punishment after death in hell. Unlike Judaism and Christianity, in Islam there can be no compromise or liberal interpretation. All of it must be accepted. To enter paradise a Muslim must accept every word of the Koran as the word of God. For Muslims the question of whether it is possible to live as Muslims in a harmonious relationship with other people of other religions can only be answered by the Koran.

Muslims believe that it is the destiny of Islam to be the one and only religion in the world. All nations are to become *Holy Nations* under Sharia Law. The stated goal according to the Koran is to accomplish this by any means possible, including war. Given the horror that is emerging from Islam under its present course, this is for the rest of the world, clearly a frightful utopian vision far detached from reality. In fact, for non Muslims the most pressing and at the same time perplexing question is: Can Islam even continue to exist at all as a viable means of religious expression in its present archaic fundamentalist form in the open, technocratic, pluralistic society of the 21st century?

If it can survive at all, then in what form will it survive? One way to approach this is to ask the questions: How much of the thought structure of the religion is based on an exclusiveness that leads to malice and never ending conflict with people of other forms of religious and social organization? Does this exclusiveness prevent Muslims from honoring others outside of its belief system? How much fulfills human potential both inside as well as outside of Islam? Can parts of its thought structure in any way be separated so that its followers can ignore its negative aspects?

These are, in fact, questions not only for fundamentalist Muslims, but also for all people of all religions who, like Muslims, consider themselves to be exclusive or *Chosen* and establish their feeling of superiority and their identity by the denigration of those with other beliefs. This includes Fundamentalist Christians and Orthodox Jews. It includes all who feel that their religion entitles them to sit in judgment of others and consider themselves *Chosen*. The greater question for those at the extremes of all religions is whether the one CREATOR of our Universe and GOD of all humankind is making the same exclusionary choices that they are.

We must search, not with arrogance, but with humility for the richness of GOD'S revelation in all religious thought. We must understand that what is left outside of this richness is not from GOD, it is of the mind of man. All is not revelation nor is all the *Word* of GOD. Nor is it *corrupted* as Islam would have it. It is simply an attempt at the truth or near the truth, but not quite at the truth.

The search for GOD'S revelation did not stop with Muhammad. It will carry on until the end of time. Until Muslims recognize this fact, there can only be stubbornness of thought leading to simmering hateful resentment. We were created by GOD to be open to His presence. We were created by GOD to think and to search for HIS revelation. For humanity this is a never-ending search. The position of Islam that the search was over 1400 years ago is wrong.

XI
The Challenge to Rabbinical Judaism
The Continuing Revelation of the Hebrew God

"And the question (was) forced upon him (Rosenzweig) as to whether there was any purpose in the synagogue, seeing that in the reality of history the struggle between the pagan world and the message of revelation was being fought out not by Judaism, but by Christianity."

Judaism Despite Christianity

The Letters between Eugen Rosenstock-Huessy and Franz Rosenzweig

About The Correspondence
By Dr. Alexander Altman, Professor of Jewish Philosophy, Brandeis University

Judaism Despite Christianity is a book of letters written in the early part of the 20th century between two great religious thinkers of our age, one a Christian, the other a Jew. In one of the letters Rosenstock-Huessy, a Christian, directs a question to Rosenzweig, a Jew, about the relevance of Judaism in world history. It was of such poignancy that when reading it, Rosenzweig decided to abandon Judaism and convert to Christianity. But then, he changed his mind.

An introduction to these letters which reads:...*there did not seem to be any place (for him) for Judaism* opens up a question that haunts the Jewish-Christian dialogue to this day: Why would Rosenzweig, a Jew, want to become a Christian, and once he did why would he then change his mind? Why would any Jew want to become a Christian?

Rosenzweig, who had not in fact been a devout Jew before his decision, decided that before converting, he would return briefly to his Jewish roots. He wanted first to experience the fullness of living and thinking spiritually as a Jew. When he did turn to Judaism, as he later wrote, what occurred was a "religious experience that happened with the force of a conversion" but it was not like a conversion to Christianity. It was an experience that brought him into a direct relationship with the God of Judaism without the intermediary of Jesus Christ. Rosenzweig was drawn back into his Jewishness. He remained there for the rest of his life.

Can both Christians and Jews learn something from this story? What was it about the question that made Rosenzweig, a Jew, decide to become a Christian? Why did Rosenstock-Huessy's question disturb him so deeply? What held Rosenzweig back from conversion to Christianity? Was Rosenstock-Huessy's question about the relevance of the synagogue in history valid? Does his assertion of its irrelevance have application in our world today 75 years later?

The question centers on the influence of Judaism as a contributing factor in the advancement of Western Civilization. Rosenstock-Huessy was saying that over the past two millennia the battle in the West against the forces of paganism had been fought not by Jewish Rabbinical introspection in the Synagogue, but by the openness of Christianity as it extended itself outward to all of man and women kind. He was saying that the dictum of Jesus Christ: *As you have loved the least of my brethren, you have shown your love to me.* had been a driving force unprecedented in world history bringing people of all tribal, national and spiritual backgrounds into a relationship with the God of all Creation, helping them to separate and destroy within themselves the opposing de humanizing and destructive forces of evil.

Rosenstock-Huessy was saying that this revelation unveiled 2000 years ago by a Jew from Nazareth was the force that had powered the Western World into the society it is today. For the first 300 years it overcame the Roman and other hostile pagan forces that were bent upon crushing it. For the next 1000 years, after the fall of the Roman Empire and through the Dark Ages, it battled the forces of Barbarian conquest. Then, with the Renaissance it opened up the human mind releasing all of its potential and allowing civilization to spring forth into a new age of enlightenment.

From the time of Rosenstock-Huessy's letters to the present day, the revelation of Jesus Christ relating to our relationship to each other and to GOD

XI The Challenge to Rabbinical Judaism The Continuing Revelation of the Hebrew God

As you have loved the least of my brethren, you have shown your love to me.

has continued to be absorbed in human consciousness throughout the world and to gain strength. In recent history, from the two great wars, to the standoff against atheistic socialism, to the war in Bosnia, to the battle against Islamic Jihad; the ideas expressed in the life and teaching of Jesus Christ have been at the forefront of the struggle.

In recent history two American Presidents have framed the threats to western society in the context of the message of Jesus Christ. It is not by accident that President Bush, a born again Christian, characterized the struggle against global terrorism as a struggle not simply against a challenge to the American democratic way of life or the preservation of two hundred and fifty years of American history, but as a struggle against an "axis of evil". On the surface this may have seemed simplistic; until viewed, as his fundamentalist Christian perspective would necessarily imply, as a struggle against the antithesis of the revelation of Jesus Christ. This antithesis has been the struggle from the very beginning of human history. It was defined by the Jews in the very first book of their Torah when in Genesis man's capacity for evil was revealed. And, it occupied the overriding theme of the rest of their Bible.

With the coming of Jesus Christ, the Jews did not reach outside of the Temple and then the Synagogue and join in this life and death struggle. In their past they had always fought for their own tribal and religious preservation, but had not made an effort to spread the ideas from their Torah to the rest of the world. At times, they had accepted some non-Jews from the outside, but just as often their armies had destroyed and left abandoned those who had challenged them and their beliefs. There was no attempt to change the world.

With Jesus as the self proclaimed last Jewish Prophet and Messiah, the new religion that he formed, Christianity, took on the great battle against evil in the world. But, the Jews rejected him. They turned inward, and as they dispersed from their homeland after 70 A.D., they hid behind their Torah in the confines of their synagogues.

Shortly after the crucifixion of Jesus, the religion of Abraham had become two Jewish religions, one, ancient Judaism and the other Christianity/Judaism. Then, Christianity itself began to change and to take on a form of its own, more separated from Judaism and in part removed from the Jesus whom the Jews had seen and heard. Four centuries later Roman Catholicism was born.

Could it be that Rosenzweig was only seeing a side of Christianity in part removed from the original purity of the thought of Jesus? If he was, then what specifically about Christianity was holding him back? Was it the dark side of the history of the Christian Church? Was it the dogma and the liturgy, the Triune God, the Nicene Creed, or the proclaimed inerrancy of the New Testament Canon of writings authorized by the fifth century catholic bishops? Could he have converted to Christianity simply by accepting Jesus Christ in his earliest form as the Jewish Messiah and the incarnation of GOD, without accepting the dogma and liturgical formality of institutionalized Christianity? Was total assimilation into present day Christianity necessary?

A more important question concerns all Jews at the time of Jesus. Why did so few, in the years immediately after the death of Jesus, do what the Pharisee Paul did? Why did more not become Jewish Christians? Was it that Jesus had extended GOD'S hand to the entire world and throughout Jewish history they had seen only themselves as His "Chosen People". Jesus had said they would have to give up everything, including the idea of being "Chosen" and be "born again" into a new life, a life lived with GOD "indwelling". For the Jews, only they were "Chosen" and God was not "within," He was outside in the heavens.

Throughout their history being Jewish had been more than just a religious belief. Jewish atheists and agnostics still considered themselves to be Jews and were considered by other Jews to be Jews. Only under extreme circumstances would a Jew be thrown out of a Synagogue.

For Rosenzweig was this tribal attachment the stumbling block? Were the interlocking Jewish/Tribal religious practices? Were the cadence, the rhythm, the emotional ties to Jewish ritual preventing him from escaping his Jewish identity? When he did experience a "conversion experience," was it real or was it just a superficial emotional catharsis taking him back to the tribal and religious ties that bound him to the Judaism of his ancestry?

The Judaism of Rosenzweig's ancestry, during the time of Jesus, was held captive by the Temple Priests. In Rosenzweig's time it was held captive by the Rabbis; as it is today. How much authority should the Priests have had 2000 years ago and the Rabbis today to tell Jews how to approach GOD and to define who GOD is and who God is not? How much of the religious practices as defined today by the Rabbis are necessary for a Jew or anyone else to know GOD?

Putting all of this aside, could there possibly have been for Rosenzweig a synthesis? Is it possible that he could have had it both ways, to be at the same time both a Christian and a Jew? For 2000 years each side has only thought in terms of total assimilation or no assimilation at all. Jews continue to reject Jesus Christ as a continuum of their vision of their God. Christians see Jews as ignorant because they have not accepted Jesus Christ as the Messiah. Jews look at the early Christians as just another of many Jewish sects that existed at the time of Jesus Christ. Christians look at Jews as being unyielding and stubborn and failing to recognize the revelation that occurred. Jews look upon Christians as being anti-Semitic. Christians look upon Jews as being exclusive, self-centered and unyielding. There has been no willingness to compromise.

It is not a question of whether there can or should ever be compromise between the two or whether one can or should assimilate into the other. These words detract attention from the real issue. The real issue must be addressed in another way. It is whether the revelation of the nature of the Creator of our Universe and the GOD of all humanity stopped at some past point in time or is a continuing process that began with the beginning of Jewish history, extended through the life and death of Jesus Christ and even is continuing to this day.

At issue is whether along the way both Judaism and Christianity have taken on trappings which have held them back from seeing their commonality, trappings that have turned both of them inward and are not relevant to the central issue of the revelation of the true nature of GOD. Within the religions themselves these internal requirements of belief and practice have served to solidify opposing positions, and this has deflected attention from the central issue of whether there ever can be a common understanding of the revelation of GOD'S nature.

In the early part of the 20th century when these two intellectuals were exchanging their letters, Jews had been resisting assimilation for almost 4000 years. No military, political or religious power had ever succeeded in separating them from their Jewish tribal identity and their Torah. The Egyptians, the Babylonians, the Romans, the Muslims, they all tried and failed. Rosenzweig could not be assimilated any more that could his ancestors. He could not assimilate because for him it was either the one or the other. Once a Jew, always a Jew. This historical tribal and religious tie to identity conditions the Jewish frame of mind to this day. For a Jew, it is the blood of Abraham running through his and her veins. It is an identity too strong to be cast aside.

Rosenzweig did not, however, totally dismiss Jesus. He saw Christianity in the role of a messenger of the Jews extending the Torah to the rest of the world. According to him, Judaism was the coals and Christianity was the flame. So he did acknowledge that Jesus was an agent of GOD. But the question still remains, then why couldn't he totally accept Jesus as the Christ? If Jesus was just another sect leader, then how did he become such a force? Why didn't Judaism without him become the flame, a flame that burned brightly for 2000 years and still burns even more brightly today?

From the very beginning of their history the God of the Jews had identified Himself as a God of both love and anger, and of awesome power, inscrutability and mystery. He was exclusively their God and their protector. The God of Jesus Christ was not the same as the God the Jews had identified. Much of this new definition was in contradiction to the definition of the God of the Torah. The God of Jesus Christ did not stand behind armies as they established earthly kingdoms but changed the hearts of the enemy. He did not keep people from pain, but He gave them comfort to endure it. There was no mystery to this God of Jesus Christ. Through his sayings, parables and his life Jesus Christ presented a perfectly clear view of the nature of this God. He was a God of pure love. Jesus built his ministry on one simple powerful statement dealing with compassion and love, even towards enemies. He defined our relationship to GOD saying:

As you have loved the least of my brethren you have shown your love to me.

Jesus Christ was a disappointment to the Temple Priests. They had expected a powerful mighty Messiah sent by the GOD that Moses had witnessed and all they saw was a poor Jew, the son of a carpenter. They expected a Messiah who would make their Nation powerful in the face of Roman power and all they saw was powerless preacher. They expected a royal burial and all they saw was a crucifixion. There was no promise of eternal holy ground, no permanence to the Temple in Jerusalem, no army to keep the enemy away.

But his words were disturbing. And the words of those who followed him were disturbing, so disturbing that the temple priests decided to persecute those Jews who became Christians. The self proclaimed Messiah had challenged the order of things. He had challenged the very definition of the nature of the Hebrew God.

Throughout their history the Jews have always wanted to know more about their God. They have wanted to see His face. From the moment of His revelation to Moses this has been their quest, to know more about their GOD. To find him they first developed an Oral Torah, which was passed on from generation to generation. Around 500 BCE it finally became the written Hebrew Bible.

But the Hebrew Bible did not tell them enough. They wanted to know more. They wanted to find a way to worship their God and to find His deeper meaning for their lives. They proceeded to develop another Torah apart from the scriptures of the Hebrew Bible, first as the Mishna and then as the Midrash. Along with these came elaborate rules of conduct all designed to help them worship

XI The Challenge to Rabbinical Judaism The Continuing Revelation of the Hebrew God

their God. As these rules developed, they became more and more demanding. How to dress, how to eat, how to pray, what clothing to wear were all considered a way to worship and sanctify themselves before their God and find His approval in them. Levitical Rabbinical Judaism was born.

The Torah and the rules that followed were to help Jews to worship and to know their God. But did they? Did Torah enable the Jews to know any more about their God than they knew of him when Moses came down from the mountain?

Judaism had become an inward religion dictating a required pattern of behavior to be applied only to the individual Jew. There was little or no requirement as to the behavior for non-Jews outside of Judaism. Those outside of Judaism were as if they never existed. The purpose of Rabbinical Judaism and the Synagogue was to preserve Judaism, not to conquer a pagan evil world. Judaism had no desire to extend itself outside of itself. There was no purpose to the Synagogue outside of the Synagogue.

This is what led to the question that Rosenstock-Huessy, the Christian, asked of Rosenzweig, the Jew:

Whether there was any purpose in the synagogue, seeing that in the reality of history the struggle between the pagan world and the message of revelation was being fought out not by Judaism, but by Christianity.

The question of Rosenstock-Huessy, the Christian, to Rosenzweig, the Jew, remains. It is a question that must be addressed today by all Jews, and not within the confinement of the Synagogue. It must be taken outside of the Synagogue and addressed in the openness of world society without reference to the Rabbinate.

cannot see the face of GOD. We learned that from Moses when he returned from the mountain and told His people what GOD had said to him:

My face you cannot see.

But we can see the presence of GOD after He has passed through our lives. We can also see him after He has passed through our world. We can see His presence in our history. We can only see the shadow of His form from behind after He has passed. He told Moses:

and you shall see my back....

Has there been any historical evidence of this in our world over the past 2000 years? Is there any evidence that He was here and still is today? Yes, if we will open our eyes we will see that He has been in our presence. We will see that over the centuries there has in fact been a very great struggle, one that the Apostle Paul described as being a struggle of *cosmic proportions*. It is a struggle that Rosenstock-Huessy described as *the struggle between the pagan world and the message of revelation.*

It was the message of Jesus Christ that was at the forefront of this struggle. Those Jews who continue to reject Jesus Christ saying he was an imperfect interpreter of their Torah should ask themselves the questions: If the self proclaimed Messiah who was rejected 2000 years ago was so insignificant and unnecessary, how is it that history has proved his presence on this Earth to be so powerful? How did this new and different view of GOD when absorbed into the lives of men and women have such power against the dehumanizing forces of evil over such a long period of time? What would our world be like today if there had not been a Jesus Christ? Without him, how would we now be facing these forces? How would we be living and thinking?

Rosenzweig's reference to Judaism being the burning coals and Christianity the flame was a correct descriptive metaphor of religious influence; nevertheless, at the same time it was an excuse by a Jew to avoid having to acknowledge the reality of Jesus Christ as the indwelling of GOD working through the Holy Spirit in the lives of very many men and women over 2000 years. Clearly, it took more than just *religious influence* to make happen what happened.

History has proved that Jesus Christ was the continuing revelation of the GOD the Jews had been waiting for so long to see. He was the incarnation of a GOD that exists not distant from the world confined to the Temple or the Synagogue but outside among and between and within all people in the world, each with his and her own human weakness.

Two thousand years of History has proved Judaism wrong to assume that the revelation of the nature of GOD exists only for them confined to its ancient form, that it ended with the Hebrew Bible and their exclusive interpretations of it.

What is GOD'S purpose for the synagogue over the next 2000 years? Should it remain inward, encapsulated within its Talmudic law, preserving for all time its anthropomorphic God in His ancient and exclusive form? Or, should it be to turn outward, at the same time embracing Jesus Christ as GOD'S continuing revelation to the Nation of Israel, as well as to the entire world?

XII
Three Different Approaches to Salvation

"The greater question those at the extremes must ask is whether GOD is making the same exclusionary choices that they are."

(The Author)

The world has chosen to look at the three religions of Abraham as if they were three brothers or sisters. The fact is, like siblings from the same family who are raised by the same parents, each is very different from the other. This is most noticeable in their separate understandings of the nature of the monotheistic God they worship and the personal relationship of believers to that God.

The understanding of the nature of the God each worships is not the same. How to achieve eternal life with GOD is not the same.

- For Christians it is by striving to live and think like Jesus Christ whom they believe was GOD incarnate. Their goal is to become perfect like he was. However, they believe that no matter how much they strive to become perfect like him, they remain fallible sinful human beings who can never attain total perfection. They believe it is only through the love and forgiveness of GOD that they can be at one with Him for eternity. The depth of that love was expressed by the crucifixion of His son—symbolically the ultimate sacrifice. Works alone therefore can never be enough to justify redemption.

- For Jews it is by both studying and following the law of the Torah and its commentaries. Torah study encompasses the whole Bible, including the prophets and the other writings. It also encompasses the bulk of post biblical literature, called Mishnah, Gemara, Midrash, Codes and Responsa. To the extent Jews live their lives in this way, they will be rewarded in kind after death by a God of judgment.

- For Muslims it is by following the teachings of the prophet Muhammad and believing that he was the appointed by God to give the world His word. This word is expressed not in the Christian Old or New Testament or the Hebrew Bible or commentaries but in a code of conduct found in the Koran and the Sunna, known together as the Shari'a. Muslims are required to believe that living and thinking by these writings is the way to eternal life. All other teachings outside of Islam are considered to have been corrupted. At death, as in Judaism, it is a God of judgment who will decide the eternal existence of the soul.

It can be seen that the three religions that sprang from Abraham have far reaching differences. The most significant of these deals with the most important questions any religion can ask of itself: What is the nature of GOD and what is our relationship to Him?

For most believers of these three religions, there is the conviction that they are right and the others are wrong. History has shown this to be true. It has made it abundantly clear that in the matter of salvation none of the three believes there can be any kind of compromise or even accommodation. Each believes that all others in the other traditions are excluded from a perfect eternal union with GOD; although, there is a general belief, at least among those with moderate views, that GOD will favor those from the other traditions that also grew out of the Mosaic Law.

The greater question those at the extremes must ask is whether GOD is making the same exclusionary choices that they are. If GOD is not, but is looking at some higher aspect of human thought and behavior, those who live and think at the extremes of these traditions may have to face the eternal consequences of a series of questions:

- Could some of their scriptures, Hebrew, Christian, Muslim not be of the Mind of GOD, but of the mind of man? Could they be *corrupted*?

- Is it GOD'S divine truth that eternal union with Him is reserved just for themselves?

- What does it mean if they are wrong?

- By judging others as being excluded, are they making Gods of themselves?

These are questions with an eternal dimension. By excluding all others, their answers may place at risk for eternity nothing less than our own souls.

39.
THREE MONOTHEISTIC BELIEFS

I. Christianity

"We are saved solely through him, out of grace and mercy, without any works or merit on our part".
(The sermons of MARTIN LUTHER
section I on Faith, and coming to Christ)

If righteousness is through the law, then Christ died for Naught.

(Galatians 2:21)

II. Judaism

"God created two different time periods: The first period is called the 'period of Effort and Striving.' This is the period we are living in. In this period we live a Torah life and perform Torah commandments.... This is where we earn the goodness. This period is temporary, as it ends in death. The second period, called 'the Period of Reward,' starts after death. During that time the soul will receive the goodness that it earned. This period is eternal."

(Rabbi Moshe Chaim Luzatto,
18th Century Italian)

III. Islam

"Thus it is evident how closely connected with the Maker is the leader (Muhammad)...who serves the purposes of the Maker's artistry...Surely the religion of God is Islam...Muhammad is the messenger of God.... If you want endless accomplishments with regard to your afterlife, walk on the Prophet's way.... By acting in accordance to the elevated Sunna of the Prophet Muhammad, one can make one's transient life produce eternal fruits to be the means of eternal life.

(WWW. islamanswers.net/sunna/loved.htm)

XIII
Science, Evolution and the Hand of GOD

In the beginning God created the heaven and the earth

(Genesis 1:1)

Before I formed you in the womb I knew you for my own; before you were born, I consecrated you.

(Jeremiah 1:5)

Three and a half billion years ago as the surface of what we now call our earth began to cool, a highly complex DNA molecule emerged in its primordial oceans. In that molecule was the first set of instructions for human life. Over time as mutations altered and added instructions, the molecule became more and more complex. Today all human beings share this same DNA molecule. Only the most infinitesimal differences exist between any two molecules and therefore only infinitesimal differences exist between any two human beings. This original DNA molecule along with its mutations has connected every human being through human history including Abraham, Moses, David, Buddha, Jesus of Nazareth and Muhammad, to name just a few. The life of each shared the same original genetic instructions.

As millions of years passed, the information contained in the sequence of the molecule increased in complexity. Life as we know it was on the path of its evolutionary journey. It was not, however, a journey that would bring forth permanent lives fixed in time without an end. It brought forth lives that would only exist for brief moments in time. From the moment of conception to the moment of death, the duration of life was like a spark briefly shining in the night. However, by being able to replicate life through the miracle of the division of the DNA molecule into an almost perfect copy of itself, rebirth could continue to take

XIII Science, Evolution and the Hand of GOD 147

place in like form through time. Without this replication, our human species would not exist today. The possibility of its existence would have disappeared.

Our lives are like sparks of light in a vast cosmos blinking on, coming to life, and then blinking off in death. Each of us comes to life as a bundle of energy momentarily capturing the rays of light coming from our sun. Then we die and our bodies return to their inorganic lifeless composition. The light rays of our sun are converted into everything we need for sustenance. From the moment we are conceived in our mother's womb, our very existence is dependent on this energy. We feed off the organic matter produced by this energy all of our lives. Every apple, every pear, every piece of fish or meat is made possible by this energy.

Our physical bodies are no more than organic chemical factories under the control of our DNA, capturing the energy of our sun. At death this whole process comes to an abrupt halt—the chemical process that kept us alive stops. We, and the complex instructions in our DNA molecules that made us possible, break down and slowly disintegrate into the basic elements from which they came. In time there is no marker left that says who we were. Everything returns to the cosmos. We turn to *dust*.

The sun, which acts as our source of life, is surrounded by a solar system that is enveloped in vast reaches of space by total darkness. There are many solar systems like ours in our universe, which was brought into being over 13 billion years ago. There are great constellations of stars in vast reaches of space swirling like hurricanes. There are so many stars, possibly hundreds of billions, that we cannot comprehend the number. This space lying beyond us continues to expand into the darkness. The galaxies beyond ours continue to move away from us.

The possibility of a person's existence in this universe as a unique living thinking individual with his/her own inner spiritual identity defies all odds. From the moment of fertilization of a single egg through to the period of gestation, we develop an inner identity unlike any other. It is the *me* within the physical me. This identity emerged out of billions of years of mutation and replication of our DNA molecules, which was brought about in random moments of time as conception occurred between single sperms and single eggs.

Is our existence then just the result of a random selection of almost identical DNA? Are we just a momentary flash of energy in the seemingly endless space of the Universe? Do we cease to exist when the energy is spent and it is all over? Are we only a spark that gives light and then dies?

Or, is it possible that each of us is a unique form of creation that has dimension beyond the one that we can scientifically measure by the observation of ourselves and our physical universe? Is it possible that the DNA molecular structure in each of us that evolved over billions of years through random selection has come into being as a unique creation in the mind of GOD, giving each of us the possibility during our brief period on this earth to be something beyond mere organic existence.

XIV

Was Jesus of Nazareth the Messiah? Will He Come Again?

And the Lord God commanded the man saying, of every tree of the Garden of Eden thou mayest freely eat, but of the tree of the knowledge of good and evil, thou shall not eat of it: for in the day that thou eatest thereof thou shalt surely die.

(Genesis 2:16-17)

"Humpty Dumpty sat on a wall:

Humpty Dumpty had a great fall,
All the King's horses and all the King's men
Couldn't put Humpty Dumpty together again."

English nursery rhyme from

Alice in Wonderland
by
Lewis Carroll

    As Genesis describes us; like Humpty Dumpty, we too had fallen. And like him, we were broken for all eternity. We could no longer be the way we were.

    Could we ever return to the way we were and be like we were, in *the image of GOD* before we fell into sin? Could we ever return to an eternal union with the GOD who was a part of us at the very beginning of our human existence? Could the sin that we brought upon ourselves ever be forgiven? Could the damage be undone?

Christians believe that the life and death of Jesus Christ was GOD'S call to return to the way we were, to let Him place the brokenness of our lives back together again. Those from the same Hebraic tradition, Jews and the Muslims, do not believe this. Jews believe that our sin has left us estranged from GOD. He has cast us away. They believe that this estrangement will remain until the coming of their Messiah, as literally prophesied in the Hebrew Scriptures. Muslims are not waiting for a Messiah but for the end of the world and a final Day of Judgment when GOD will examine their lives in His Book of Records. They expect that Jesus, whom they look at as the second greatest prophet next to Muhammad, will then again appear. For those of the other main world religions, the Hebraic idea of original sin and estrangement from GOD is not a part of their understanding of man's spiritual nature. They do not acknowledge the duality of human nature and the force of evil as it was described in Genesis.

For the Jews, from the beginning of their history, and with the presence of Jesus Christ for the Christians from the beginning of theirs, the story in Genesis of the fall of man presented a vivid description of that part of the nature of man that was alien from GOD. Genesis told how sin had led to an estrangement from GOD. It declared that the result was for mankind an endless cycle of pain and suffering.

Any study of history shows this duality in the nature of man to be true. The hundreds of millions who have suffered over the ages in the hands of their fellow men is testimony to man's inhumanity to man. The horrors of history both past and present show clearly this duality of man's nature as it was described in Genesis. The Human Being, among all others in the animal kingdom, has shown without interruption through history a unique propensity to degrade and destroy.

Today, Christians view the life and death of Jesus Christ as GOD'S call to make right what had gone wrong. For them it was a divine intervention by GOD. GOD showed men and women a way that they in their imperfection can be at one with GOD in His perfection both here on earth as well as for eternity. The coming of the Messiah had the purpose of removing man from the damnation into which he had fallen, giving him the possibility eternal union with GOD.

During the time when Jesus Christ lived and in the immediate period after his death, his purpose was not so well defined. It took time for the universality of his message to be understood. Many at the time thought he was the Jewish Messiah, others did not. He did not, in fact, build his ministry on a proclamation that he was. He identified his presence as being beyond the limitations of the expectations of the Hebrew prophecies. He often was circumspect as to whether he was.

XIV Was Jesus of Nazareth the Messiah? Will He Come Again?

He avoided the Talmudic arguments as to whether or not he was. He would answer the question of whether he was with words like: Who do you say I am, or Who do they say I am?

There is a question as to whether Jesus Christ himself believed that he was. Verses in the Gospels show him making this proclamation; however, the argument among many Christian scholars as well as non Christians is that these verses are in fact not historic in the sense that they are not a verbatim record of what Jesus actually said. It was the early Christian followers who interpreted his presence as being that of the long awaited Jewish Messiah. They needed to legitimatize the messianic Jesus among the many other Jewish prophets who had over the years suddenly come on to the scene and then had just as suddenly faded away. During the period when the Gospels of Matthew, Mark, Luke and John were being written, to make a Talmudic case for Jesus being the Messiah, they used the prophetical biblical evidence at hand.

Looking back at the life and death of Jesus Christ, there is no question that he claimed a divinity that transcended Jewish prophecy and the Jewish historical religious experience. It was a claim of being at one with the GOD of all creation. He demonstrated a power and authority not less than that of GOD Himself. It was a power and authority that extended beyond his crucifixion. And, it revealed a God with an entirely different nature from the God defined in the Hebrew Bible.

It is clear from a study of scripture that Jesus Christ viewed the meaning of his life beyond the confinement of the definitions of what a Jewish Messiah was or was not expected to be. He did not view himself as a King who would restore the nation of Israel. Nor did he view himself as an apocalyptic divinity to mark the end of time. He distanced himself from the legalistic complexities of prophetic Hebrew scripture. This may have been the reason he often answered in such an ambiguous way when being asked the question of whether he was the Jewish Messiah. He viewed himself as the fulfillment of GOD'S plan for all mankind and not just the fulfillment of one prophecy or another for the Nation of Israel.

The conclusion can be made that Jesus Christ may have understood himself to be the Jewish Messiah, but he did not build his ministry on a proclamation that he was. Both the New Testament Canon, as well as the other writings not included in the Canon, such as those that were found at Nag Hammadi in 1945, show that he viewed himself beyond the messianic fulfillment of Hebrew prophecy.

The vision of Jesus Christ was a vision of a new and different kind of personal relationship with GOD. It was not distant, as was the Hebraic relationship. His vision even extended so far as to bring GOD into oneself, as was demonstrated in the Last Supper, a sacred act that later became the Holy Sacrament of the Eucharist.

When Jesus Christ appeared, many of the Jews were expecting a nationalistic Messiah who would be anointed by GOD himself and who would restore the Kingdom of Israel. In their scriptures he was described as a King of the line of David. He would lift up Jerusalem to its glory and lay the foundation for a theocracy that would rule GOD'S Kingdom on earth. This national ideal saw the Messiah establishing here on earth the Kingdom of GOD. It would take place under the miraculous intervention of the Messiah. He would reestablish Jerusalem as its center and gather the dispersed. His Kingdom would be eternal. With it would come the conquest and subjugation of the heathen who would be driven from Jewish land.

Another parallel line of thought existed among the Jews. In it the Messiah is described in terms of being like a Son of Man appearing on the right hand of GOD in the clouds of heaven, inaugurating a new age, not by national victory but by the exercising of the divine right to judge the whole world. This was the apocalyptic ideal, based principally on the Book of Daniel. A future age was to be ushered in by the Divine Judgment of mankind preceded by the resurrection of the dead. The Messiah, pre existent from the beginning of the world, would appear at the consummation, when there would exist a heavenly Jerusalem which would be the abode of the blessed.

This apocalyptic idea also existed among the Jews independently, without a Messiah, that is the idea that the end of the world would come and there would be a final judgment. This would be a day of reckoning when pious Jews would be recognized for their piety.

With Jesus Christ, none of this came to pass. There was no ultimate manifestation of GOD'S Kingdom on earth. A new King did not appear to restore the Nation of Israel. Nor did the end of the world occur. All that the Jews witnessed was the son of a carpenter from Nazareth speaking about a new and different kind of God from the one they recognized in their Hebrew Bible, and even re defining many of the scriptures on which rested all of their arguments as to what the Messiah would or would not be.

The Jews therefore remained skeptical of this claim, and do to this day. Their belief that every word of their Hebrew Bible is literally the Word of GOD held them back from accepting the universality of a messianic Jesus.

They asked then and today ask the same question: If he was the Messiah sent from GOD, why was he not able to establish the Kingdom of Israel? In fact, history was quickly moving the other way. The Romans were gradually eliminating the Jewish presence in Jerusalem. There would be no hope for a unified nation, just the opposite. The Jews were being dispersed. Jesus clearly had not restored the Kingdom of Israel. And what about the *End of Time* when those who had spent their lives in the study of the Torah would be separated from those who had not, and rewarded with GOD'S eternal grace? He did not bring that either.

The early Christians attempted to counter at least the apocalyptic argument by saying there would be a Second Coming of Jesus Christ and then an apocalyptic period when these things would take place. The newly converted Jewish Christians, as well as the converted gentiles accepted this, and at least for the first one hundred years after the death of Jesus Christ, eagerly awaited the Second Coming.

In view of the justifiable skepticism of Jews during Jesus' time, as well as today, based on their Talmudic arguments, the question must be addressed by Christian scholars: Why were the early Christians writers so quick to support the argument that Jesus Christ was the Messiah? Why did this in the early years of Christianity become such an important part of Christian doctrine? Why is it so important today? From our perspective in the 21st century, looking back at the influence of the life of Jesus Christ on the world over the past two thousand years, his being a Jewish Messiah seems for many a less important issue.

The reason was that for the early Jewish converts to Christianity this claim was absolutely essential in order to establish a Jewish belief in Jesus Christ. Without a tie into the Messianic prophesies of the Hebrew Bible, the divinity of Jesus Christ would have been open to question. It must be remembered that for the first fifty years the church was not Gentile but Jewish. Gentile conversion was only a gradual process that came later on. Most of the early Christians had been devout Jews before becoming Christians. They all had a thorough knowledge of the Hebrew Scriptures. Even for the non-pious Jew, studying the Torah and other sacred books was an important part of life. A Jew would spend his whole life in the study of the Hebrew Bible. In order to argue their case among their fellow Jews, it was important for the Jewish Christians to prove Jesus Christ was the Messiah based on a Hebrew Scriptural foundation. Even his lineage had to be traced to David. Everything had to be supported from the original divine source, the Hebrew Bible. The early Jewish Christians needed to see a fulfillment of the prophecies that they knew and understood and in which they believed.

Nevertheless, as the early Christian Church wrestled with this concept, there were different messianic interpretations. The concept was not one that could be clearly defined based on Hebrew scripture and commentary. Jesus Christ himself had added to the confusion by his ambivalence.

Among the early Christians there were basically three interpretations of the role of Jesus Christ as the Messiah:

1. Jesus began his messianic work when he was baptized by John.

2. Jesus began his messianic work at his resurrection and ascension to GOD'S right hand.

3. Jesus would begin his work as the Messiah with his Second Coming.

As the years passed, these interpretations lost their importance so that today it is the Christian view that Jesus of Nazareth from his birth was without question the long awaited Jewish Messiah. It is also the Christian view that Jesus himself interpreted his role as being that of the Jewish Messiah.

The messianic and apocalyptic idea had grown out of the history of the Nation of Israel. From its very beginning this history had been a painful one. In many ways it was no different under the domination of the Roman Empire. Throughout this suffering, there was the idea that at some future time GOD would *even the score* and then evil in the world would be defeated and Jews would receive their just rewards in heaven. The end of the world would take the form of a cataclysmic event when GOD would recognize those Jews who had, over the ages, been his loyal subjects.

The early Jewish Christians were confronted with the same painful existence. The concept of an Apocalypse and the Second Coming of Jesus Christ was one that gave them hope during their time of trial. They had come from a religion that stressed temporal rewards for behavior that pleased GOD and temporal penalties for transgression. As time passed they saw that their righteousness was not being rewarded. Evil had not been vindicated. GOD'S enemies were not being overthrown. They only saw persecution by the Romans, as well as by their fellow Jews. Most of their fellow Jews did not accept Jesus as the Messiah The Jewish Christian converts therefore found themselves alone and isolated.

For these Christians the idea of an apocalyptic period when GOD would destroy the ruling powers of evil and restore the righteous gave them hope. This idea had for Judaism itself taken a firm hold by the year 200 B.C., although it extended back to the writings of the Prophets. Notable is the idea of judgment referred to in Isaiah 2:12. For the Jews it was anticipated to be a period marked by a cosmic cataclysm when GOD would destroy the world. It would mark the end time and the ushering in the Kingdom of GOD.

During the early period of Christian persecution this idea was quickly accepted and taken over by many of the followers of Jesus. It was ultimately incorporated into the orthodoxy of Christian faith as well as the Canon of accepted writings—The New Testament—so that today it is accepted by many Christians as an article of faith. The Book of Revelation became the final proclamation of Christian doctrine relating to the Second Coming, the end of the world and the final judgment.

The Disciples of Jesus looked upon him as being the fulfillment of this apocalyptic biblical prophecy. For them, however, there was a problem. It was that Jesus had come, but there was no end of time.

There was only one interpretation that they could make of this—that there would be a second coming. This idea was readily accepted by many in the early Jewish Christian community and the gentile converts. In time, it was fully incorporated into orthodox Christian belief. After the crucifixion of Jesus, one of the Disciples, John, in his exile on the island of Patmos about 95 A.D., using the imagery from Ezekiel and Daniel, wrote the Book of Revelation which gave a thorough description of the event. With this book, the idea took on a dimension well beyond the traditional Jewish one.

This Hebraic and Johannine prophecy would, for the early Christians, lay the foundation for their firm belief in the Second Coming of Jesus Christ. At that time, the messianic as well as the apocalyptic predictions of the Hebrew Bible would all be fulfilled at once, and the powerful evil forces would be defeated. Christians would be ushered into the hands of a loving GOD in heaven. Non-Christians, that is, those who did not profess a belief in Jesus Christ, would be left behind.

It is the view of many Christians today that there will be a Second Coming of Jesus Christ. They believe that in time the Apocalypse will occur according to the Hebrew biblical prophesies as further reinterpreted in the New Testament in the Book of Revelation. Then, there will be a *Day of Judgment*.

The Book of Revelation caused a great deal of controversy in the early Christian period and barely made it into the Canon we now call the New Testament. The presupposition it made as to the *End of Time* and who will be saved and who will not was from the very beginning attacked by many Christians. Recent scholarship into the discoveries at Nag Hammadi as well as historical conclusions based on other information as to the underlying power struggles that took place among the Christian bishops during the second through fourth centuries, as doctrinal matters were being settled, raise questions as to whether the idea of an Apocalypse and a second coming was a part of the teaching of Jesus Christ at all and therefore should have been included as part of Christian orthodoxy.

Most striking is the incongruence between the idea of a future apocalyptic judgmental period and the message of Jesus Christ. This, for Christians, gives rise to an irreconcilable tension. Through spiritual rebirth and the grace of a loving GOD, before they physically die, most Christians believe themselves to be *born again* into a union with GOD in the here and now. As the Apocalypse calls for a postponement of this union until there can be a *final judgment*, there arises a doctrinal inconsistency. In the 21st century, the very idea of the *dead* being resurrected from their graves is difficult to grasp. The two ideas are theologically incongruent: the one; immediate acceptance by GOD through rebirth, and the other; the raising of the body and the person from the dead and then future judgment

This theological problem, for Jews as well as Christians, is made all the worse by the fact that there were recorded actual reappearances of prophets in the Hebrew Bible and the New Testament. Over the past 2000 years there have been reappearances of the Virgin Mary. Jesus Christ was said to have spoken to Paul long after Jesus died. Modern science has confirmed a number of cases where there has been communication with those who have physically died. Of note is the well-known Elizabeth Kubler-Ross case where a deceased patient some time after death returned. If we must wait for the Apocalypse and the Second Coming, how could all this have happened?

In the New Testament, Jesus did talk about a future judgment time, but not in Gospels such as the 5th Gospel of Thomas that were excluded from the Canon by the Roman Catholic Church. The question must therefore be asked: Was the *End of Time* recorded in the New Testament only there because the early Christian writers wanted it there? And, did they want it that way only in order to explain away their inability to understand more deeply the message of Jesus Christ. Were they too closely tied to the Hebrew Bible?

There was never nor is there today any ambiguity for the Jews. As has been stated, the Hebraic concept of the Apocalypse and the coming of the Jewish Messiah are based on the prophecies of the Hebrew Bible and its commentaries. At that time there will be a separation of those who, during their lives on earth have been observant; those who have lived the Torah life, and those who have not. Entrance to heaven will only take place after the occurrence of the Apocalypse, not before. This was the belief of most practicing Jews during the time that Jesus Christ lived. It is the belief of Jews today.

XIV Was Jesus of Nazareth the Messiah? Will He Come Again?

Two thousand years have now passed, and there has been no Second Coming of Jesus Christ. Nor has there been an Apocalypse. Hope continues that this will take place though, especially among evangelical Christians. Because of the theological incongruity of the concept itself, however, many Christians today are asking the question: Did the early Jewish Christians simply expropriate this idea from the Hebrew Bible, given their need to rationalize it, as a result of the *First Coming* not fulfilling all of biblical prophecy? Is the Second Coming then in fact an inauthentic part of the Gospels? Further confusion arises in Matthew 16:28 where Jesus says,

Verily I say unto you, There will be some standing here, which shall not taste death, till they see the Son of man coming in his Kingdom of God.

This statement, taken literally, means that his followers would see the end of the world during their generation. Of course, this did not occur. Christians over the centuries who take the Gospels as the Word of GOD have always been disturbed by Matthew 16:28. It is inconsistent with other parts of the Gospels. Could Jesus have meant that after his death, he would return, not during a future apocalyptic period, but in the hearts and minds of people? He would then lead them into a rebirth into the Kingdom of GOD, not in some distant dimension, but here on earth?

Many Christians still await the *Second Coming* and have in fact moved its expectation to the forefront of their belief system. A recent development has been the belief, primarily among evangelical Christians, that Christians and Jews will be brought together in the last days. Then, those Jews who welcome Jesus Christ as their long awaited Messiah will pass on to heaven along with their Christian brothers and sisters, and those Jews who do not accept Jesus as the Messiah will go to hell. The 21st century geopolitical significance of this is found in the strong and vocal American evangelical Christian support of the God given right of the Nation of Israel to occupy the territory of the Holy land and in particular the city of Jerusalem where the Second Coming is to occur.

Could it be that the canonical references of Jesus Christ to a Second Coming were wrongly interpreted and therefore wrongly recorded because of a thought process of the early Jewish Christians rooted in the prophesies of the Hebrew Bible and based on a *need to believe*? Did they only hear what they wanted to hear? Did they interpret the words of Jesus Christ only the way they wanted to interpret them? The 5th Gospel of Thomas, which may very well predate the Gospels placed in the New Testament canon refutes the idea of a Second Coming and an Apocalypse.

Whether or not Jesus Christ spoke of his Second Coming and an Apocalypse cannot be proved or disproved. What is open for debate now in the 21st century is what he really said when he lived. Orthodox Christianity stifled this debate for 2000 years claiming that all matters relating to the scriptures were settled.

If we look at the prophesies of the Hebrew Bible and the New Testament statements relating to the end of time from the perspective of modern science, we are left with the fact, fully recognized today, that there may be at the end of our world as we know it a catastrophe of overwhelming proportions. At that time, it is evident those of the human species who are alive then, other than those able to colonize other planets—which at the present is a remote possibility—will perish. The scientific reasons for this possibility were not understood 2000 years ago as they are today. Then, the workings of the physical Universe and the interdependence of life on our planet were a mystery.

Until the turn of the 20th century, the Canon of writings found in The New Testament for almost all Christians remained the inerrant WORD of GOD. The description of the Apocalypse and the idea of a second coming of Jesus Christ were considered to be sacrosanct. They were to be accepted on faith. The images that grew out of early Christian doctrine, defining a physical separation between heaven and earth, were required to be accepted on faith. Any thinking that did not fit into these ideas was considered heretical. Much of Christianity continues to hold to these ideas today.

These ideas, held as sacrosanct since the very beginning of the Church, are now being challenged. This challenge is not just an academic or theological one. It is a challenge, the outcome of which will have a far reaching influence on the question of how future generations are to view themselves and the world in which they will continue, or not continue, to exist. This challenge came with the discovery at Nag Hammadi in 1945 of the lost "Gnostic" Gospels.

These writings, and in particular The Gospel of Thomas, show Jesus Christ talking about himself, as well as heaven and earth, in a different way. He spoke of heaven as if it were non-dimension in space and time and in fact even as if it were a part of earth. He spoke of the non-physical aspect of the human form—which he a demonstrated by his reappearances after his crucifixion. These were and continue to be ideas alien to traditional church doctrine; but, interestingly, fall in line with modern scientific theory which recognizes space as multidimensional, time as purely a man made construct enabling him to understand himself and the Universe in ways that he can mathematically measure, and the human form not as physical mass but as energy particles without mass, or more specifically moving energy surrounded by vast space. The very idea of heaven as being someplace else where one physically "goes up to" therefore quickly looses its meaning as does the idea of an "end" or a "beginning" of time. Thus, the orthodox Jewish and Christian idea of one going "up to" heaven at the "end of time" rings hollow.

Three recorded statements about heaven. purportedly made by Jesus Christ, are worth noting. They show a progression in thought that could not have been understood when the Gospels were written and compiled, but can be understood now in the 21st century:

From the authorized Christian New Testament

The Kingdom of Heaven is like a mustard seed.... A mustard seed is smaller than any other; but when it has grown, it is bigger than any garden plant....

(Matthew 13:31-32)

From the Nag Hammadi Library: The 5th Gospel of Thomas

The kingdom is inside of you, and it is outside of you. (3)

What you look forward to has already come, but you do not recognize it. (51)

It will not be a matter of saying 'here it is' or 'there it is'. Rather, the Kingdom of the father is spread out upon the earth, and men do not see it. (113)

It is interesting to observe that the Matthew description does not speak to a heaven here on earth. It simply adds descriptive definition to a metaphysical reality that exists somewhere else. It is therefore no more than a further clarification of the biblical Hebraic non-descriptive and murky definition of heaven. Nor does it place us in heaven. It describes heaven as someplace in our conventional understanding of *space* apart from us. The 5th Gospel of Thomas, however, describes an entirely different kind of heaven, and it places it on and within our plane of existence. It tells us everything about heaven we would ever want to know. It challenges us to break through our traditional Hebraic way of thinking and find it within ourselves. It forces us to find rebirth, to shed the old and become the new.

The Thomas Gospel descriptions are not found in the Hebrew Bible or the Koran or in Roman Catholic Christian Orthodoxy, and for very good reason. These are all religions of final judgment and passage to a heaven in some far distant place at the time of the Apocalypse. Passage for those with these beliefs; Jews,

Christians, and Muslims can only come as a future event and then only for those who have pleased a judgmental God. As noted, Hebrew biblical definitions of what it is are murky and impossible to define. The description that Muhammad made in the Koran gives more definition. It describes a sumptuous banquet with virgins for the pleasure of men who have been devout Muslims.

These and many other definitions left open by the Hebrew Bible and the New Testament Canon were challenged with the discovery of the 5th Gospel of Thomas in 1945 in Upper Egypt. Outside of the Egyptian city of Nag Hammadi it was discovered along with more than fifty other early Christian texts, many unknown since antiquity. They were found in an ancient six-foot jar unearthed from a hillside. After 1600 years the seal of the Christian Canon cast by the Christian Church in the fourth century was broken.

In response to a fourth century edict to destroy all but the authorized Christian canon of writings, a group of monks near that town took the so named *unauthorized* and *heretical* writings out of their library, placed them in a six foot earthen jar, and buried the jar in a hillside where it would remain for 1600 years.

The early Christian bishops who had the greatest influence on forming the theology that would become the foundation of the Roman Catholic Church had, to a large extent, rested their case on the inerrancy of the Hebrew Bible as well as certain new writings about Christianity. They alone were to decide what to include and what to exclude in the New Testament. These bishops, by and large, represented a Roman Christian consensus and not that of the provinces. As they were debating, clearly one of the Gospels that must have troubled them the most was the 5th Gospel of Thomas. They branded it as *heretical* and ordered it destroyed.

The author Elaine Pagels in her book *Beyond Belief The Secret Gospel of Thomas* remarks:

"I was amazed when I went back to the Gospel of John after reading Thomas, for Thomas and John clearly draw upon similar language and images, and both, apparently, begin with similar *secret teaching*. But John takes this teaching to mean something so different that I wondered whether John could have written his Gospel to refute what Thomas teaches.... I was finally convinced that this is what happened."

It should be noted that The 5th Gospel of Thomas was written long before the Gospel of John. The gap in time may have been as much as fifty years.

To understand why early Christianity took this turn, it is necessary to look not only at this Gospel, but also at the many others and to examine the question of why they were declared *heretical* and ordered by the bishops to be destroyed. This includes all of those found at Nag Hammadi.

Strong personalities often shape history, especially when they have carefully assembled political power. This was the case with early Christianity. In sorting out what writing would be accepted for the New Testament Canon and what would not, a bishop named Athanasius, intent on bringing all Christians under the supervision of one office, in the year 367 proclaimed twenty-seven books to be The New Testament. At the same time he called upon Christians everywhere to "cleanse the church of every defilement" which are "filled with myth, empty, and polluted."

Bishop Athanasius in his selection showed a predisposition toward the inerrancy of prophetic Hebrew Scriptures as the foundational framework for Christian belief and toward the Gospel of John as the one Gospel that in effect encapsulated that prophetical belief. He would make sure that this for the early Christian Universal (Catholic) Church became the center of its belief system.

Once the writings were chosen, from that moment on the tenets of Christian theology were sealed. From then on there was only one door leading to salvation and that was the one leading into the Universal Roman (Catholic) Church.

The hierarchal structure of the Church based on apostolic succession was fixed for all time. Only those bishops who were a part of the one holy and apostolic church had the authority to interpret the word. To make sure that there would be no temptation to make changes, a council of bishops was convened at Nicaea in 325 and an authorized creedal statement was written. This was a complex set of belief concepts about the nature of both **GOD** and the divinity of Jesus Christ. Thereafter, all who offered viewpoints apart from these creedal statements were labeled as *Heretics* and *Schismatics* and denied participation in the one Universal Church. Over the years, some so labeled were even burned at the stake.

The Emperor Constantine, the first Roman Christian Emperor who reigned during this period, was quick to accept the authorized Christian Canon and the creedal statements that grew out of them. It was a way to unify the Roman Empire through a universal anti-pagan Church during a time of imperial turmoil. The Spoken creedal phrases repeated at every worship service such as "one Holy Catholic and Apostolic church" brought unity and strength to a slowly fragmenting Roman Empire. The books of the New Testament declared by Athanasius to be the only acceptable books relating to the life of Jesus Christ and also the creeds have not changed to this day. Around them was formed the belief system of the Christian Church over the centuries.

The authorized Gospels which became a part of The New Testament and the formulation of the Nicene Creed were the end result of a bitter battle among strong personalities and political groups, each bent on forging its own brand of Christianity. The thinking that won out came from the efforts of two individuals, beginning with a second century bishop named Irenaeus, and then finally in the fourth century a bishop named Athanasius. Athanasius, the architect of the authorized Canon of New Testament writings as well as the Nicene Creed formulated at the council of Nicaea in 325 was tenacious, extremely gifted politically and from the biographical facts known about him even could be described as megalomaniac. His objective was to unite Christendom under one rule with one iron clad interpretation of the life of Jesus Christ, primarily based on the literal meaning of the Gospel of John.

The Nicene Creed was accepted by the Emperor Constantine who had attended the council. It soon became the architecture of Christian belief and has remained so to the present day. Those who opposed it, estimated to be as much as one half of Christendom at the time, were expelled from the council. General opposition throughout the Christian community was eliminated by an edict from Constantine issued just before the meeting that all "heretics and schismatics" were to stop meeting and to surrender all property they had to the Catholic Church. As time passed, the New Testament writings and the Roman Catholic creedal theology that grew out of them was assumed to be sacrosanct. The conclusions at Nicaea were assumed to have come from the Holy Spirit. They could not to be questioned.

The issues at the council were very broad in nature; however, there were several that formed the core of the debate. Their resolution in favor of Athanasius had a far-reaching effect on future Christian doctrine. Their resolution served, with Constantine's active support, to assure the growth of Christianity into a well organized and popular world religion. Among scholars today, this has raised the question of whether the resolution of some of these issues may have been primarily for political purposes. This is the reason for the intense interest in the Nag Hammadi discovery. Until then, scholars had only been able to speculate in vague terms as to what these issues really were.

A very general summary of the opposition position follows:

- Every person alive has the divine within.

- We received our being from the divine, the same source as Jesus.

- Jesus is not our master.

XIV Was Jesus of Nazareth the Messiah? Will He Come Again?

- We can become like him as equals.
- Jesus came to show us the light each of us has within.
- Self-knowledge is knowledge of the divine within.
- All those who find the light of the divine within are saved.
- Those who don't die as if they never were.

Was Athanasius no more than a religious and political fanatic who pushed through the council a dogma that did not in fact reflect the true meaning of the life of Jesus Christ? Was he held back in his understanding of Jesus Christ by his strong desire for the growth of Christianity throughout the Roman Empire? Should other views of Jesus Christ have been included? Was an almost total reliance on the Gospel of John to define Christianity correct? Who really wrote the Gospel of John and how much of it was from the mouth of Jesus Christ?

When we look at Athanasius from a modern psychological perspective, we see in his actions and his personality some disturbing signs. The telltale symptoms of religious fanatics are:

1. Absolute intolerance of dissent
2. Belief that if you are not with us you are against us
3. Belief that one's cause has been blessed by GOD
4. Belief that one's actions are commanded by GOD
5. Belief that the cause is not just good but the only good
6. Use of reinforcement techniques such as repetition of simple phrases
7. A doctrine riddled with contradictions

It will be left to the religious historians to answer these questions. The fact remains that Athanasius and those who supported him blocked out a different view of Jesus Christ, and then with the backing of Constantine enforced their own brand of Christianity on the world, a brand that has dominated ever since

Since the discovery of the 5th Gospel of Thomas in 1945 at Nag Hammadi, Christianity has been forced to reexamine the rational for the selection of the writings that formed the New Testament and also, as a byproduct of this examination, the creeds themselves. We now see that in the process of establishing the system of theology that would become the Roman Catholic Church, the bishops suppressed many important resources relating to what Jesus Christ may have said. The Nag Hammadi discovery revealed that there existed a much wider range of Christian thought within the first one hundred years after his death than was previously recognized.

Many Christians today who repeat the Nicene Creed during their worship with words describing Jesus Christ as *begotten not made, of one being with the father* who is *seated on the right hand of the Father* and who will come *in glory to judge the living and the dead* do not give these words a second thought. Nor do those who are not Roman Catholic know that as their churches are not considered by Roman Catholicism to be the *one holy and apostolic church,* therefore they themselves live in ignorance. Many Christians, when they repeat the words set down 1600 years ago saying that they *look forward to the resurrection of the dead,* do not in their hearts believe this. They speak of their dead Christian relative or friend who has just passed on as being at present in heaven. They do not give much thought to what Athanasius really meant 1700 years ago.

Nor do they have a clear idea of what position Jesus Christ would have taken as to the constitution the three part Trinity which grew out of the Nicene Creed, a concept that had no Old or New Testament foundation but was formulated after the Council meeting. So, they are left to ask: Do we pray to Jesus Christ or through Jesus Christ, or do we pray directly to GOD?

They are not aware of the fact that there were many other ideas about the life and death of Jesus that were never given a chance. They are not aware of the fact that many of these issues were looked upon in a different way by close to one half of Christianity during Athanasius's time.

To find another point of view of major importance, we must turn to the nemesis of Athanasius, The 5th Gospel of Thomas. The Church over the centuries knew about the 5th Gospel of Thomas. Even though by edict all but the authorized New Testament Gospels were ordered destroyed, some fragments of the Thomas Gospel continued to exist. The official church position always was that these fragments were associated with a discredited early religious movement called Gnosticism and therefore were heretical and of little value. The complete manuscript found at Nag Hammadi showed that the Gospel of Thomas was not in fact a Gnostic Gospel in a heretical sense, but it was an authentic account of the life of Jesus Christ, either predating or written at the same time as the New Testament Gospels, and possibly written by a Jewish follower of Jesus who lived in Ephesus or in Antioch, the capital of Syria, or it may have been written even

XIV Was Jesus of Nazareth the Messiah? Will He Come Again?

earlier by his brother Judas (not Judas Iscariot). In any event, there is sufficient evidence to suggest to scholars that the person who wrote it traveled with the disciples of Jesus and may even have been one of them.

The Nag Hammadi writings show Jesus teaching about a different kind of personal relationship with GOD from that shown in the authorized Gospels. The writings speak of heaven in a different way. They speak of the Apocalypse in different way. They speak of the Second Coming of Jesus Christ in a different way. They show that Jesus Christ offered union with GOD; not just to those who believed in him, as the Christianity of Athanasius based on John's Gospel insisted and orthodox Christianity insists to this day, but to each and every person born on this earth who finds the *light* of GOD within him or her self. This is identified as the same light that Jesus Christ found within himself. It is identified as the image of GOD hidden in man, an image that has been there, as described in Genesis, ever since the creation of man. It is an image that is within every person from birth. This is a far different view from the sinful and corrupted view of man as seen by Orthodox Christianity. It is a contradiction of the description of man as seen in the Gospel of John.

To quote again from Elaine Pagel's book:

"What John opposed...includes what the Gospel of Thomas teaches—that GOD'S light shines not only in Jesus but, potentially at least, in everyone. Thomas's Gospel encourages the hearer not so much to believe in Jesus, as John requires, as to seek to know God through one's own, divinely given capacity, since all are created in the image of God".

The 5th Gospel of Thomas is too long to quote here in full. It is not in narrative form as are the canonical Gospels, but is presented as a series of 114 statements attributed to Jesus Christ. Some of the statements parallel those in the canonical Gospels. What follows are selected words from some of the statements that run contrary to the canonical Gospels. They may surprise many readers as they already express the ideas of many modern day Christians in the 21st century, even though the orthodox beliefs of their churches may say otherwise. They also have some parallels with the mystical Judaism of today.

(3) Jesus said...the Kingdom in inside of you, and it is outside of you. When you come to know yourselves, then you will become known, and you will realize who you are.

(13) Jesus said, I am not your master.

(17) Jesus said, I shall give you what no eye has seen and what no ear has heard and what no hand has touched and what has never occurred to the human mind.

(18) The Disciples said to Jesus, Tell us how the end will be. Jesus said, Have you discovered then, the beginning that you look for the end? For where the beginning is, there will the end be. Blessed is he who will take his place in the beginning; he will know the end and will not experience death.

(24) He said to them, There is light within a man of light, and he lights up the whole world. If he does not shine, he is in darkness.

(28) Jesus said,...I found none of them thirsty. And my soul became afflicted. For the sons of men, because they are blind in their hearts do not have sight; for empty they came into the world, and empty too they seek to leave the world.

(41) Jesus said, Whoever has something in his hand will receive more, and whoever has nothing will be deprived of even the little he has.

(51) His disciples said to him, When will the repose of the dead come about, and when will the New World come? He said to them, What you look forward to has already come, but you do not recognize it.

(70) Jesus said, That which you have will save you if you bring it forth from yourselves. That which you do not have within you will kill you if you do not have it within you.

(77) Jesus said, It is I who am the light, which is above them all. It is I who am the all. From me did the all come forth, and unto me did the all extend. Split a piece of wood, and I am there. Lift up the stone, and you will find me there.

(94) Jesus said, He who seeks will find, and he who knocks will be let in.

(97) Jesus said, The kingdom of the father is like a certain woman carrying a jar full of meal. While she was walking on the road, still some distance from home, the handle of the jar broke and the meal emptied out behind her on the road. She did not realize it; she had noticed no accident. When she reached her house, she set the jar down and found it empty.

XIV Was Jesus of Nazareth the Messiah? Will He Come Again?

(108) Jesus said, He who will drink from my mouth will become like me. I myself shall become he, and the things that are hidden shall be revealed to him.

(111) Jesus said, The heavens and the earth will be rolled up in your presence. And the one who lives from the living one will not see death.

(113) His disciples said to him, When will the kingdom come"? Jesus said, "It will not come by waiting for it. It will not be a matter of saying 'here it is' or 'there it is.' Rather, the kingdom of the father is spread out upon the earth, and men do not see it.

It can readily be seen from these statements that the differences between the teachings of Jesus Christ found in the New Testament and in particular the Gospel of John and those found in the 5th Gospel of Thomas reach to the very core of some of the most significant questions facing Christianity today. They are central to today's understanding and misunderstanding of Jesus Christ by Judaism, Islam and other religions in the world. They reach to the very definition of our personal relationship to the Creator of the Universe and to all fellow human beings. They challenge us to reconsider the ancient idea of the presence of the Kingdom of GOD as if it were in a far off place. They force us to look at judgment as being not at some future time but in this time at every moment in every life. They challenge not only the exclusivity of Orthodox Christianity, but also the exclusivity of all other Orthodox religious thought. They challenge us to think more deeply and give broader definition to the words in John 3:16, *whosoever believes in him (Jesus Christ) shall not perish but have everlasting life* and ask us to use the words:

Whosoever shall find within him or her self the divine light that Jesus Christ found within himself will never be separated from God but will be reborn into HIS presence to be in oneness with HIM for all eternity.

(Author's words)

Because of the wide differences in interpretation of scripture brought on by the Nag Hammadi discovery, important questions relating to the teaching of Jesus Christ as they relate to present day orthodox Christian thought call for examination. This examination is in fact being done by eminent biblical scholars, archaeologists, and historians—honestly inquisitive human beings. And this time it is being done without the accusation of heresy, as was always the case in ages past.

Few Jews today are concerned about or even aware of this conflict and debate within Christianity, or do they choose to look at Jesus in any wider context than that of the Jewish Messiah. For them the study of the Torah remains their primary concern and therefore the question remains: According to the Hebrew Bible was Jesus Christ the Jewish Messiah sent by GOD as a fulfillment of prophecy or was he not? They believe he was not. To them it is clear from a rabbinical examination that Jesus of Nazareth did not fulfill biblical prophecy. The rabbinical conclusions are based on a literal interpretation of prophetic scripture as well as rabbinical commentary. For them, these scriptures are the Word of GOD, and they do not prove that he was the Jewish Messiah. Only the words of the Torah are perfect. All else—The New Testament as well as the 5th Gospel of Thomas—is imperfect knowledge coming from Hellenistic and other outside influences.

For all Orthodox Christians he was the Messiah. Their belief is based not on obscure and unfounded blind faith but on Christian interpretations of scripture developed over the ages. These interpretations are from fragmentary, but nevertheless compelling evidence in various passages of the Hebrew Bible. For them, a literal interpretation of every reference is not necessary nor the rabbinical disagreement. They believe that the ambiguity and often conflict over the many references to the coming Messiah put forth by the Rabbis should not be taken as reason to doubt. As the Apostle Paul writes:

When in former times God spoke to our forefathers, He spoke in fragmentary and varied fashion through the prophets. But in this final age he has spoken to us in the son…the stamp of GOD'S very being.

(Hebrews: 1:1-3)

Jesus Christ time and again corrected the Hebrew Bible. As he did so, he would use the personal pronoun *I*. According to the Jewish faith only GOD can correct the Hebrew Bible and only GOD can use the personal pronoun *I* when doing so. Therefore, this can only come with the Messiah. The argument between Christians and Jews therefore becomes a circular one.

There is an aspect of the Christian claim that contradicts and extends beyond the rabbinical argument. As we have seen, it is that the earthly presence of Jesus Christ cannot be narrowly confined to the messianic vision of the Hebrew prophets and their apocalyptic predictions. This raises the question:

Did the life and death of Jesus Christ have a greater purpose? Did he come, not just to save the Nation of Israel, but also to save the world?

Surely the transformation of the western world over the past 2000 years from the darkness of paganism into our present age of enlightenment based on Chris-

XIV Was Jesus of Nazareth the Messiah? Will He Come Again?

tian values did not take place by itself. The spiritual power released upon mankind by Jesus Christ was without doubt the principal driving force. Without it, the decaying Roman Empire would have left us with an entirely different world. A question is often posed by historians: What would the world be like today if it had not been for the presence of Jesus Christ?

Would pagan barbarism have swept through all of Europe and stayed there? What would have held it back? Certainly not insular Rabbinical Judaism. Would Roman and Greek classical thought have been extinguished? Would Islam in the seventh through ninth centuries have spread like a contagion so that today Europe would be one giant Islamic clerical state under the rule of the Koran and bent on conquering by force the entire world? Could there have been a Renaissance? Even if the Muslims had not been totally successful, would barbaric Scandinavian Vikings be today altruistic Social Democratic Norwegians, Danes, and Swedes? Would there have been a U.S. Constitution? Would there have been a Marshall Plan? Would the United States and Europe have stood up to the despotism of a Nazi Germany and a Soviet Union? After the Second World War, would there have been a reconstruction of a Japanese nation or would it have been totally humiliated and crushed with its women raped and its men murdered? Would there have been a Roman Catholic and later Protestant Church to set an example for what the word *charity* means as it is extended into the world beyond those of its own kind?

The course of history was changed not by the sudden adherence of mankind to a new set of rules—The Ten Commandments—or a universal church creed, but by an inner conversion experience that transported people into a new way of thinking. It was a movement that gradually swept through all of society and influenced all of human behavior at every level. Although the Roman Church did have an influence, the change did not come, as some Roman Catholic Christians would insist, from its exclusive presence as the *Body of Christ*. The course of history was changed slowly as human consciousness shed its view—and its fear of an Hebraic fearful and judgmental God—and accepted a belief in a God of Love and forgiveness, a God who valued each person for what they were as they were and for what they could creatively become. History was changed, as Thomas described it in his Gospel, from men and women finding the *light within*.

In the very beginning of the Torah, Genesis describes the condition of man after his eyes were opened to knowledge of both good and evil as one of being estranged from GOD. Adam and Eve had disobeyed GOD and were sent away from Him. Where Adam was at one time a part of GOD and in His image, he was now cast away. From that moment on GOD existed far off in another dimension. There, he would look down on Adam and Eve and their offspring as a punishing as well as rewarding God, like a father looking down on His children. They would spend their lives trying to please Him, but they could never rise to GOD'S call for perfection. The punishment therefore would always far exceed the reward. For the Jews, this was and continues to be the understanding of the nature of the God of the Hebrew Bible and their relationship to him. It also explains for them the inscrutability of an unfathomable God.

To understand Christian thought and the God of Jesus Christ, we must return once again to the English Nursery Rhyme. If all the Kings horses and all the Kings men could not put Humpty Dumpty back together again, who could? Could GOD take something that was irreparable and restore it to the perfection of what it was before? Could He bring man back to the state in which he had existed before he was corrupted by the knowledge of evil? Could GOD bring him back from a life of alienation from Himself? Could He reverse the words in Genesis 2:17...*thou shalt surely die*—and replace them with the words *thou shall never die*. Jesus Christ said yes GOD could, but then Jesus Christ set a condition. He said:

I am the way

Many of the early Christians missed the full message of Jesus Christ. They missed it because they were concentrating on the wrong picture. They were concentrating on the picture of Jesus as the Jewish Messiah. They were concentrating on the Apocalypse. They were concentrating on the second coming of Jesus Christ. They were concentrating on a fear of a judgmental and retributive Hebrew Bible God. They did not see Jesus Christ as the incarnation of a God of pure love and themselves as having the possibility to be at one with the God that Jesus Christ had redefined. It was easier for them to concentrate on the wrong picture. It was easier for them simply to profess a rhetorical belief in Jesus Christ and then settle into their religious orthodoxy. It was easier than modeling their lives after the life of Jesus Christ and searching for the *light within*. Almost all Christians still miss this message today.

The life and death of Jesus Christ showed us that we are no longer broken by sin. By GOD'S grace we are put back together again. We are restored in the image of HIS perfection, like Humpty Dumpty before the fall. This comes to us not by our good works but by HIS grace. Jesus Christ showed us that a God of perfection loves us, even as we are. In spite of our inadequacy, HE sees us not as sinful human beings but as we were in our perfection and perfect union with HIM before we opened ourselves to sin.

Jesus Christ identified himself as the way to enter the presence of GOD, not at some future moment in time during an apocalyptic period but by rebirth now, here on earth. This is what he meant when he said that you must lose your life to gain it.

He came as a final revelation to say there is no need for the Apocalypse prophesied in the Hebrew Bible. Nor is there a need for a Second Coming. He said GOD is here with us now, with each of us who will accept Him. GOD is with us through the Holy Spirit. This is how The Kingdom of GOD has come to earth. Each of us has within the same light that Jesus had in him. If we can find that light, we can walk the same path that Jesus walked. People throughout the world, who have walked in this path, people like St. Francis of Assisi and Mother Teresa were ushering in His Kingdom on earth. And there are countless others who have done and are doing the same. Many are unknown. Some do not even know Jesus Christ; they are from other religions or have none at all, but they have found His light within themselves. These caring, loving individuals are all too few, but then Jesus said the path is narrow. This is what Thomas in his Gospel is telling us.

It is a path that leads to a knowledge of GOD'S purpose for our lives. Jesus told us about this path during the short period of time he was with us. He told Thomas it is not a path that argues whether or not Jesus of Nazareth was the Jewish Messiah. It is not a path strewn with apocalyptic and messianic argument and debate. It is not a path that pits Orthodox against Gnostic Christians. It is not a path that says only through apostolic succession in the Roman Catholic Church can we know the truth.

Jesus took all of this away from the Roman Catholic bishops, from the Jewish Temple Priests, from the Rabbis, and from today's' evangelical preachers. He took it away from the Mullahs too who fear Allah, and only considering Jesus of Nazareth a prophet, are afraid for fear of eternal damnation to believe that they should look to Him and not to Muhammad for the ultimate truth.

It is an uncluttered path that leads to a God of love and love only. HE showed us the path through the example of Jesus Christ, which can be the model for our lives. Jesus Christ set the example for our thoughts and our actions. Jesus Christ said we can become a part of a loving God right now here on earth, the GOD who created us in HIS image, or we can turn our backs on HIM. The choice is ours.

He gave us the choice to prevent an Apocalypse of our own making. He gave us the choice to enhance or degrade the life and the natural environment. When GOD gave man the power to subdue nature, He also gave him the power to destroy it. He gave us a choice, we can worship false Gods or we can worship

HIM, the one true GOD. The false Gods will destroy us and our world. They will lead not only to our own individual destruction but also to the destruction of the human species and the earth on which we live.

We must look at the confusing and often contradictory prophetic predictions of the end of time pronounced in ages past and question whether these were no more or less than an expression of a people searching for an explanation for the pain and suffering that they were experiencing. They lived in a world overwhelmed by evil. Their lives often appeared to be influenced by sinister forces beyond their control. More often than not, their religion gave them no protection. They saw sinners being rewarded and the good being punished. All they had for solace was their dream of a time when the world would end and those who had kept the faith would be rewarded.

Jesus Christ offered a way to experience a life free from pain and suffering. He did not eliminate pain and suffering, but he gave us a way to live with it, and to benefit by it.

Modern science has shown us that there may indeed be an end to the world for the human species, but it will not be an end caused by an angry God. It will be an end caused by a natural cataclysmic event such as an asteroid. Or, it will be an end caused by man himself as he overheats, degrades, and pollutes his environment, and poisons or manipulates living creatures, including man himself.

What the prophets of the Hebrew Bible did not understand is that we bring upon ourselves both individually and as a society our own pain and our own destruction. They saw man as powerless to change this. It was logical for them to blame God and to talk about an apocalyptic period. They did not understand that GOD does not punish, we punish ourselves when we separate ourselves from GOD; when, as the 5th Gospel of Thomas tells us, we do not find him.

The God that Jesus described to Thomas, unlike the God of Hebraic, Koranic, and Christian orthodoxy does not free us with dream like solutions, such as an Apocalypse, from the individual responsibility to overcome the evil in this world. He does not offer to separate good and evil miraculously at the end of time. Nor does He begin with the presupposition of man's innate sinfulness and inadequacy. He starts with the presupposition of man's goodness and ability to overcome evil. He is the one GOD who points to each of us to make this separation by ourselves and with HIM within to become co-creators of HIS Kingdom here now on earth.

Is this what GOD was trying to tell us with the discovery of the long lost 5th Gospel of Thomas at Nag Hammadi in 1945; that we have all gone astray; Christians, Jews, Muslims, and all others, that we have opted for the easy way out? Was

HE trying to tell us that to save ourselves and to save the world HE created for us, each of us on our own must separate him and her self from the comfort and paralysis of our own particular man-made religious orthodoxy and find HIM within?

XV
Not the God They Think They Know

The GOD OF ALL CREATION is testing the three world religions that sprang from the blood of Abraham. All are failing the test. He is saying to each of them:

I am not the God you think you know.

Each declares: "I am right, you are wrong, I know GOD, you don't." Each bases his declaration on dogmatic appendages to ancient texts written down in ages past by the hand of man and declared the inerrant WORD OF GOD. Taking on the role of GOD himself, each stands in judgment of the others. Each has created its own vision of GOD.

Christian Evangelists use their literal interpretation of New Testament texts to pass judgment on all those who do not profess a rhetorical belief in Jesus Christ. They see American society as perverted and adrift, overtaken by evil forces. They look forward to the end of the world as foretold in the Book of Revelation when GOD will destroy it; and they will then be separated from those who do not believe. The unbelievers destined for eternal damnation will include the likes of Gautama Buddha, Mohandas Gandhi and Dr. Jonas Salk, as well as those loving husbands and wives, fathers and sons, and mothers and daughters who perished in the World Trade Center Towers but were not professed *believers* in Jesus Christ. They refuse to acknowledge that GOD may be looking at each of us in a different way, with only the first clues to a deeper meaning as to our relationship with Him coming from scripture. They confine their inerrant view of Jesus Christ to the fragments of scripture authorized by the Roman Church that were written down by the early Christian writers of the New Testament decades after his crucifixion.

Conservative and Orthodox Jews turn a blind eye to the message of Jesus Christ, considering him irrelevant, even after having witnessed his transforming power as it challenged an inhumane pagan world of 2000 years ago and turned it into the 21st century enlightened western society in which we now live. They continue to worship the distant all-knowing, judgmental, powerful, fearful, inscrutable ancient God of their Torah, holding fast to their insular tribal religion, refusing to acknowledge a Christian God of love and a far broader covenant extending not only to their own Jewish people but to all of mankind. Zionists declare the soil of Israel as having been given by Yahweh himself to the self-proclaimed Nation of Israel and shed their blood for this cause. They stubbornly expand their territory, starting up settlements in Palestinian areas, believing it is their Judea, a land given to them by none other than GOD himself, knowing full well the universal Muslim hatred it is causing. As this hatred intensifies, Israel turns its back on the teaching of Jesus Christ to love even your enemies and as a national policy looks for its revenge for Palestinian atrocities to the biblical injunction from the Book of Leviticus:

Fracture for fracture, eye for eye, tooth for tooth, as he has caused disfigurement of a man, so shall it be done to him…For I am the Lord your God.

Muslims look at their God as a distant God of awe to be feared. They consider everyone outside of Islam as *infidel* and all scripture outside of the Koran to be *corrupted*. They say that only their Koran is the true Word of GOD, and they look forward to an Islamic theocratic world under Islamic law. Brain washed by their mothers, fathers, and clerics into an euphoric religious frenzy, young Muslims use their bodies in ritual suicide to kill Jewish *infidels* by strapping on to themselves explosives filled with fragments of metal. They blow themselves up killing and maiming innocent bystanders, even those of their own belief, with the conviction that their suicide will transport them directly to the court of Allah where there will be beautiful virgins to greet them. Other Muslims world-wide enter a Jihad against non-Islamic nations killing and maiming *unbelievers* by committing the same ritual acts of suicide spurred on by the same dream of direct entry into eternal sexual paradise.

These are the extremists of the three religions and they have taken the center stage. They preach that the only measure of certainty for eternal union with GOD is a blind belief in the inerrancy of their scriptures: the Torah, Mishna and Midrash for the Jews, The Old and New Testaments for the Christians, the Koran, Sunna and Sharia for the Muslims. They each consider themselves the only *elect* in the eyes of GOD with all others outside their own religious traditions, as well as inside who do not agree with them, destined for eternal pain and suffering. They drown out, even within their own traditions, any possibility for individual religious diversity by way of a liberal interpretation of scripture. They place their own fundamentalist stamp of approval on their own version of Christianity, Judaism and Islam for the entire world to see.

Is there a common thread of belief that runs through all three of these religions that can be studied as the underlying reason for all of them failing the test? When we study them closely, we see in each great truths with deeply positive meanings for humankind which certainly cannot be traced to the cause for failure. In the Christian New Testament the failing cannot be found in the Sermon on the Mount of Jesus Christ. In the Hebrew Bible it cannot be found in the Ten Commandments or the 23rd Psalm, which says: *The Lord is my shepherd, I shall not want.* It cannot be found in the rules of charity described in the Koran or the meaning of Ramadan.

But if we look more closely to the very beginning of the Torah, we see troubling signs. In Genesis after the thundering statement to Moses that *Thou shalt have no other Gods before me,* we see the heavy hand of a God who says:

He that smiteth a man, so that he die, shall be put to death.... He that stealeth a man and selleth him shall be put to death.... He that curseth his father and mother shall be put to death....

The rules continue to be laid down throughout the Hebrew Bible and over time become more and more demanding. Eventually there are 613 of them and they cover every aspect of the life of an observant Jew; from the *Tefillin* that one must wear on one's head to the making of *pilgrimages* to the Temple to the *uncleanliness* of *menstruous women* to the treatment of *lepers.*

The God of the Hebrew Bible over the course of Jewish history becomes a demanding God who asks for total obedience. He makes heavy demands on the individual Jew. In the Hebrew Bible and its interpretations He lays down rules that must be followed. When He says that you must *love* me, He implies that you must also obey me. Love and obedience join together as one. Their absence is expressed as fear, fear of a vengeful and vindictive God. If GOD is not obeyed, He becomes angry. Then, He punishes.

We see in the Hebrew scriptures an all-powerful God whose anger is to be feared. In the 90th Psalm we read the words, *So we are brought to an end by the anger and silenced by the wrath...All our days go under the shadow of thy wrath...Who feels the power of thy anger, who feels thy wrath like those that fear thee?*

But, at the same time we see a God of compassion and of mercy. The twenty third Psalm says: *The Lord is my shepherd, I shall not want....* and *I will fear no evil, for thou are with me; thy rod and thy staff, they comfort me.*

Can these two sides to the nature of the Hebrew God be reconciled? How can we understand wrath and mercy at the same time? After the destruction of Jerusalem by the Babylonians, the prophet Jeremiah in his book of Lamentations struggles with this problem. He says that *the Lord had afflicted her (Israel) for the multitude of her transgressions* and that *He hath cut off in his fierce anger all the horn of Israel.* He says that God *has utterly rejected us; thou art very wroth against us.* Then he places GOD'S wrath in a personal dimension by saying that *God is surely against me.* Just as suddenly he changes the drift of the monologue and says*: Yet he will have compassion according to the multitude of his mercies.*

If GOD is *surely against* Jeremiah, how can He at the same time be *compassionate* and *merciful* toward him? How can GOD be a punishing God on the one hand and a merciful God on the other? Can He ever be pleased? How are we to know when in His *anger* He will come down and rain total destruction upon us? If it is because we have not pleased Him, how do we please Him? Is it by following the 613 rules, or does He require more than that? Can we ever please Him enough?

The God that Jeremiah saw is the same as the God that Jews, Christians, and Muslims worship today, an incomprehensible schizophrenic God. This is the 21st century God of the Hebrew Bible, the Christian Old Testament—as well as parts of the New Testament—and the Koran. This is the God of many Jewish scholars who question whether GOD was punishing the Nation of Israel as a result of some form of disobedience by the horrible act of the Holocaust. This is also the God of Jerry Falwell, Pat Robertson, and other Christian Evangelicals who proclaimed that by the World Trade Center disaster, God was punishing America for its wicked ways; just as He punished the Nation of Israel in ages past for its wicked ways. This is the God who permeates the consciousness of much of the world. It is the God whose worship today is patterning the behavior of many Jews, Christians, and Muslims towards each other.

We must stop to ask ourselves the question: Are we worshiping a false image? Did this Hebraic definition of the nature of God come from the CREATOR OF OUR UNIVERSE or did it merely come from the hand of man? How much of His nature at the time it was defined was conditioned by the psyche of a tribal nation living in a barren desert surrounded by mortal enemies? Was this just another pagan God, pieced together by a desert tribe in search for a protector? Was the Nation of Israel only looking for a God who would assure its own survival? Why would the GOD of the Universe favor the Jewish tribe at the expense of their enemies? Why would He stand behind David protecting him as he wantonly killed his enemies? The Psalms speak of vengeance and destruction of *my enemies*. How do we define the *enemy*? Is it possible that I could, at the same time, be their *enemy*? Should only I be protected? What of those who were destroyed? What of their loved ones? Did their lives have no meaning other than to be GOD'S sacrifice? Were they all irrelevant?

The idea that in GOD'S eyes everyone else is irrelevant remains strongly imbedded in our western thought patterns to this day. For Jews this means all of those outside of their special covenantal relationship with GOD. For Christians it is those who do not *believe* in Jesus Christ. For Muslims it is all infidels. This is the underlying logic that justifies the thoughts and actions of religious extremists as well as the many millions who silently support them.

In the Hebrew Bible, we find a picture of a God who gradually grew out of the early Hebrew tribal experience and came into being as a reflection of the need for a God who could lead it through dangers as it developed into a religiously cohesive and unified nation. He was their protector from the dangers of living in a primitive world. He was their assurance of survival. Our Nations of the world face different challenges today. Should we look to the same kind of God? Can we rely on the same kind of God?

If the GOD OF ALL CREATION is testing the three world religions that sprung from the blood of Abraham, is this misunderstanding of His nature what is making them all fail the test? Can this failure be traced to this common view of GOD as expressed in the common source of all three religions, the Hebrew Bible? Can we find here the beginning of the answer to the riddle?

All religions, in their earliest stages, ascribe human qualities to their Gods. For the Jewish Tribes he took on the persona of a father. The Jewish nation was like a child looking up for protection to a father. In their scriptures he was even called "father." In the eyes of the young Nation of Israel, like a father he was protective but at the same time stern and disciplinary. Like a father he was seen as mighty and powerful, as vengeful, as capricious, as quick to anger, as judgmental, as unfathomable and as sometimes merciful. These were all human traits the Jewish people could understand as they gave shape and form to their God. And, as a father would do with a child, he made a covenant with them. Like a father, though, he remained the powerful figure in control of the covenant. If you do this, then I will reward you. If you disobey me, I will punish you. I will be the one to decide, not you.

XV Not the God They Think They Know

As the early Jewish tribal society became more complex and as it developed into a nation, the nature of their God became more complex. It became a reflection of the experiences of their prophets, philosophers, and priests as they tried to reconcile the events of their daily existence with unknown and frightening forces beyond their comprehension. But their God remained essentially the same as he was from the very beginning; mighty and powerful, vengeful, capricious, quick to anger, judgmental, unfathomable, and only sometimes merciful. This was the God who filled the oral and then ultimately the written record of Hebrew existence. He became at first the God of the Oral Torah, then of the written Torah or Hebrew Bible, then the Christian Old Testament and then in the 7$^{th.}$ Century after Jesus Christ, the Koran.

This was not the God of Jesus Christ. The God of Jesus Christ was not vengeful. He was not capricious. He was not quick to anger. He did not punish. He said we punish ourselves when we turn our backs on Him, when we reject Him. He was however judgmental, but He made a clear distinction. He said we are not to judge nor even speculate how He is to judge; only He can judge. He was more than sometimes merciful; He was always merciful. And, He was not unfathomable. His nature was shown in clear and certain terms by the life and death of Jesus Christ.

It was this Hebrew concept of the nature of GOD, over 1500 years in the making, which Jesus of Nazareth challenged. But, it was not a concept easy to change. The Jews would not give up their concept of the nature of their God. He had become too much a part of their lives and their daily existence. To accept a God of a different nature would have meant changing the very foundation of their tribal culture. To change called for a totally different thought process. They would even have to give up their special covenantal relationship with their God. Nor could the change be made piece meal, it had to be total. One had to be *born again*. Jesus told them how far reaching the change would have to be when he said they would have to hate even their mothers and fathers in order to come to him. He called for a complete break from the God of their tribal and personal identity.

The early Christians had a problem abandoning their image of the God of the Hebrew Bible. Even though they did become *born again* into this new vision of God presented by Jesus Christ, they found it difficult to view differently the nature of the God they had believed in all of their lives. The reason for this was that they all had been devout Jews. Many, such as Paul and Peter, were intellectually gifted Jews. Others were common people. For all, before Jesus came into their lives, the God of the Hebrew Bible was the only God they had ever known.

The description of that God in the Hebrew Bible was the only description the early Jewish Christians had ever known. They were taught to believe that the words of their scriptures were inerrant, were from GOD Himself. Furthermore, they believed Jesus to be the Messiah foretold in their Hebrew scriptures. He was the fulfillment of those scriptures. In fact it was those scriptures that gave him validity. So the early Christian community did what every society always does when a new idea is introduced. It amalgamated the past concept of the Jewish God into the new one given by Jesus Christ.

But there were contradictions. How could they be reconciled? In time, an answer was found. After over 300 years of fierce debate and political maneuvering among Christians of differing interpretations of the meaning of the life of Jesus Christ, two concepts of the nature of GOD were incorporated into a formalized Roman Christian doctrine called The Trinity. The Jewish God and the Jesus God were incorporated as two separate Gods in a single Christian Trinitarian God (Father, Son and Holy Ghost); one God being the father God of the Old Testament—the Jewish Father God—the other God being the God as Jesus Christ—the Son of the Jewish Father God. But this did not entirely solve the problem. How could GOD be loving on the one hand and vengeful and capricious on the other? How could He be a merciful God on the one hand and a punishing God on the other? The debate goes on to this day. Over the years, the early Christian Church Fathers finally settled for an inscrutable God, one sometimes impossible to understand.

What does this ancient Hebrew biblical concept of the nature of GOD and the Trinitarian Christian concept of the *Father* have to do with the problems and conflicts among the three religions in our world today? It has everything to do with them. This archaic concept of the nature of GOD is the motivating force behind the responses of the three religions towards those within their belief systems as well as those outside of them. Whether it is the eye for and eye retaliation of Israel, the world terrorism of Jihad against infidels, or the judgmental condemnation of Evangelical Christianity, all can be traced to a personal identification with the God of the Hebrew Bible.

This is not to say that the Hebrew Bible has not had a far-reaching and positive influence in our world. Its wisdom set the very foundation for the forward development of western society. It was the foundation for Christianity. It defined the human condition. It showed the predicament of man in the face of a perfect Creator. It pictured man as a creature quick to define evil but not always able to make the distinction between it and goodness.

XV Not the God They Think They Know

What Jesus Christ did was redefine the nature of the God of the Hebrew Bible. When Jesus Christ would say: *The scripture of old says, but I say...*, it was a clarification of Hebrew scripture. He was pointing not just to the errors but also to the shades of gray. The God of Jesus Christ was not in all aspects in conflict with the God of the Hebrew Bible. The conflict lay rather in the assertion by the Jewish Priests of that time that the Hebrew Bible was inerrant and their priestly interpretations were unquestionable.

We become like the God or Gods we worship. There is a dynamic motivating interaction that takes place. For those at the extremes of these three religions, it is the God of the Hebrew Bible who drives their thoughts and actions. The persona of this God they revere determines their behavior. For the others, those who are not the activists, it takes the form of silent agreement and compliance. If my God is vengeful, I can think vengeful thoughts and be vengeful. If my God is capricious, I can think capricious thoughts and be capricious. If my God is quick to anger, I can be angry and lash out with my anger. If my God is judgmental, I can think judgmental thoughts and be judgmental. If my God is unfathomable, I don't have to explain my actions, I too can be unfathomable. If my God is only sometimes merciful, I can withhold my love as I wish; I can be only sometimes merciful.

With Jesus Christ the concept of the nature of GOD had changed. The final veil of the face of GOD had been lifted. But not all accepted it; not the Muslims, not the Jews, not even all of the Christians. Many Christians to this day have not abandoned the Hebrew God. Their bible studies center on the Old Testament. They consider the words of the Old Testament to be inerrant. Many others remain in the process of moving away from Him.

Western civilization broadly speaking has, however, moved away from this God. It has taken 2000 years to work through the last vestiges of a belief in a vengeful, unmerciful, powerful Old Testament God. For every St Francis of Assisi there was a Savonarola. But, the message of Jesus Christ prevailed. The God Father of the Trinity became more like the God Jesus. Through all of the backsliding, the positive message of love and respect for human dignity still prevailed. It is the reason the western world moved forward. It is the reason we have an enlightened world today.

The Jews stayed with their Hebraic God until the enlightenment of the 19th Century in Europe when parts of Judaism began to integrate into Christian political and economic society. This movement has continued, particularly in the United States with the advent of Reformed Judaism. Under the influence of western European Liberalism, the Christian idea of social justice for all members of society in its broadest sense beyond the tribal community began to pull many Jews away from the enclosure of their Rabbinical Orthodox biblical past and their definition of their Hebrew God. Many today have moved past their Christian brothers and sisters and hold to an even broader view of social justice.

This has not been the case with Islam. Over the course of the centuries Islam, as a religion, remained isolated and frozen in thought. It remained calcified as to its understanding of the nature of the God taken by Muhammad from the Hebrew Scriptures.

For 1400 years, from the very beginning of Islam to the present day, this ancient religion has been frozen in time with limited contact with the western world. Except for the brief period of the Crusades there was little interest on the part of Europe. The subjugation of those who did not convert to Islam was always a local affair. The cries of those persecuted Christians and Jews, as well as others as far away as India, living in the path of its conquests were not heard by the rest of the world, as the world then was not interdependent as it is today. The brutal methods of warfare and subjugation remained largely unknown. Christianity and Judaism slowly disappeared from what is now called the Middle East.

In recent history the first signs of conflict between Islam and the West came with the recognition of the State of Israel in 1948. From then on each year the reality of the meaning of Islamic belief in its God for the West only gradually became apparent. Finally, by the enormity of its horror, the destruction of the World Trade Center Towers marked a turning point in world consciousness and an understanding of the dangers inherent in Islamic thinking. The non-Islamic world finally began to realize that fundamentalist Islamic extremism presents a serious danger in a pluralistic interdependent world that is moving quickly into the 21st century and beyond. It was the West's liberal view toward freedom of thought and religious belief that held it back from understanding this for so long—and continues to hold it back even today.

In a remote city in the Arabian Desert 600 years after the death of Jesus Christ, Muhammad framed his vision of the perfect society based on his observations of the spiritual and social depravity of the Pagan world around him. It was a violent world. It called for a strong militaristic leader.

Muhammad would therefore model himself after the great Prophet Kings of the Hebrew Scriptures: David, Solomon, and especially Abraham. In these prophets he saw the hand of a powerful and protective God, the kind of God who would lead Islam to victory in battle over all unbelievers. This was the kind of God who would, through the angel Gabriel, dictate to him the inerrant holy book of Islam, the Koran.

XV Not the God They Think They Know

Muhammad found his answers about the nature of the God who would become the God of Islam not in the Christian New Testament but in the Hebrew scriptures. The God of Jesus Christ would only be referred to where it suited Muhammad. His theology would be a revision of Hebrew scripture. It would begin with the very beginning of man in the Garden of Eden. It would even borrow from the Jewish scholar's interpretations, the Midrash.

Even though Christianity had been in existence for over 600 years when Muhammad began to receive messages from the Angel Gabriel and speak the Koran to his disciples, Christian values were largely unknown among the tribes of the Arabian Desert. Unlike Judaism, none had impacted the society immediately surrounding Muhammad. Nor would Muhammad have considered Christian values a practical way to approach the problems that he faced. Therefore, the Christian God did not become the God of the Koran.

The religion of Muhammad has not changed since then. Islam sees the West as it did during its initial expansion when Muslim armies conquered infidels wherever they went, subjugating and slaughtering those who were in disagreement. The Davidic God of conquest remains its model. Islam today views the outside world in the same terms as it did 1400 years ago, as a world of pagan infidels. The thought patterns of Islam are the same as they were when the religion was formed. It thinks this way because its clerics have kept Muslim thinking deterministically confined to their own vision of GOD as defined in the Koran. Through fear of eternal punishment, Muslims cannot think of any other kind of God.

More frightening is the fact that Muslim clerics world-wide in mosques and schools are teaching young Muslims that they have been given a mandate to repeat the Pagan, Christian, and Jewish conquests of the past and that Allah will favor them eternally if they devote their lives to this end.

Islamic thought has been calcified into a 7th Century mold. As long as the Koran is considered the word of GOD, it cannot change. Islam cannot shake itself from its beliefs, because the Koran prevents Muslims from seeing the world in any other way than the way that the Koran describes it.

The social and economic progress throughout the world that has been carved out over the past 2000 years by men and women bowing down to a different kind of God, the one revealed by Jesus Christ, cannot be acknowledged. Muslims cannot admit that for 2000 years this new vision of GOD and not the one described by Muhammad in the Koran has been the great driving force behind world history leading to the advancement of human civilization. When Muhammad shut the door on the God revealed by Jesus Christ, he isolated Islam into the singularity of the ancient God described in the Hebrew Scriptures. All that is left now for Islam is to hate the infidel West and resent it for the fruits of its new vision.

This hatred is being waged against the backdrop of a secular western world that in the perception of Islam is fast losing its connection with the sacred. It sees the West as a consumer driven society that has strip-mined the mystery of life from the souls of its people. Rather than rigorously cultivating inner life according to the Koran and Sharia, it sees the West as obsessively pursuing mindless sensual pleasures that force attention towards the most mundane. Islam sees these distractions in western secular society as an impediment to a focus on the sacred; with the result being an inability to understand the complex higher values given by the Koran and Sharia. With little imagination and a shortened attention span, it sees those in the West as unable to understand the beauty in the Arabic poetry of the Koran, unable to comprehend its deeper meanings. Islam sees the West as weak, superficial, and unable to prepare for the hard choices that must be made in order to follow the discipline of its one true religion.

Islam is wrong in its blanket perception of the West. Its clerics have been blinded by their fundamentalist extremism. Many of their observations are, in fact, correct, but like their evangelical Christian counterparts, they cannot acknowledge the dynamism of a pluralistic open society, the creative undercurrents that lie beyond their observation. They are held back by their doctrinaire religious beliefs from seeing the goodness and creativity of human beings living outside of Islam. They are unable to make such an acknowledgement for fear that their God will condemn them to eternal damnation. An open rational view of human behavior and a different view of their God would spell the end of Islam.

Beyond the human suffering that Islam has in the past and will inevitably in the future bring upon itself and others, there is a question as to whether Islamic intransigence really matters in a world moving as fast scientifically and socially as it is today. Those at the extremes always want to take control and often they do, but not for long. The history of the West has shown that it is the peacemakers, the pragmatic problem solvers, and those with new constructive ideas that in the long run make the difference. These are the people who take the talents their Creator has given them and use them for His purposes. They are the ones who clean up the pieces, set the broken bones, put back together the broken lives and open the future, after the extremists have become exhausted. They are the sons and daughters of GOD. And, they are from all faiths and some with none at all.

There is little that Islam can do to change itself. This is because Muhammad built his theology on two tragic errors. The first was that the Koran in its entirety is the inerrant word of God and therefore cannot be changed. The other is that the God of the Koran was modeled after the Hebraic God of the Old Testament, and not the New. It is this Hebraic image of God that has given rise to the view of Muslims that all who are not with us are our enemies who must be conquered and changed. They are infidels who are living corrupt lives and are worshiping false Gods. This in turn has in recent years spawned 5th columns of terror throughout the world bent on destroying all who disagree with Islamic theology.

If Islam cannot move forward in its recognition of a different kind of God, can Orthodox Christianity and Judaism? Can the monotheistic ancient God of the Torah as well as the Triune father God of Christianity be seen in another way? Can a broad metaphysical interpretive view of God as expressed in the life of Jesus Christ without the appendages of the God of the Old Testament be acknowledged? The answer to these questions will determine the future of world history.

The answer for the future of Judaism, Christianity, and Islam as well as all other world religions lay in the validity of their perception of the Creator of the Universe. There can only be one reality to our Creator. In time, whether that is one hundred years from now or ten thousand, the GOD that mankind looks to can be only one GOD, the one Creator of all. As in the past, religions that do not reflect the will of the one Creator of all will perish.

In time the way human beings deal with each other as well as with the physical world around them must be a reflection of the will of that one Creator. If it is not, the human species will cease to exist. Nothing is more important for the human species than to unravel the paradoxes of past religious belief and discover the will of the One Creator. There is only one nature to our Creator. We must not be held back by our perceptions of Gods constructed in ages past. We must not stop until we find the one GOD who will define our future.

Man from the beginning of time has been in search for the nature of his Creator. This quest did not come to an end with the Koran and Sharia or the last book of the Hebrew Bible or the authorized Canon of New Testament writings. It will go on regardless of how much effort is made by those at the extremes to hold it back. Man has shown that by his very nature he is willing to leave the comfort of the past for the uncertainty of the future.

We have a God given right to question the nature of the Creator as He was defined in ages past. His image is not something any Rabbi, Imam, Ayatollah, Pope, Priest, or Pastor can dictate. GOD gave each of us the intelligence to find out for ourselves.

Nor will man be content with placing GOD out there in some other place at a distance from himself. He will want to find GOD in the here and now within himself. This is not a new idea. It is the metaphysical meaning of the Christian sacrament of the Eucharist. The Eucharist is an act of acknowledging GOD within. It is the act of believing that GOD exists within me. He is a part of me. I am a part of him.

It is an act that says we must invite him in. We must take the initiative. We cannot grow, work miracles, and evolve unless we have become co-creators with a God who is a part of us, who is within. We, along with GOD, then become the authors of our own existence.

Scientific discoveries in the 20th and 21st century have presented an additional challenge to the picture of the nature of the God presented in the Hebrew Bible. Quantum physics has uncovered a new and different level of reality against which all religions must now be examined. These discoveries have shown us that matter is not what we perceive it to be and we in our physical form exist in another dimension right now. They show us that we have no physical form, as we understand it. We are nothing but energy. The ultimate definition and source of this energy exists in some other dimension. We are in our essence a reflection of something else.

Could it be that this is what Jesus Christ was referring to during The Last Supper? There may be more to the Eucharist than the disciples of Jesus ever imagined. Jesus Christ told us what the Vedic seers had declared, we are in the womb of GOD now, not at some future period of time on some future judgment day but now, in His endless dimension of eternity.

The God of Jesus Christ calls us from that dimension back to this one for servitude towards our fellow man. Christians are called upon by GOD to show their love towards Him through individual and collective acts of love and kindness towards others. These acts are a reflection of GOD in one's life. Unlike with tribal religions, these acts are not limited to one's own family, clan, nation, or particular religious persuasion. They demonstrate a love that extends even to mortal enemies.

Unlike the God of the Hebrew Bible and the God of the Koran, the God of Jesus Christ does not call for subservience to Himself nor is He a God to be feared. He welcomes each of us into a mystical union that changes us and brings us, at least temporarily, into His non-material dimension. It is a dimension that anyone can enter. No one is left out. No one is irrelevant.

In this dimension, we are born again into oneness with Him. It is a dimension where He overlooks our individual weaknesses and values us for our individual strengths. There, we are at one with Him and He is at one with us. It is a dimension that renews us. But, it is not a dimension where we can remain. While we are living, our place is not in His dimension. In His eyes it is not there where we are to find our own relevance. It is here on earth among all of humanity, and not just among those of our own kind, but also among those of all kinds. He said that as we have shown our love to the least of His people, we have shown our love towards Him.

We must return to earth to do His work.

XVI
A Challenge for the Religions of Abraham in the 21st Century and Beyond

Sometime in the dim past of human history, painters began the great painting. The first brush strokes were made. Cave walls suddenly became the backdrop for the deepest reaches of the human mind. The nature of God was being revealed.

At first this GOD was not as He later became, a God to be feared. He was not even a *He*. This GOD had no shape or form. This was a God with no gender or anthropomorphic identity. It was the GOD the cave painters had observed outside of the cave in the heavens and the earth filling everything with its greatness. Inside the cave and inside the minds of the painters and inside the minds of those who entered the cave with their torches to see the spectacle, this was a GOD of wonder, of awe.

Then, after tens of thousands of years, suddenly the brush strokes changed. A Hebrew tribe living in a barren desert looked at the canvass and reinterpreted the brush strokes from the past. A different view of God was revealed. He was now in human form and He had the same emotions as human beings. Also, He was now a God to be feared.

But the picture was not finished. Just as suddenly, fifteen hundred years later, the canvass changed again. A young man from Nazareth appeared reinterpreting the nature of the Hebrew God. He had no quarrel with the way his ancestors had defined the human predicament as a struggle between good and evil, but he did not agree with the way they had defined GOD'S view of man in relation to that predicament. So, he added new brush strokes to both the painting in the cave and to the Hebrew painting. He said that GOD was more than a God of wonder and awe. He was a God of pure love. He said that man was made in the image of a GOD of pure love. He also said that GOD was not a God to be feared, nor was HE a punishing God with a nature like that of a human being.

XVI A Challenge for the Religions of Abraham in the 21ˢᵗ Century and Beyond

Six hundred years later there was another change. An illiterate merchant named Muhammad claimed that he was receiving messages from the angel Gabriel defining the one and only true nature of GOD. His God was copied from the Hebrew painting, but in many ways He was an even more demanding and fearful God—and more punishing.

The Hebrew Bible and the Koran were each written to set out for all time the Word of GOD. What was written could never be changed until the end of time. For the followers of these two religions the picture was finished.

This was not the case for the early followers of Jesus Christ. After his crucifixion, Christians embarked upon a quest to know Him. For them, the painting was not yet finished. Three hundred years of debate only opened up new questions about the person claimed to be the Messiah prophesied in the Hebrew Scriptures, who He really was and what He really said. To settle the issues once and for all, a canon of writings was set out by the bishops of the newly formed Universal Christian (Catholic) Church. In a compromise these bishops decided to include in the Canon both the Hebrew picture of God from the Hebrew Bible and the one painted by Jesus Christ in the New Testament even though in many ways they contradicted each other.

All writings outside of this canon of Old and New Testament writings and all ideas opposing the creeds built upon them were then declared heretical. All heretical writings were ordered destroyed. The bishops too wanted to finish the picture.

But, questions remained. Many believers in Jesus Christ saw GOD calling upon them to continue to search for GOD'S revelation. For them, the picture was not finished. In fact, for them parts of it as set out by the bishops were flawed. The picture painted by the bishops did not have a purity of structure and form like that of the early cave painting, but distortions that gave rise to opposing and dissident elements of structure and form.

In a great painting there can only be one underlying truth that is revealed by its underlying structure and form. For GOD'S Great Painting this is the revelation of HIMSELF to us as well as the revelation of HIS demand on us. This is the two-part meaning of HIS canvass. This is what mankind has been trying to paint from the beginning of his consciousness.

Like any great painting GOD'S Great Painting has a structure and form that demands all of our attention. To begin to understand it we are called upon to commit all of ourselves to it. It cannot be understood by superficial observation. It can only be understood deep in the quietness of the mind. There can be no distraction. Meaning is not found on the surface, only beneath the surface.

Making up the unifying structure and form of all great paintings are the brush strokes. These brush strokes showing the human understanding of God, first appeared on cave walls as colors and forms. With the development of language and writing, they jumped off the walls of caves and onto scrolls and the pages of books. The picture of GOD and our relationship to Him was now being painted in words. Words were being used to express ideas.

As each of the three religions of Abraham rushed to finish the painting, the words, and their meanings, became frozen in time. These words were looked upon as being from GOD and without error. The paint was allowed to harden on the canvass. Other words like *heresy* and *blasphemy* became a part of the language. Those who did not agree with the religious authorities were *damned* for all eternity.

Among those who came to see the first cave paintings the feeling of awe soon turned into another kind of feeling. The figures on the cave walls took on a power of their own. They became objects of belief. This switch from idea to object was not only confined to the earliest periods of human consciousness. It also took place in Jewish, Christian, and Muslim belief.

For Christianity the words from the scrolls and books that had expressed the original ideas became objects of belief. A religion that began with only two hieroglyphic icons, the cross and the fish, became a religion of majestic cathedrals lined with statuary, frightening demons rising out of an inferno, a human-like Sistine Chapel God of ferocious power, angels with wings, relics and mummified saints. Iconic images depicting the word meanings of Christian scriptures that began as ideas of belief had turned into a proliferation of objects of belief. It was easier to look at the original Christ images as objects of belief than to search inward for the ideas they had at one time represented.

But, for some Christians the picture nevertheless continued to change. The objects that had lost their meaning were cast aside. GOD cannot be hidden behind a facade. HE calls on us to go to the other side and search for HIS revelation. Discoveries in the present often contradict assumptions from the past. New assumptions replace old ones.

In a great painting one brush stroke is laid upon another, and in the chiaroscuro of the colors and tones, as errors are covered over, a new texture and shade emerges along with a new visual truth. The errors are hidden, never to be seen again. One true unifying artistic creation emerges. This has not been the case with the scriptures found in the Hebrew Bible or the Christian record of the life of Jesus Christ or the Muslim Koran. For most of those who follow these reli-

XVI A Challenge for the Religions of Abraham in the 21st Century and Beyond

gions, the words remain inerrant, frozen in time. Over the course of history, only the brave have come forward to challenge them.

The first stroke was made by the hand of the cave painter, not by the hand of GOD. Nor were the words creating what all three of the religions of Abraham defined as the Word of GOD made by the hand of GOD. The paints on the palette were always mans'. Some human beings claimed that GOD Himself was holding their hand and mixing the paints, but that was only their claim. What was interpreted to be the Word of GOD, and what passed for revelation was often no more than an expression of human wants, desires, emotions, and biases, conditioned by a changing world. In the end, individual views and interpretations as well as expediency often won out. No one has ever seen GOD face-to-face.

It could have been close to being finished, but it isn't. Today, thousands of years after the first mark on the cave wall, GOD'S Great Painting is seen as a confusion of errors, contradictions, and omissions. Those brush strokes made in error over the ages were not covered up. Some brush strokes contradict others. Some stand out like a cacophony of thought challenging others. Some are hardly decipherable. This confusion draws our attention away from the underlying structure and form of GOD'S Great Painting. We miss HIS message.

We humans are proud and do not like to cover up old ideas and admit that we were wrong. It is hard for us to unlearn what we so confidently thought we knew, to shed the protective cover that for so long has been our protection. We fear that if we change one brush stroke, all of the others too will have to be changed. Then, like a painter forced to wipe the canvass clean we will have to start all over again. It is easier for us to keep the picture as it was. The canvass that we have painted revealing the nature of our Creator therefore appears as a confusion of many irreconcilable brushstrokes, laid not one on top of the other but side by side.

We cannot capture the meaning of HIS message if we concentrate our vision on each and every word and the dogma that has grown out of them. Nor can we begin to see the overall beauty and meaning of HIS message. We are prevented from understanding the underlying structure and form. We miss HIS truth.

Today, GOD is calling upon each of us to find and to cover up the past errors in the religions that came from Abraham. HE is asking us to fill in the omissions. HE gave us the intelligence to do this. HE endowed us at the very beginning of our creation with the ability to discern. This ability was not reserved for any special person or group of people; priests or pastors, popes or bishops, rabbis or mullahs, it was given to each of us, to each and every human being.

We are called on by GOD to search into the depths of our minds and to paint over the brushstrokes made in error and to replace them with new brushstrokes taken from a new mixture of colors laid on a clean palette. New and different brushstrokes that will illuminate GOD'S real meaning. HE calls upon each of us to correct and to add to the picture. HE calls on each of us to finish the painting ourselves.

For those willing to open their minds to HIS presence, HE is ready to help them finish HIS Great Painting, a painting revealing HIS True Being. Those who do not let HIM help miss the revelation that HE wants them to have. They miss seeing HIS presence in the underlying structure and form of HIS great canvass. They miss seeing the subtleness of the chiaroscuro.

They only see a confusion of brush strokes on the surface of a canvass painted in ages past, a canvass which in fear of a judgmental God, himself created by these ancient brushstrokes, they have blindly accepted.

They see a canvass in which they have taken no part.

XVII
The Origin of anti-Semitism
The Story of Jacob and Esau

Which ones can make the claim to be loved like Jacob; the Jews, the Catholics, the Presbyterians, the Baptists, or is it the Muslims? Which were from the very foundation of time destined to be the *Chosen* ones? Which were not?

The God of the Hebrew Bible made a distinction between the two brothers. Jacob He loved, Esau He hated. The Nation of Israel that sprang from Jacob He loved. All other Nations and all other people He hated.

It was a distinction not made on merit or lack of merit, on being good or being evil. It was not related to what either brother did or did not do to please the Hebrew God. It was a distinction made seemingly without reason. It was a distinction made before their birth, before either one even had a chance to make his own choices. Jacob was included in GOD'S grace. Esau was excluded, cut off. The Nation of Israel was included in GOD'S grace. All others were cut off.

Is the story of Jacob and Esau as it was recorded in Genesis simply a primitive tale of little relevance today, or does it remain a part of our 21st century world? Should we dismiss this story about the beginning of a special covenantal relationship between GOD and the Nation of Israel as just an elitist notion?

For the Jews this is a story that established their belief that they were elected by GOD to be His *Chosen* people. Later, for Christians the belief in election and predestination looked to this story for its meaning. When the Prophet Muhammad was receiving his messages from the Angel Gabriel six hundred years after the death of Jesus Christ, the distinctions between Jacob (Yaqoub) and Esau (Ishaq) were not made, but the idea of superiority was there and this story formed the basis for his belief that only those who accepted the Islamic faith were to be among the *Chosen*. He (Allah) was able to say in the Koran:

> *Fight those who do not believe in Allah…they are in a state of subjection.*
> (Sura 9.29)

O you who believe! Do not take the Jews and Christians for friends;...Allah does not guide unjust people.
(Sura 5.51)

And the Jews say...And the Christians say...Allah will destroy them; how they are turned away!
(Sura 9.30)

The Children of Israel. All this—the evil of It—is hateful in the sight of your Lord.
(Sura 17.38)

This was a story that had a lasting impact, first on Judaism, then on Christianity, and then on Islam. Was it really from GOD Himself; or, did it merely grow out of the mind of an early Jewish patriarchal tribal nation looking for a personal God for its own protection? When Jacob and Esau were born, was GOD present at all? Did Jacob get the upper hand not because he was loved by GOD but simply because he was devious and deceitful? Were the early Jewish writers merely transferring their own emotions of love and disappointment toward their male offspring into an anthropomorphic paternal God of their own definition and by so doing giving him their own human frailties, having him be like any father, favoring one son over another?

The answers to the above are unimportant. What is important is the lasting impact this story has had on western thought and how this is leading to conflict in the interdependent geopolitical world of today.

It is a story that begins in Genesis and extends through the Old Testament and then into the New. It builds in intensity, as the idea of GOD'S covenant with the Nation of Israel becomes more and more a part of Jewish religious thought. It is simply the story of two brothers. The role of GOD behind the scene at first does not in fact appear. The full written explanation of the why of GOD'S choice between Jacob and Esau only appears fifteen hundred years after their births, in the Book of Malachi when we find a confusing yet definitive explanation. The Prophet writes in the person of GOD Himself:

Was not Esau Jacobs's brother?...yet I (God) loved Jacob, and I (God) hated Esau.

(Malachi 1:2-3)

Malachi makes it clear that GOD not only favors the Nation of Israel, even with all its faults, but He dismisses all other nations and their people as marginalized. As with Esau, He turns His back on them.

Malachi's revelation that GOD chooses as He wishes to choose, favoring whom He wishes to favor did not stop with the end of the Jewish Bible. The words of Malachi were brought into the Christian New Testament. The Christian idea, of the *chosen ones* being only those who believed in Jesus Christ as the Messiah, was born.

The Apostle Paul and later the Roman Catholic Church placed this idea of exclusivity and superiority in the forefront of Christian theology where it has remained ever since. It was called Election and Predestination and it was to be available only to believers in Jesus Christ. With the presence of the Messiah, no longer would any kind of special relationship be available for the Jews. GOD had turned His back on those in the Nation of Israel who did not accept Jesus as their Messiah. The covenant that had only been available to Jews and the *particularity* of individual Jews in the eyes of GOD had ended. They were to be like Esau, separated from the love of GOD.

The Apostle Paul looked to the messianic prophecies of the Hebrew Bible for his claim that only those who believed in Jesus Christ were favored by GOD. He began his argument with the story of Jacob and Esau. We see a reference to Malachi in Paul's Letter to the Romans where he says:

> As it is written, Jacob have I loved, but Esau have I hated.
> (Romans 9:13)

He ties this in with the concept of election when he says in Romans:

For the children being not yet born, neither having done any good or evil, that the purpose of election might stand, not of works but of him that calleth.

(Romans 9:11)

Then, to make sure that this special place, as it had been over the years for the Jews, would apply regardless of Christian human frailty, he again quotes again from the Hebrew Bible:

I will have mercy, and I will have compassion on whom I will have compassion.

(Romans 9:15)

In his Letter to the Ephesians he then makes the final claim:

According as he has chosen us in him before the foundation of the world, that we should be holy and without blame before him in love, having predestined us into the adoption of children by Jesus Christ, to himself, according to the good pleasure of his will...

(Ephesians 1:4-5)

Sixty years after the death of Jesus, Paul had drawn a line in the sand. Only Christians can stand in the place of Jacob.

This challenge to the Jews did not end there. There was yet to come another challenge. The Prophet Muhammad said both Judaism and Christianity were misguided religions. Their writings were corrupted. He drew another line in the sand. Muhammad was to be the new Jacob, chosen by Allah Himself and the Nation of Islam under Sharia Law the new nation. All others were the Esau. They were irrelevant. It was the will of Allah.

With each of the three religions making the same claim, the idea that only *we* were chosen by GOD took on a new and potentially dangerous dimension.

For Judaism the idea of being the *Chosen* people had become the foundation for the belief that there existed a covenant between GOD and the Nation of Israel. Individual Jews were to share in this and be singled out as being separate from others. This is the belief of Jews to this day. For Christianity with the writings of the Apostle Paul, election and predestination became the foundation for the idea that Christians are separate from all others and some, if not all, are predestined to exist in GOD'S grace. For Muhammad writing six hundred years after the death of Jesus Christ the idea of being superior and separate became the rational for the belief that all of those outside of Islam are infidels and are doomed to either a lower status—People of the Book—or, for all others, eternal damnation.

The biblical Jewish, Christian, and Muslim scriptures quoted above came from ages past and therefore may today seem archaic and benign, but they are not. As they were in the past, they are very much alive today in our world. They have become an important part of the thinking process of 21st century Jews, Christians, and Muslims. If GOD could favor Jacob and turn his back on Esau, why shouldn't we be able to act in the same manner? Why shouldn't *Chosen* Jews or *Sharia* Muslims or *elected* Presbyterians, Baptists, and Roman Catholics consider themselves separate and superior to all others?

XVII The Origin of anti-Semitism The Story of Jacob and Esau

In recent years the Jewish concept of being *Chosen* has become the justification for the idea of the land of Israel being *their* God given land. Jews remain GOD'S *Chosen* people with a right to that land. Jews define themselves by the word *particularity*, which is as being different and superior as to their religious beliefs.

For Christianity the concept of election and predestination became the justification for the Inquisition and the Crusades. It fueled hatred over the centuries among competing Christian theological positions, as it does to this day, each Christian group believing that only its members are among the elect. Over the centuries it provided the rational for Christian anti-Semitism. As for Islam, from the time of Muhammad to the present day it has fueled the hatred of Muslims toward Jewish and Christian *infidels*.

It allowed many German Catholics and Lutherans to look silently down with disdain on German Jews as the Holocaust unfolded. After all, had not Paul quoting Isaiah (29:10), referred to the Jews as "those of whom God has given a sluggish spirit, eyes that would not see, and ears that would not hear" (Romans 11:8)?

If GOD could devalue Esau and view him as a non-person, why shouldn't they, as elected and predestined Christians, be justified in viewing the Jews as non-people? Why shouldn't they look at the Jews as being separate and inferior? In the mind of GOD, as with Esau, Jewish lives had little value. Their Christian theology told them the Jews, like Esau, were irrelevant. Jewish lives had no place in eternity except among the damned. The Apostle Paul had said so. Without remorse, the Jews could be exterminated. It is not surprising that the world witnessed the Holocaust.

German Christians must not be the only ones singled out. The Holocaust was only a boil coming to the surface and erupting telling us of an underlying disease permeating all three religions. It is the disease of superiority, judgment, and arrogance. It existed then and continues to exist just as powerfully today. Jews, Christians, and Muslims must each recognize their own culpability. The idea that certain human beings "other than our own" have little or no value and we like Jacob are superior and favored by GOD is woven into all three. It is a disease that goes back to the very beginning of Judeo Christian Islamic scripture, to the story of Jacob and Esau.

The story of Jacob and Esau is just as pernicious a force today as it was over three thousand years ago. The idea that only those of our own particular religious belief system have higher value in the mind of GOD is firmly imbedded in the subconscious of each. This, to a great extent in the world of the 21st century, is influencing the thoughts of Jews, Christians, and Muslims towards each other. It is also influencing their actions. These feelings today are the primary underlying cause of today's world conflict.

Those who don't believe this is true need only open the morning newspaper.

Concluding Statement
The Legacy of Past Religious Belief for the 21st Century and Beyond

"What is Life?
It is the flash of a firefly in the night,
It is the breath of a buffalo in the wintertime,
It is the little shadow that runs across the grass
And loses itself in the sunset."

(A Blackfoot Indian Chief as he was dying)
Circ 1890

    The words above were spoken to an American missionary by a Blackfoot Indian Chief as the Blackfoot Indian Chief lay dying. They express a sense of wonder at the magnificence of GOD'S creation. They speak to no moral rightness or wrongness. They are simply the reflection of a dying human being in his last hours, acknowledging the existence of his creator.

    These two men coming together on the American prairie were bound together by a common inescapable human link; however, each viewed the world around him from an entirely different perspective.

    The American Missionary came from a society with a belief system built upon ancient Hebrew scriptures and prophecies. An essential part of his value system was the belief, made explicitly clear in the very first book of the Hebrew scriptures, that it was man's God given right to subdue nature for his own purposes.

The Blackfoot Indian Chief came from an earlier form of social organization dating back to the very beginnings of mankind, perhaps extending as far back as 250,000 years. He came from a value system that looked at nature not in terms of domination or subjugation but in terms of harmonious accommodation. It was a value system that held to the belief that mankind was placed on earth to live in harmony with nature.

His was a pre-agriculture civilization of hunters and gatherers. It looked at the world, the stars, the mountains, the plants, the animals, from an entirely different point of view. It was a view that saw all of nature at one and in harmony with the mystery of the Creator of the Universe. It was a nature not to be subdued or dominated by man, but to be revered and looked upon with respect and awe, even as in the poem of the Blackfoot Indian Chief, to the very smallest part—the flash of a firefly in the night.

The Blackfoot Indian Chief has now been gone for over 100 years, yet his eyes are still with us in his last words as we too picture this scene in our own minds. We see more than just a picture of a dying human being painted in words. We see our own never-ending search for GOD.

The world today has little of the sense of awe that the Blackfoot Indian Chief expressed. Not only are we caught up in our religious history, but also we are caught up in the frenetic pace of our lives. We have lost sight of the wonder of GOD'S creation all around us. We look for our answers not to the firefly in the night and the breath of the buffalo in the wintertime, but to our reliance on reason and modern science.

We look to Quantum Physics to extend our knowledge farther and farther into the smallest parts of matter. We use our advanced instruments and our analytical knowledge to break down matter into its smallest composition. But as we do this, we are left with mathematical constructs that behave in less and less predictable ways and only open up new and profound mysteries. We also extend our knowledge the other way, out into the vast depths of space in our Universe, and as we do this we are left with the same uncertainties. As scientists delve into these mysteries, they long for a *Unified Theory* that will bring this all together, knowing all along that there will always be another side to the reaches of their knowledge.

Our world has undergone far-reaching changes since the Blackfoot Indian Chief lay dying. We not only know more about the physical universe around us but we also know more about what makes human beings act the way they do. Both the social sciences as well as the physical sciences have moved forward at exponential rates of speed.

This has not been the case with religion. We have not seen the same far-reaching changes. In fact, we have often seen a stubborn resistance to change. Advances in religious thought are held back by the rigidity of past belief, which is grounded on the inerrancy of ancient religious texts.

Those belief systems most intent on resisting change carry many different labels, the most prominent being that of Orthodox, Ultra-Orthodox, Conservative, Fundamentalist, and Evangelical. In all cases; however, there is a common denominator. Presuming the superiority of their belief system over all others, believers proclaim that only they are right and everyone else is wrong. The beliefs of all others outside of their own belief system are devalued.

These *believers'* generally hold to certain common convictions and follow certain practices in order to establish in their own minds the superiority of their own particular belief system. On the surface these can seem benign, and even necessary for individual religious fulfillment; however, they can also lead to unintended consequences. These consequences can lead to pain and suffering among those both within and outside of a particular belief system.

Some generally followed are:

- Only we have an understanding of the true nature of GOD

- Only we will be at one with GOD after death

- Only we have a true covenant with GOD

- Only we have been endowed with a mission as the moral catalyst for all humanity

- Only our rituals and observances have value and are the path to GOD'S grace

- Only our scriptures come from GOD and are without error

- We are surrounded by an alien, hostile, threatening, and immoral world

- All society outside of our own religious belief system exists in ignorance

- All society outside of our own religious belief system has been overtaken by evil

- Those who hold ideas other than our own have been overtaken by evil

- There will be a messianic age concurrent with an End of Time when only we will be saved by GOD

All of these beliefs and practices to one degree or another can be found in Judaism, Christianity, and Islam. None of the three Hebraic religions can escape the criticism that, in one way or another, they enable their own believers to say: "I have value in the eyes of GOD and you don't because you don't believe what I believe."

With this separateness come both intended as well as unintended consequences. We can see this in our recent history. Some examples are:

- The silent superiority of Lutheran and Roman Catholic Germans—as well as many others in the west—who, during the Hitler era, looked at Jews and their religious beliefs and practices as being misguided. For them Jews *held ideas other than our own* and therefore were *overtaken by evil*. As the Holocaust unfolded, many German Christians who believed that *only we have a true covenant with GOD*, silently stood by, seeing Jews as having little value as human beings.

- Jewish intellectuals at that time who, rejecting the divinity of Jesus Christ, preached the rabbinical idea of their own *particularity*, a word the rabbis used to describe all Jews, which defined them as unique among all of civilization—because of their Torah and its definition of covenant. Believing in this, these Jews openly considered their religion not only to be superior to Christianity but also a religion *endowed with a mission as the moral catalyst for all humanity*.

- In more recent times, evangelical Christians who believe that both The Old Testament and The New Testament *scriptures come from GOD and are without error*, and therefore interpreting the Gospel of John 3:16 in its most narrow sense, openly condemn those in society who do not express a rhetorical belief in Jesus Christ, saying that they will not be saved at death but will pass on into the fires of hell.

- Muslims throughout the world who believe that every word of the Koran *comes from GOD and is without error* and therefore as instructed in the Koran, harbor hatred and resentment toward the enemies of Islam, namely Christian and Jewish *infidels*, as well as Hindus and others. They believe that their hateful thoughts and actions are encouraged by Allah, to include the murder of all enemies of Islam, even by means of suicide if necessary.

In each of the above we see one group of believers assuming superiority over another, and we see an unwillingness and inability to change. Each religious group proclaims that *only we have an understanding of the true nature of GOD.*

Concluding Statement The Legacy of Past Religious Belief for the 21st Century and Beyond

This feeling of superiority acts as a negative force freezing old religious patterns of thought and works against the acceptance of new religious ideas originating from outside the bounds of the narrowness of a particular group's religious orthodoxy.

These responses can affect geopolitical events with broad and far reaching geopolitical results in both positive and negative ways. Politicians, religious leaders, and intellectuals may be at the forefront; however, it is the general population with its underlying beliefs that become the underlying driving engine of change.

For Jews the idea that *only we have been endowed with a mission as the moral catalyst for all humanity*, led to the Socialist movement at the turn of the 19th Century. This Jewish utopian idea of social consciousness as it spread throughout Europe ultimately led to social democratic reform in many of the European countries. It also was largely responsible for the world's experiment with International Communism, a system that tragically released the darkest side of human nature. In the United States, this social consciousness gave political impetus to the International Trade Union Movement as well as other forms of social activism. The idea of Judaism acting as a force toward social goodness as well as the idea of the *particularity* of Jews and the special place of Jewish thought continues to exist in the United States as a liberal political dimension of Reformed Judaism.

For evangelical Christians the identical idea of one's religion being *the moral catalyst for all humanity* in recent years has expressed itself politically in exactly the opposite way. Resting their case on the breakdown of morality in American society, in the 2000 Presidential election the Evangelical Christian *Moral Majority* exerted considerable political influence and turned the election in favor of a Republican Presidential candidate holding to a conservative ideology in line with the evangelical Christian conservative political agenda. This conservative agenda in its interpretation of *social consciousness* was in stark contrast to the recent historical one of Judaism just described

This conviction that only *our* particular religion as interpreted by *our particular group* can be seen as *the moral catalyst for all humanity* is often based on the belief that certain supporting scriptural texts, as well as certain interpretations of them, are from GOD and therefore are without error. This can manifest itself in many different ways.

Many Jews today believe that the Torah and the Midrashim comments that grew out of it are from GOD. They believe that *only we have an understanding of the true nature of GOD*. In fact, when a Rabbi is interpreting the Torah, in Judaism it is GOD who is speaking. This authority has led some Rabbis to pronounce that the land of Israel was given to the Jews by GOD, and the restoration of the Temple there is directed by GOD.

Muslims, as has been noted, believe that the words of the Koran were given to Muhammad by Allah himself. The Sharia law that grew out of the Koran is sacrosanct. Sharia law is Allah's law for all humankind. A Muslim must live his life under Sharia law. Islam is to be *the moral catalyst for all humanity.* Therefore, the conquests of Islam cannot rest until the world has become a clerical state under Sharia law.

Christianity has followed much the same pattern. The idea of being *the moral catalyst for all humanity* is central to all Christian belief. Also, there is an emphasis on the "*particularity* of the individual believer—covered by the complex and often debated concept of predestination.

The idea that *Only our scriptures come from GOD and are without error,* taken to an extreme, can be seen in the approaches to two concepts common to Evangelical Christianity, namely the concepts covering the end of the world and evolution.

Evangelical Christians believe that *there will be a Messianic age concurrent with the End of Time when only we will be saved by GOD* and they eagerly await for this time, which they call the Apocalypse.

As for evolution, in their arguments against Darwinian, as well as the more recent scientific theories of evolution, they refute all but the biblical creation account. Archeological and anthropological discoveries are to be ignored. Carbon dating is from the devil. Darwinian evolution was a hoax. Man began as Adam. Eve came from the rib of Adam. The Universe was created in six days. GOD flooded the world because He was angry with mankind. Only Noah and his family were saved.

These Christians look outside of themselves with myopic eyes seeing scientific progress as something to be feared and rejected. They look with suspicion at all other religions open to a modern scientific view of evolution and those in them who believe in any other way.

From the very beginnings of man's search for a knowledge that would free him from the cycle of birth and death he had woven into his history a written record of his beliefs. Whether is was the dialogues of Plato, the classical Hindu scriptures of the Vedas, the Koran of Muhammad, the Hebrew Bible or the Canon of the Christian New Testament writings, the expression of religious thought at some point of its development took a written form. Fundamentalist religion says that this was the word of GOD and it cannot be changed. It refuses to acknowledge that any of it could be from the mind and hand of man.

If this were merely an academic exercise, it would have little relevance for the world of today, but this is not the case. In fact, it has become the cause of much of the present world conflict, and it promises to be the cause of future conflict. It has in a sense taken over the conflict of the past century between the two political ideologies, Communism and Capitalism, and grown to express itself in the form of international terrorism with potential dangers even greater than those previously faced.

Pointing to the inerrancy of their scriptures, fanatical factions within nations and in some cases the nations themselves brazenly justify their actions as the will of GOD. They claim to be exclusive or *Chosen*.

The texts supporting the arguments over which these conflicts have arisen represented the efforts of past civilizations to explain the nature of GOD based on their ancient level of understanding of themselves and the world around them. Much of what was written has limited relevance in the world of today if taken in literal form.

A case in point is a famous passage in the Hebrew Bible:

It shall be done to him as he has done; fracture for fracture, eye for eye, tooth for tooth; the injury and disfigurement he has inflicted upon another shall be in turn inflicted upon him.

(Leviticus 24:20)

and in the Koran:

It is life for life, eye for eye, and nose for nose, and ear for ear, and tooth for tooth, and reprisal in wounds....

(Sura 5.45)

This may have been a legitimate way for Hebrews to control a tribal society in the desert 3500 years ago, and Muslims their society in the Arabian desert 600 after Jesus Christ, but clearly it is not the way human beings should respond to each other in our modern age where in an escalation of violence planes can be flown into buildings, suicide bombers can blow themselves up in night clubs and atomic bombs can be detonated in major cities.

Modern day Jews will argue that this Leviticus passage is now for them in the 21st century interpreted only in a legalistic sense; however, recent events in Israel prove that this is not the case. The same can be said for Muslims who will point out that their Koran goes on to say:...*but he who forgoes it, it shall be an expiation for him....* The dangerous outcomes of these archaic thought patterns cannot be passed off in such an intellectual fashion. Once these ideas are fixed in the minds of the believer, they remain in the subconscious.

An example of scriptural thought patterns acting as a driving force in decision making is the Palestinian/Israeli conflict over the settlements in the West Bank near the city of Jerusalem. This land for Orthodox Jews was mandated to them by Yahweh in their scriptures. As they aggressively expanded these settlements in defiance of world opinion, Palestinians respond in turn with suicide bombings. Then, Israelis in turn respond with the killing of Palestinian terrorist leaders as well as innocent Palestinian civilians caught in the crossfire.

We need to acknowledge the power that scripture has over our thoughts and actions. We are rapidly becoming one world of one human race. No longer can we hide behind our past tribal, national, and religious identities as a justification for our actions. The time has come for religious scriptural self-examination. Not only Christians, Jews, and Muslims, but all peoples of the world of all religious beliefs must examine the validity of their beliefs and ask the following two questions:

- Are we being held back in our social development as a world community by our belief in the inerrancy of ancient religious texts that no longer relate to our new knowledge?

- Is it possible that many of these texts have more to say to us, but by holding fast to the inerrancy of their language, we are missing new and deeper meanings?

Here is where debate among religions of all peoples of all nations should be taking place, not over the inerrancy of any scripture of any kind. The past has given us glimpses of GOD'S revelation, not a lock on the truth. As human beings we entered the world with the commission to search for the truth.

To find the truth there are two questions that every religion must address:

- Does the GOD we worship ask us to honor each other?

- How do we honor each other?

This today is the challenge to all people of all religions. Each of us must take this road in search for GOD. Whatever the traditional religious background, all of mankind from its very beginning has been moving towards this same goal. We should not be held back now by ancient religious texts. They should enhance our knowledge, not restrain it.

Concluding Statement The Legacy of Past Religious Belief for the 21st Century and Beyond

Many Christians believe that in the life and death of Jesus Christ, GOD redefined His very nature and how He views each of us. They interpret the words of Jesus Christ as saying that GOD'S love extends to all of humankind. As to our weaknesses, Jesus Christ said that with man and women perfection is not possible but by GOD'S grace salvation for everyone is possible. He said that GOD'S love and his redemption extend to all of us, to the good and the bad, the weak and the strong. Most importantly he said that our worship of GOD is expressed here on earth by our love towards each other. He called for a love no longer to be confined to family or tribe or to those of our own particular religious belief system. It was to extend to all people.

Since the presence of Jesus Christ on this earth, there has been a never-ending quest by theologians, scholars, and philosophers to understand the meaning of his teaching and of his life. Of one thing most would agree. He showed mankind a monotheistic God far removed from the pagan Gods of the time, and in many ways, unlike the God of the Hebrew Bible. And it was a God far removed from the God Muhammad revealed 600 years later in the Koran.

Also, he defined a different relationship between his fellow Jews and GOD. He asked them to totally abandon much of what they had, since the beginning of their history, believed to be the Word of GOD. He asked them to abandon the beliefs of their mothers, their fathers, and to follow him.

These new definitions were written down by many writers in the century after his death and later brought together in the fourth century by the Bishops of the newly established Roman Christian Church in a canon of writings called The New Testament. The question of what really came from Jesus Christ and what came from the hand of man was settled by a Council of Bishops. Then, like the Torah for the Jews, this canon of writings for the Christians was declared The Word of GOD, not to be changed in any way, only to be interpreted.

Until the turn of the 20th century, for most of Christendom, the belief in the inerrancy of these New Testament texts and the dogma that grew out of them remained inviolate. Although there had always been individuals who questioned these beliefs, it was not until early on in the 20th century that scholars began to actively question the texts and the dogma. Then, in 1945 there came a startling development. Near the Egyptian town of Nag Hammadi in the Upper Nile, a six-foot jar was discovered in a hillside. It contained over fifty ancient texts. One, The Gospel of Thomas, which some scholars now declare predates the New Testament Gospels, was found. It challenged much of the accepted belief of Christians about what GOD expects of them and how they can become at one with HIM. It redefined the concept of heaven. It refuted the idea of the Second Coming and the End of Times. It even redefined in many ways who in fact Jesus of Nazareth said he was.

Challenges to accepted religious belief in the last century, not only based on Christian New Testament writings, but also the Hebrew Bible (Christian Old Testament and Torah) have come from many other different directions. Some are from archaeological discoveries and some from the physical sciences. The expansion of knowledge relating to our world and our universe has been exponential and this is clashing with orthodox biblical belief.

As this debate over the inerrancy of scripture continues, there is arising an entirely new issue that is largely being ignored. In recent years we have heard scientists question whether our human species, given its present pace of resource use and the accompanying environmental degradation, can survive for as long a period as it has already existed. The fragility of our earth is illustrated in the photographs that have come back to us from our astronauts. Our scientists are warning that the earth may not be able to sustain us if we continue to pollute and destroy. Clearly, issues such as this call for a reassessment of our relationship to our natural environment, as well as to each other. They also call for a reassessment of the adequacy of the role of religion in addressing the future.

The religions grounded on the Hebrew Bible should be examining these issues. They are not. Rather, they are wasting their time and energy in a constant battle as to who is theologically right and who is theologically wrong, who is saved and who is not. As far as the future of the world is concerned, arguments over apocalyptic prophecy take center stage. There is an assumption that the day will come when the world will no longer be. GOD is viewed as the destroyer. He will end it all as He did with the world in Noah's time, but this time totally.

The question must be asked of those who believe in an Apocalypse. Is yours a self-fulfilling prophecy, which over the centuries has rested on a false foundation, that of man's God given right to *dominate nature*? What if the Blackfoot Indian Chief was right and all of nature should be looked at as being at one in harmony with the mystery of our Creator? What if GOD intentioned a continuation of HIS creation here on this earth towards the beauty of HIS perfection and we humans are a part of that perfection? Is apocalyptic thinking a death wish for all of humanity? By their own belief in the End of Times are they, the sons and daughters of Abraham, subliminally setting the stage for the end of the human species? Are they selfishly saying to future generations: We want it all now. We don't have to care about the future of the world. GOD will be destroying it anyway.

Those of the tradition of Abraham believe that man was told by GOD that he has dominion over nature, he can dominate it and to use it for his own purposes. The Book of Genesis tells man that he is to:

rule over the fish of the sea and the birds of the sky and over the cattle and over every creeping thing that creeps on the earth.

(Genesis 1:28)

From the beginning of his history this is what man did, and it allowed him to prosper. It is only in the last century as scientists have observed the irreparable damage being done to the world that man has looked back and realized that the power to dominate nature also gave him the power to destroy it. To his horror he is seeing that by degrading and destroying the environment that surrounds him he is setting out the pathway to his own extinction. Humankind is seeing the first glimpses of the end of the human species, not coming from a punishing God in some apocalyptic act of final judgment, but from himself.

Could this assumption that originated in the ancient Hebrew Bible and became such an important part of the theology of Judaism, Christianity, and Islam be wrong? Have we been misguided by the words of these ancient texts? Were the words of the Hebrew Bible that laid the foundation for Judaism, Christianity, and Islam directly from GOD or were they merely from an exceptionally gifted and introspective people living in a desert wilderness looking for the answers to their existence? Are other assumptions made in the Hebrew Bible, The Christian New and Old Testaments and the Koran wrong? Should we be searching for greater knowledge elsewhere?

There may be a great deal that modern man can learn from the Blackfoot Indian Chief and those who lived before him. The Blackfoot Indian Chief looked at all of nature as being at one and in harmony with the mystery of our Creator, a Creator who intended a continuation of everything in His creation here on earth, a creation forever moving towards perfection. The Blackfoot Indian Chief would have had no quarrel with parts of the Book of Genesis, but he would not have agreed with all of it. He too believed that what GOD had created in the world was all *Good*. For him, GOD was a creator of beauty. HE was a creator of the mystery of life. HE was also a God who looked upon every man, every woman, every bird, every animal, every living thing, even to the very smallest—*every creeping thing that creeps upon the earth*—as an interdependent and sacrosanct part of the mystery of that creation. The Blackfoot Indian Chief saw each and every living thing, as well as non-living thing, to be honored and respected, not to be ruled over or dominated.

For the Blackfoot Indian Chief the breath of the buffalo in the wintertime was the spirit of GOD saying to him:

I am here with you. See me in the beauty of my creation. Die in peace.

The words in this book are addressed to everyone, from those with the same faith as that of the Blackfoot Indian Chief to those holding complex faiths grounded on ancient writings and philosophical discourse. They are also addressed to those with no faith at all. They give due credit, but largely leave aside for other writers the positive role that religion has played over the course of history towards the advancement of human civilization, and rather concentrate on the shortcomings of religious belief in the world of the 21st century. They come to the conclusion that the underlying cause of world conflict today is religious belief.

The three Hebraic rooted religions, Judaism, Christianity, and Islam, exist suspended in a time warp going back thousands of years. They are unable to change. It is for this reason that they are unable to act in concert as a positive force toward the advancement of human civilization. In very many ways each has become an impediment to advancement.

As for Christianity, many of the ideas in this book are in opposition to accepted Christian doctrine as it was grounded by the early church bishops in the authorized New Testament texts. The message sides more with the revelations taken from the Nag Hammadi findings, and in particular The 5th Gospel of Thomas. Knowledge gained from this Gospel was used in the argument against the inerrancy of the New Testament as well as the Hebrew Bible and the Koran. It was also used as an argument against all institutionalized religion.

The Jesus portrayed by Thomas said that GOD does not limit His presence to those of any single earthly religion. He said that the relationship between human beings and GOD is direct and without the need for any religious institutional intermediary.

He told Thomas that GOD exists in the here an now and not in some far off dimension looking down on human beings and judging them as to whether or not they are following the laws and observances called for in their religious texts. Nor will there be a final judgment day. He said GOD exists at every moment within and around each and every one of us. We are a part of Him and He is a part of us.

There is a caveat though. Jesus told Thomas that the road might not be an easy one. For some it will be very painful. He said we cannot find GOD within until we have cast aside from our lives everything of this world that by defining our wants and desires is distracting us. We must first know in the depths of ourselves on what side we have placed our lives, what God or Gods we have allowed to define us. He said it is only after we have done this that we can then begin the search to the depths of our very being to find answers to the most penetrating questions about ourselves, questions that we may never have dared before to ask, questions about who we really are. Only then can we discover the one GOD who is within. Only then can we reach HIM. Jesus told Thomas, only then can HE reach us.

According to the Thomas Gospel, the God we find within will not be the anthropomorphic God of the Torah. Nor will He be the God of the Christian Old Testament or much of the Christian New Testament or the God of the Koran. He will not be a judgmental God. He will not be a God capable of anger. He will not be a God to be feared. He will not be a God who requires us to obey 613 commandments or to pray five times each day. He will be a God of awesome power and pure love who requires us to show this same love to each other.

This is not the definition of the God revealed in Hebrew, Muslim, and Christian religious texts. Christians have come close to the Thomas definition in the New Testament, but they nevertheless continue to hold on to the Hebraic definition of the angry, judgmental, and fearful father God of the Old Testament. They define Him that way as the inscrutable father God of their Trinity.

The time has come for humans to face a number of questions: Have these three religions wrongly defined the nature of our Creator? If the thoughts and actions of those following these religions are being conditioned by their belief in this ancient God, is this patterning their behavior towards each other and the world around them? Is this a primary cause for present world conflict? Does it threaten future human existence? Was Thomas right? This book has been an exploration of these and other questions, but it has left it to the reader to decide the answers.

I wrote this book with the same feeling of awe of GOD'S creation that was expressed by the Blackfoot Indian Chief. There is no other way that a person of any faith can approach the WORD of GOD.

My thoughts are from my own search, and like those of the Blackfoot Indian Chief, they come from my own personal view of all that surrounds me. There is little difference though between us. I have the same sense of awe as I see in the depths of my mind the

> "...flash of the firefly in the night
> ...breath of the buffalo in the winter time
> ...little shadow that runs across the grass
> And loses itself in the sunset".

This is as far as I have come to an understanding of my own view of GOD. You may find after reading this book that you have traveled farther along the path.

Sexuality and the Religions of Abraham

inerrant *adj.*, inerrancy *n.*
"not wandering, not erring, making no mistakes, infallible"
Webster's New World Dictionary

The use of the masculine form *mankind* to designate the human species and the words *HIM*, *Him* and *His* to designate GOD are used throughout this book only to avoid having to invent words that are gender neutral.

GOD'S nature in the Hebrew Bible was revealed using images and symbols that could be understood within the social conventions of an historical time period. This was a period when men were considered to be the intellectually dominant members of society. Women were subject to them, and as leaders were seldom heard from. Abraham was a man. Moses was a man. David was a man.

The dominance of the male begins at the very first page of Jewish/Christian as well as Muslim history. The Book of Genesis reads in 1:26:

And God said; let us make man in our image, after our likeness.

And then in: 2:21-22:

And the Lord God caused a deep sleep to fall upon Adam, and he slept; and he took one of his ribs, And the rib, which the Lord God had taken from man, made he a women.

Many of those who believe in the inerrancy of every word of the Bible and the Koran will declare that since GOD made *Man* in His own *image*; therefore, GOD must look like man. And, as woman was *taken out of man*, she therefore must be secondary to man.

The words in Genesis referring to GOD making man in his own image are GOD'S revelation to men and women of the human species that they were created like HIM, not in bodily form, but in mind. The words mean that each of us is a reflection of the mind of GOD. We are a part of HIM. HE is a part of us.

The Genesis story does not stop there. It goes on to explain that not all of us are like HIM. WE have a capacity that He does not have. We have the capacity to choose evil. Therefore, our human nature is not all like HIM. This is the revelation coming from Genesis. It is a story explaining the duality of human nature. This is its meaning. It has nothing to do with sexual dominance or difference.

The words of the Torah for centuries were not written, but were passed from generation to generation by word of mouth. Storytellers revealed what they considered to be GOD'S message, using the language of Myth. Many of the biblical images found in the Torah—including the Garden of Eden itself—extend back another 2000 years into early Sumerian times, before the Jewish people had existed as a unified tribe. Many other images grew out of the mythology of prior generations of other tribes and nations in the Mesopotamian area.

The early Jewish writers used these images to explain the revelation of GOD as they interpreted it within the context of their own understanding of themselves and their relationship to Him. Theirs was a culture of dominant men, as other cultures had been. Males therefore were dominant in their Myths.

Males were dominant when Jesus Christ preached, but he made no distinction between Man and Woman. He looked with equanimity on both. Women played an important role in his life, and in fact women defined much of his ministry.

For Islam, 600, years after Jesus, Muhammad adopted the Hebraic view of male and female.

It was the Apostle Paul, not Jesus Christ, who defined the role of women in the early Christian Church. He gave the Christian community hard and fast choices as to how to behave. These choices were deeply rooted in his pharisaic religious bias. They were also in sympathy with the prevailing social structure of the Roman society from which conversions were taking place. Paul's rhetorical hardball was intended for a far less enlightened audience than we see in today's world. We must therefore view the statements of Paul in the context of the period in which he lived and the challenges he faced. We must view them in the context of his own pharisaic background, his temperament, and his own questionable sexual orientation.

Men and women in the 21st century and beyond must search for the ultimate truth about GOD and their relationship to GOD, without the literal constraints of past mythology. They are physiologically different, but their souls are not. They were both made in the image of GOD. Like Adam and Eve after the fall, both men and women have a capacity for good as well as for evil. They have to make choices every day of their lives between good and evil. Both were given the freedom to contribute to society according to their abilities as mothers and fathers and mentors—as well as Priests, Pastors, Mullahs, Rabbis, CEOs, Artists, Electricians, Plumbers, and Presidents.

We are all, each of us, GOD'S chosen ONES in a *human society* with no sexual dividing lines. Each of us was born into this world to add to it, to use for GOD'S purposes what He has given us, each according to his or her individual ability. Biological sexual form—or even orientation—is not relevant.

Jesus Christ told us in the 5th Gospel of Thomas (24) and the Gospel of Matthew (25:15-30) that what matters in the mind of GOD is what we make of our lives. If Judaism, Christianity and Islam do not elevate their theologies and the scriptures that support them to acknowledge this, in time they will cease to be.

Comments on the Bibliography

Each of the seventeen essays in this book deals with a contemporary Jewish, Christian or Muslim religious issue that is important for an understanding of the underlying causes of world conflict. Some essays are followed by *Reflections* that serve to support the subject being covered.

The words and viewpoint in the essays and reflections are a mix of many ideas, but most are strongly the author's. Their content, therefore, is presented without attribution.

Wherever a quotation is used, the source is identified. All biblical quotations were taken either from the King James Bible or The New English Bible. Quotations from the Koran were taken from the electronic version of The Holy Qur'an, translated by M.H. Shakir and published by Tahrike Tarsile Qur'an, 1983, revised January 2000 as well as other unknown sources. All poetry quotations, except that in the introduction, were taken from *The Treasury of American Poetry*. The Lewis Carroll Humpty Dumpty (Dumpy) verse from *Alice in Wonderland* quoted in Part XIV was taken from an Internet Lewis Carroll page. The poem from the dying Blackfoot Indian Chief quoted in the Introduction is from an unknown source.

Some information was taken from fictional accounts of history and some not. Where fictional accounts were used, such as from the book, *Galileo's Daughter*, which describes the early resistance of the Roman Catholic Church to the advances in the sciences, and *Desire of The Everlasting Hills*, which describes the survival of Christianity after the fall of the Roman Empire, the author believes using such fictional accounts, for the purposes of this book, are an accurate account of historical events.

Direct quotations were only made where the author determined that they were from scholars considered to be among the most respected in their particular fields of study. In all cases the name of the scholar is given along with the quotation.

Although scholarship standards on religious matters in academic publications tend to be high, the author found that in almost all popular publications there exists a rigidity of belief and a strong bias. This is a bias that serves to crowd out moderate voices. It is found at the popular publications of Judaism, Christianity, and Islam. It is most pronounced in what is popularly known as Christian and Islamic Fundamentalism as well as Conservative and Orthodox Judaism. This bias to a large extent determines what is allowed and what is excluded in both the mass media and the publishing marketplace. The result is that religion in general is presented to the public only at the extremes, or at least it is heavily influenced by the extremes.

The author found another kind of bias more far reaching than that confined to popular extremist views. It too extends across the mass media and the publishing industry. This is the bias of *religious political correctness*. It is a pervasive bias against any kind of open religious discussion contrary to predefined religious views. It stifles discussion in the name of religious tolerance. It exists in the United States under the guise of *freedom of religious expression*, but in fact it produces exactly the opposite result by stifling this expression.

This bias does not exist equally among all religious traditions. For example, it is particularly apparent in the United States with respect to any form of criticism of Jewish religious practices and beliefs or the Torah (Hebrew Bible) and the dark side of Zionism as a causal factor in world conflict. On the other hand, criticism of the religion of Islam is fair game. Almost all writing about Islam is highly critical and places it in a cynical light. The same applies to Roman Catholicism. Again, the reader is only given a picture of the dark side. A recent example is Dan Brown's *The Da Vinci Code*. Here Catholic history with wild poetic license is portrayed in an extremely cynical light. There is little mention in popular literature of the transforming influence of Roman Catholicism on western world history.

Judaism presented a special problem for the author. Almost all self criticism is internal and among and between Jewish scholars. It is in a sense hidden from the general public. The internal debate is very much confined to the Torah. Any cross-religious Christian or Hellenistic or eastern religious thought is absent and even denigrated. For example, within Judaism, any acknowledgement of the positive transforming power of Jesus Christ on western civilization over the millennia is totally absent.

Evolution in Jewish thought is kept within Judaism as an internal affair. External philosophical ideas are looked upon with suspicion and arouse a self-defensive stand. This is not the case in the Christian dialogue which not only recognizes the importance of the Jewish historical experience—Christian Old Testament—but also to some extent has been open to other influences such as the influence of Hellenistic (Greek philosophical) and even eastern religious thought.

Comments on the Bibliography 219

Islam presented much the same problem for the author as Judaism. There is the same kind of resistance to any kind of cross religious influence. Islam, however, exists under a far more static condition and with far greater restraint than Judaism, principally because it is more rigidly tied into the Koran and it has not been exposed to the secular western world. Islam is not a religion of self-criticism either internally or externally. By definition it is a static religion. The Koran cannot be challenged. The penalty for disbelief is eternal damnation.

Writers in the West generally view Islam as if it exists in a time warp out of the past. This view is largely filtered through the perspective of western intellectuals. Positive aspects of Islam are disregarded. Hopefully, this book will stimulate an intellectual response from moderate Muslims in defense of Islam. The author in fact came upon many aspects of Islam that could be viewed as very beneficial for western society. Given the current world religious crisis and the association of world terrorism with Islamic belief, a dialogue with Muslims would be very constructive.

With regard to the sciences, the author found that the only perceptible bias is coming from evangelical Christianity based on its non-evolutionary creationist stand, a stand that neatly dovetails into its—and Orthodox Jews as well as all Muslims—apocalyptic argument saying that GOD will destroy the world. The scientific arguments in this book, which are opposed to this evangelical creationist and apocalyptic stand, are based on the biographical sources listed. These sources are considered generally by the scientific community to be current and authoritative.

Lectures at Florida Atlantic University are presented without outlines. This is not the case with those of The Teaching Company where extensive outlines and bibliographies are furnished. These lectures are available from The Teaching Company in audio and video form. Reference is not made in the book to specific lectures; however, individual lectures that were of particular importance in drawing conclusions are enumerated. It is the author's intention to encourage readers to listen to these lectures, read the source material and draw their own conclusions.

QuickVerse Essentials Version 6 (Parsons, 11640, Arbor St., Suite 201. Omaha, Nebraska 68144) was used extensively for calling up biblical scripture and researching both Orthodox Christian commentary as well as traditional scholarly commentary on biblical subject matter. Examples are the author's research done to answer questions such as; whether Jesus regarded himself as the Messiah, the origins of the Doctrine of the Trinity, how Jewish belief in future life developed, and the Jewish concept of the *Day of Yahweh*—day of judgment

(Isaiah 2:12). For further study of these and other subjects, it is suggested that readers conduct their own similar research through sources such as QuickVerse.

Three sources; the Internet, *Halley's Bible Handbook*, as well as QuickVerse were used more to gain an understanding of what religious believers of different convictions consider to be historical as well as theological truth as opposed to *the* truth. Each comes with its own extreme bias.

Examining the role of religious belief as a cause for world conflict without including an examination of the overriding historical presence of Jesus Christ over two millennia is inescapable. The question of how those who followed Jesus Christ caused conflict then and continue to do so now, becomes all-important since his was a ministry of peace and non-conflict. To find answers the author examined the *conflict producing shortcomings* of institutional Christianity against the backdrop of a questionable rightful or wrongful historical interpretation of the life and teachings of Jesus Christ, as presented in the canon of writings authorized by the Roman Church in the fourth century A.D.

It is now an accepted fact—although confined to the world religious academic community—that the early Roman Catholic Church stifled the ideas of at least half of early Christianity and then, with Eusebius' 10 volume *Ecclesiastical History*, rewrote early Christian history to support their exclusive view of Jesus Christ. In doing so, the Church systematically defamed the leading individuals in all of the early opposition movements, calling them *Heretics*. They then ordered all of their writings destroyed. It has only been in recent years that the ideas of movements such as the Ebionites, Valentian Gnostics, and Marcionites, to name only a few, have been painstakingly rediscovered to show how biased the early church was. This was well documented in Walter Bauer's 1934 ground breaking book entitled *Orthodoxy and Heresy in Earliest Christianity*. Since then, scholarship in this area has been intense. That fact remains, however, that these revisionist ideas have not penetrated organized Christianity. In fact, organized Christianity—including the Roman Catholic Church—is fighting them tooth and nail.

A writer with considerable influence on Roman Catholicism was the Apostle Paul. The author therefore included a study of the influence of the Apostle Paul on the early Church. This included an examination of the influences on his life that may have affected his writings, to include his pharisaic background as well as his possible homosexuality. Reflections 24 through 37 are the author's attempt to single out those statements made by Paul that in the author's opinion are likely to have reflected what Jesus actually said.

Every attempt was made to leave open to readers their own conclusions as to who Jesus of Nazareth really was and whether in fact he has been over history and is today being rightly or wrongly interpreted. Whether it involves the Nag Hammadi Library findings or the letters of the Apostle Paul, it is left up to the reader to decide what is authentic and what is not.

The reader will find that criticisms of Christianity in the book are as numerous as those of Judaism and Islam. The central idea that archaic religious beliefs in each tradition to one degree or another must bear much of the blame for present world conflict is the overriding theme. It is the rigidity of all of our belief systems that goes to the core of the problem. The author concludes that the anthropomorphic judgmental, fearful, yet merciful father GOD found in the Torah, Hebrew Bible (Christian Old Testament), much of the Christian New Testament, and the Koran is the patterning force behind the behavior of those believing in this God. This underlying image manifests itself as a sub conscious force of enormous strength driving our aberrant behavior towards each other. We pattern our thoughts and behavior after the God or Gods we worship.

Are the three religions based on the Torah flawed? Is the Torah definition of GOD not GOD? Were the Jews deceived by the words of the deceiver? (see reference to Genesis 3:5 in Part IX) Have Christians and Muslims, who adopted this GOD image from the Torah also been deceived? The author asks the reader to decide these questions for him or her self. Each of us must face the question of whether his or her beliefs taken from the past are false or are true.

Unfortunately, the answers to these questions, because of the strong general bias in religious information referred to above, are not being openly debated. They should be. As the 21st century moves forward, many of the answers can no longer wait.

For each of us, our moment of physical existence on this earth is brief. For the human species, our moment of human existence is only a flicker in the infinite dimension of time and space. There is no guarantee that the human species will continue to exist for ever. During our time on this earth, each of us is offered the unique possibility of becoming something beyond mere organic existence, something beyond our physical selves that can bring the human species closer to GOD'S purpose for it.

The author found little evidence that the general public, through the organized religions of the world and their spokespersons, is fully aware of this. To some degree religious academia is, but not organized religion.

Patterning our thoughts and actions after false Gods is holding us back. Our ignorance is holding us back. As a result, we as individuals are suffering. Humanity is suffering. Planet earth is suffering. We must find the true GOD of our creation and pattern our thoughts and actions to be in *oneness* with that true GOD. This is the most important thing any of us can ever do in our lives. The author found that so far, Judaism, Christianity, and Islam have not given us a true picture. Nor will they let it change.

We must find that GOD. It is the author's belief that how we direct our lives towards that true GOD will determine not only what we as individuals will become but also what will become of the human species.

Bibliography

Abdullah Al-Kadhi, Misheal. "Jesus Second Coming and Grace." http://www.sharif.org.uk/jesus4.htm.

Adler, Alfred. *Understanding Human Nature*. Greenwich, Connecticut: Fawcett Publications, 1927.

Aikman, David. "The Great Revival: Understanding Religious Fundamentalism." *New York Times*, August 4, 2003.

Angier, Natalie. "The Origin of Religions, From a Distinctly Darwinian View." *New York Times*, December 24, 2002.

Austin, Bill. *The Back of God*. Wheaton, Illinois: Tyndale House, 1980.

Barzun, Jacques. *From Dawn to Decadence, 500 Years of Western Cultural Life*. New York: Harper: Collins Publishers, 2000.

Bauer, Walter. *Orthodoxy and Heresy in Earliest Christianity*. Philadelphia: Fortress Press, 1971.

Bennett, James. "Crossing Jordan, The Exit That Isn't On Bush's Road Map." *New York Times*, May 18, 2003.

———. "Tourism of Sacrilege? Religious Leaders and visitors have opposing views about Jerusalem's Dome of the Rock." *New York Times*.

Berger, Arthur S. LLB. "Life After Death? We Are the First Generation to Know." Lecture sponsored by the Lifelong Learning Society of Florida Atlantic University. Boca Raton, Florida.

Berger, Dr. Allan. "Anti-Semitism: Ancient and Contemporary." Lecture sponsored by the Lifelong Learning Society of Florida Atlantic University. Boca Raton, Florida.

———. "Major Jewish Religious Thinkers of The 20th Century." Lecture sponsored by the Lifelong Learning Society of Florida Atlantic University. Boca Raton, Florida.

Berman, Paul. "The Philosopher of Islamic Terror." *New York Times*, March 23, 2003.

Bethke Elshtain, Jean. *Just War Against Terror*. New York: Basic Books, 2003.

Bishop, Eileen. Heightened Dissension within LCMS Remnant of Terrorist Attack, Lutheran Life National News, 10/5/02.

Bly, Robert. *Iron John*. New York: Vintage Books, 1992.

Borg, Marcus. *Jesus & Buddha, The Parallel Sayings*. Berkeley: Seastone, 2002.

Cahill, Thomas. *Desire of The Everlasting Hills*. New York: Anchor Books, 2001.

Cary, Professor Phillip. "Kant: Morality as the Basis of Religion Philosophy and Religion in the West." Lecture from the class on *Philosophy and Religion in the West*, Eastern College, recorded by The Teaching Company Limited Partnership.

———. "Kant: Reason Limited to Experience Philosophy and Religion in the West." Lecture from the class on *Philosophy and Religion in the West*, Eastern College, recorded by The Teaching Company Limited Partnership.

———. "Platonist Philosophy and Scriptural Religion Philosophy and Religion in the West." Lecture from the class on *Philosophy and Religion in the West*, Eastern College, recorded by The Teaching Company Limited Partnership.

———. "The Jewish Scriptures: Life with the God of Israel Philosophy and Religion in the West." Lecture from the class on *Philosophy and Religion in the West*, Eastern College, recorded by The Teaching Company Limited Partnership.

———. Lecture class on *Augustine: Philosopher and Saint*, Eastern College, recorded by The Teaching Company Limited Partnership.

———. "Plato's Inquiries: The Gods and the Good Philosophy and Religion in the West." Lecture from the class on *Philosophy and Religion in the West,* Eastern College, recorded by The Teaching Company Limited Partnership.

———. "Plato's Spirituality: The Immortal Soul and the Other World Philosophy and Religion in the West." Lecture from the class on *Philosophy and Religion in the West,* Eastern College, recorded by The Teaching Company Limited Partnership.

———. "Plotinus: Neo Platonism and the Ultimate Unity of All Philosophy and Religion in the West." Lecture from the class on *Philosophy and Religion in the West,* Eastern College, recorded by The Teaching Company Limited Partnership.

———. "Schleiermacher: Feeling as the Basis of Religion." Lecture from the class on *Philosophy and Religion in the West,* Eastern College, recorded by The Teaching Company Limited Partnership.

Chopra, Deepak. *How To Know God.* New York: Harmony Books, 2000.

Collins, John J. *The Scepter and The Stars: The Messiah of the Dead Sea Scrolls and other Ancient Literature.* Anchor Bible, 1995.

Crab, Larry. *The Safest Place on Earth.* Halifax, Nova Scotia: World Publishing, 1973.

Dali Lama. *How to Practice The Way to a Meaningful Life.* New York: Pocket Books, 2002.

Davey, Monica. "Episcopalians Give Nod for Gay Bishop." *New York Times,* August 4, 2003.

Eck, Professor Diana. "Creating a World: Two Cultures of Ancient India." Lecture given at Harvard University, recorded by The Teaching Company Limited Partnership.

———. "Gandhi: All Religions are True." Lecture given at Harvard University, recorded by The Teaching Company Limited Partnership.

———. "The Upanishads: Teaching on Wisdom." Lecture given at Harvard University, recorded by The Teaching Company Limited Partnership.

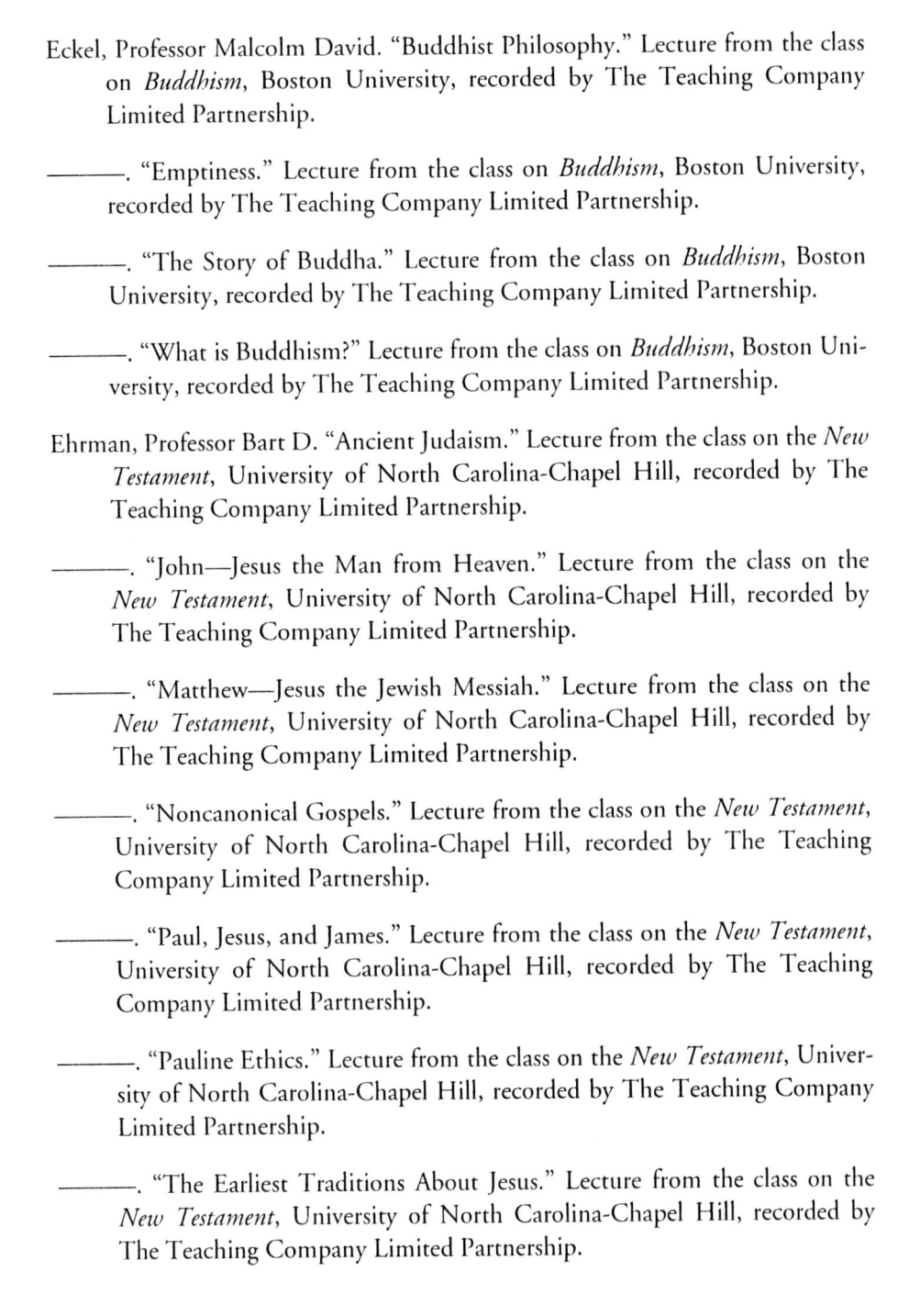

Eckel, Professor Malcolm David. "Buddhist Philosophy." Lecture from the class on *Buddhism*, Boston University, recorded by The Teaching Company Limited Partnership.

———. "Emptiness." Lecture from the class on *Buddhism*, Boston University, recorded by The Teaching Company Limited Partnership.

———. "The Story of Buddha." Lecture from the class on *Buddhism*, Boston University, recorded by The Teaching Company Limited Partnership.

———. "What is Buddhism?" Lecture from the class on *Buddhism*, Boston University, recorded by The Teaching Company Limited Partnership.

Ehrman, Professor Bart D. "Ancient Judaism." Lecture from the class on the *New Testament*, University of North Carolina-Chapel Hill, recorded by The Teaching Company Limited Partnership.

———. "John—Jesus the Man from Heaven." Lecture from the class on the *New Testament*, University of North Carolina-Chapel Hill, recorded by The Teaching Company Limited Partnership.

———. "Matthew—Jesus the Jewish Messiah." Lecture from the class on the *New Testament*, University of North Carolina-Chapel Hill, recorded by The Teaching Company Limited Partnership.

———. "Noncanonical Gospels." Lecture from the class on the *New Testament*, University of North Carolina-Chapel Hill, recorded by The Teaching Company Limited Partnership.

———. "Paul, Jesus, and James." Lecture from the class on the *New Testament*, University of North Carolina-Chapel Hill, recorded by The Teaching Company Limited Partnership.

———. "Pauline Ethics." Lecture from the class on the *New Testament*, University of North Carolina-Chapel Hill, recorded by The Teaching Company Limited Partnership.

———. "The Earliest Traditions About Jesus." Lecture from the class on the *New Testament*, University of North Carolina-Chapel Hill, recorded by The Teaching Company Limited Partnership.

———. "The Greco-Roman Context." Lecture from the class on the *New Testament*, University of North Carolina-Chapel Hill, recorded by The Teaching Company Limited Partnership.

———. "The Historical Jesus—Sources and Problems." Lecture from the class on the *New Testament*, University of North Carolina-Chapel Hill, recorded by The Teaching Company Limited Partnership.

———. "The Early Christians and Their Literature." Lecture from the class on the *New Testament*, University of North Carolina-Chapel Hill, recorded by The Teaching Company Limited Partnership.

Fisher, Ian. "Israelis Worry About Terror, by Jews Against Palestinians." *New York Times*, August 19, 2003.

Friedman, Thomas L. "Dinner With the Sayyids." *New York Times*, August 10, 2003.

Friese, Kai. "Hijacking India's History." *New York Times*, December 30, 2002.

Gawain, Shakti. *Creative Visualization*. New York: Bantam Books, 1982.

Gittelson, Dr. Abe. "Contemporary Jewish Movements." Lecture sponsored by the Lifelong Learning Society of Florida Atlantic University. Boca Raton, Florida.

Glynn, Professor Simon. "The Politics and Philosophy of Globalization: Impact on The World Today." Lecture sponsored by the Lifelong Learning Society of Florida Atlantic University. Boca Raton, Florida.

Goodstein, Laurie. "O Ye of Much Faith! A Triple Dose of Trouble, 'Crises in hierarchy, doctrine and identity bedevil three major world religions.'" *New York Times*, June 2, 2002.

Gould, Stephen Jay. *The Structure of Evolutionary Theory*. Boston, Massachusetts: Harvard University Press, 2002.

Gozier, Andre, O.S.B. *15 Days of Prayer with Meister Eckhart*. Liguori, Missouri: Liguori Publications, 2000.

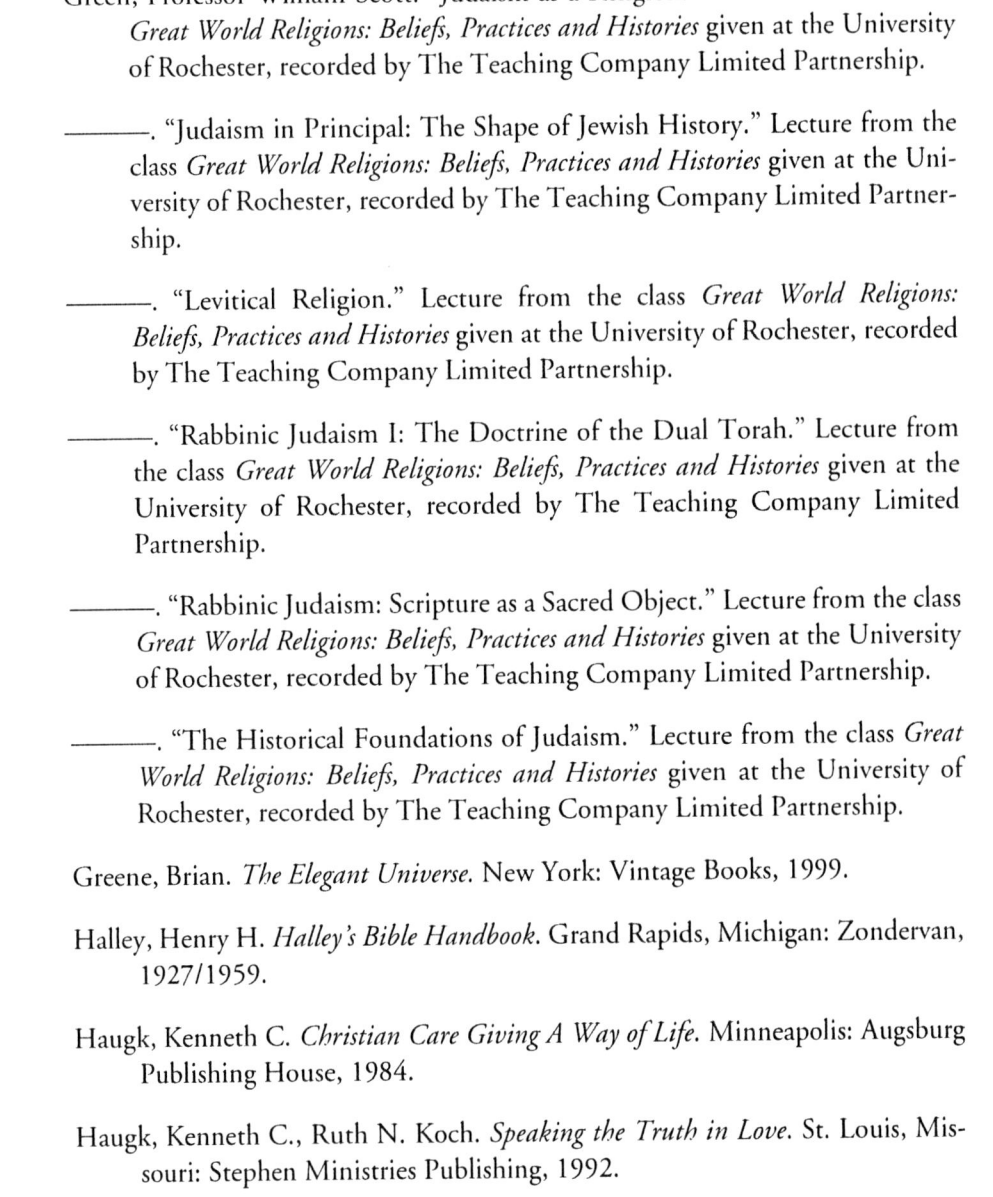

Green, Professor William Scott. "Judaism as a Religion." Lecture from the class *Great World Religions: Beliefs, Practices and Histories* given at the University of Rochester, recorded by The Teaching Company Limited Partnership.

———. "Judaism in Principal: The Shape of Jewish History." Lecture from the class *Great World Religions: Beliefs, Practices and Histories* given at the University of Rochester, recorded by The Teaching Company Limited Partnership.

———. "Levitical Religion." Lecture from the class *Great World Religions: Beliefs, Practices and Histories* given at the University of Rochester, recorded by The Teaching Company Limited Partnership.

———. "Rabbinic Judaism I: The Doctrine of the Dual Torah." Lecture from the class *Great World Religions: Beliefs, Practices and Histories* given at the University of Rochester, recorded by The Teaching Company Limited Partnership.

———. "Rabbinic Judaism: Scripture as a Sacred Object." Lecture from the class *Great World Religions: Beliefs, Practices and Histories* given at the University of Rochester, recorded by The Teaching Company Limited Partnership.

———. "The Historical Foundations of Judaism." Lecture from the class *Great World Religions: Beliefs, Practices and Histories* given at the University of Rochester, recorded by The Teaching Company Limited Partnership.

Greene, Brian. *The Elegant Universe.* New York: Vintage Books, 1999.

Halley, Henry H. *Halley's Bible Handbook.* Grand Rapids, Michigan: Zondervan, 1927/1959.

Haugk, Kenneth C. *Christian Care Giving A Way of Life.* Minneapolis: Augsburg Publishing House, 1984.

Haugk, Kenneth C., Ruth N. Koch. *Speaking the Truth in Love.* St. Louis, Missouri: Stephen Ministries Publishing, 1992.

Hawking, Stephen W. *A Brief History of Time.* New York: Bantam Books, 1988.

———. *The Universe in a Nutshell.* New York: Bantam Books, 2001.

Hayes, Richard B. *The Faith of Jesus Christ*. Grand Rapids, Michigan: William B. Erdman's Publishing Company, 1983.

Hendricks, Professor Robert. "Buddhism in India and the Beginnings in China." Lecture given at Dartmouth College, recorded by The Teaching Company Limited Partnership.

———. "Religion in Ancient China (Before 500 BCE)." Lecture given at Dartmouth College, recorded by The Teaching Company Limited Partnership.

Huntington, Samuel P. *The Clash of Civilizations and the Remaking of World Order*. New York: Simon & Shuster, 1996.

John Paul II, His Holiness. *Crossing The Threshold of Hope*. New York: Alfred A. Knopf, 1994.

Johnson, Professor Luke Timothy. "An Apostle Admired and Despised." Lecture from the class on the *Apostle Paul*, Emory University, recorded by The Teaching Company Limited Partnership.

———. "Life and Law: Galatians." Lecture from the class on the *Apostle Paul*, Emory University, recorded by The Teaching Company Limited Partnership.

———. "Life in Christ: Second Corinthians." Lecture from the class on the *Apostle Paul*, Emory University, recorded by The Teaching Company Limited Partnership.

———. "Paul's Influence." Lecture from the class on the *Apostle Paul*, Emory University, recorded by The Teaching Company Limited Partnership.

———. "Problems of Early Christianity." Lecture from the class on the *Apostle Paul*, Emory University, recorded by The Teaching Company Limited Partnership.

Kieschick, Gerald B. *The State of the Synod*. Lutheran Church—Missouri Synod, 9/25/02.

Koterski, Father Joseph. Lecture class on *Natural Law and Human Nature*, Fordham University, recorded by The Teaching Company Limited Partnership.

Lewin, Kurt. *A Journey Through Illusions.* Santa Barbara, California: Fithian Press, 1994.

Lewis, C. S. *Mere Christianity.* San Francisco: Harper Collins, 1952.

Lichtenstein, Dr. Murray. "Bible and Babel: Hebrew Bible." Lecture sponsored by the Lifelong Learning Society of Florida Atlantic University. Boca Raton, Florida.

———. "How "True" is The Bible?" Lecture sponsored by the Lifelong Learning Society of Florida Atlantic University. Boca Raton, Florida.

———. "Judaism and Islam." Lecture sponsored by the Lifelong Learning Society of Florida Atlantic University. Boca Raton, Florida.

Lind, Michael. "The Right Still Has Religion, 'George Bush is president today because the religious right vetoed the nomination of John McCain.'" *New York Times*, December 9, 2001.

Maltz, Maxwell M.D. *Psycho-Cybernetics & Self-Fulfillment.* New York: Grosset & Dunlap, Prentice Hall, 1960.

May, Rollo. *Love and Will.* New York: W.W. Norton Company, 1969.

———. *Man's Search For Himself.* New York: W.W. Norton Company, 1953.

———. *Power and Innocence, A Search for Sources of Violence.* New York: W.W. Norton Company, 1972.

———. *The Courage To Create.* New York: W.W. Norton Company, 1975.

Moorehead, Alan. *No Room in the Ark.* New York: Harper & Brothers Publishers, 1957.

Moyers, Bill. *Facing Evil.* A Co-Production of Public Affairs Television, Inc., KERA/Dallas, 1988

Myrdal, Gynnar. *Challenge To Affluence.* New York: Vintage, 1962.

Packouz, Rabbi Kalman. "Soul is Essence of Being Human." *Sun-Sentinel*, November 1, 2002.

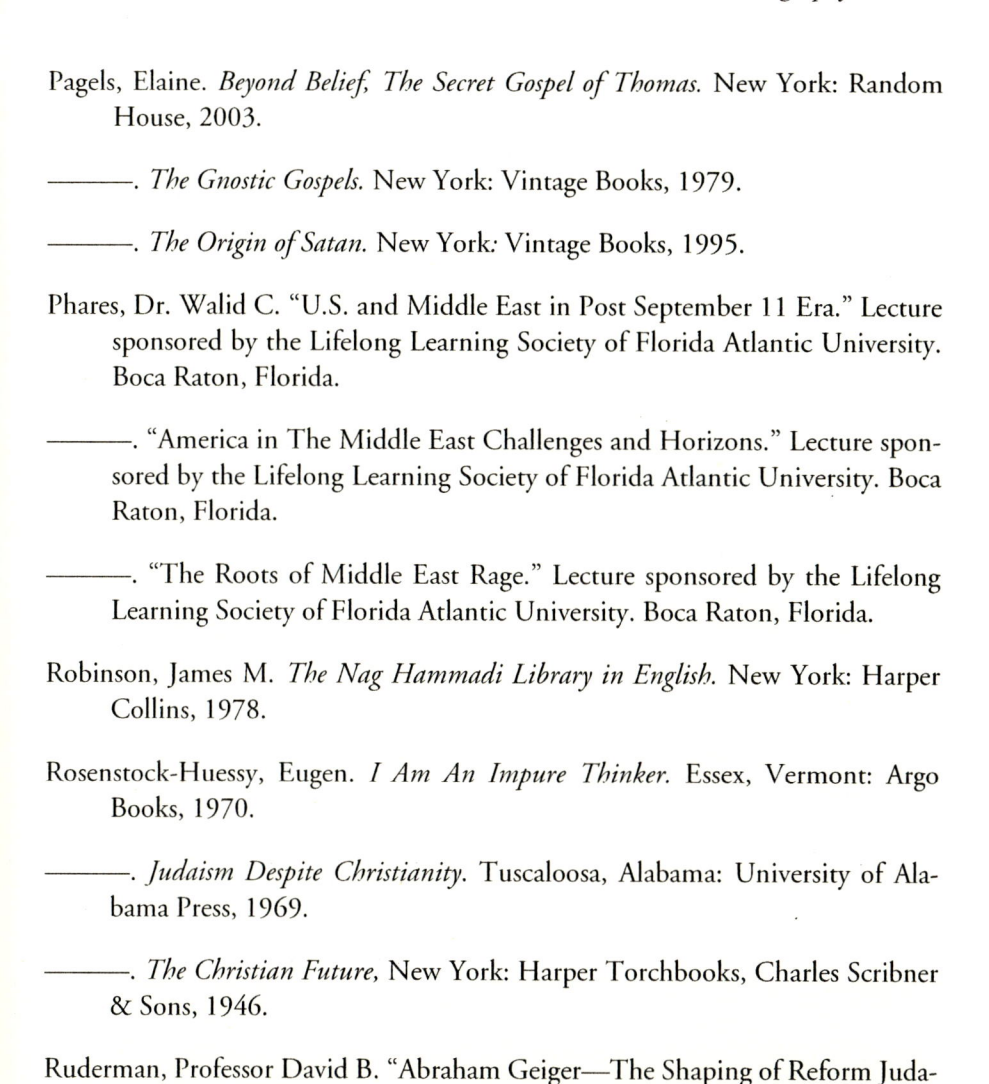

Pagels, Elaine. *Beyond Belief, The Secret Gospel of Thomas.* New York: Random House, 2003.

———. *The Gnostic Gospels.* New York: Vintage Books, 1979.

———. *The Origin of Satan.* New York: Vintage Books, 1995.

Phares, Dr. Walid C. "U.S. and Middle East in Post September 11 Era." Lecture sponsored by the Lifelong Learning Society of Florida Atlantic University. Boca Raton, Florida.

———. "America in The Middle East Challenges and Horizons." Lecture sponsored by the Lifelong Learning Society of Florida Atlantic University. Boca Raton, Florida.

———. "The Roots of Middle East Rage." Lecture sponsored by the Lifelong Learning Society of Florida Atlantic University. Boca Raton, Florida.

Robinson, James M. *The Nag Hammadi Library in English.* New York: Harper Collins, 1978.

Rosenstock-Huessy, Eugen. *I Am An Impure Thinker.* Essex, Vermont: Argo Books, 1970.

———. *Judaism Despite Christianity.* Tuscaloosa, Alabama: University of Alabama Press, 1969.

———. *The Christian Future,* New York: Harper Torchbooks, Charles Scribner & Sons, 1946.

Ruderman, Professor David B. "Abraham Geiger—The Shaping of Reform Judaism." Lecture from the class on *Jewish Intellectual History: 16th to 20th Century,* University of Pennsylvania, 2002, recorded by The Teaching Company Limited Partnership.

———. "Abraham Heschel—Mystic and Social Activist." Lecture from the class on *Jewish Intellectual History: 16th to 20th Century,* University of Pennsylvania, 2002, recorded by The Teaching Company Limited Partnership.

———. "Mordecai Kaplan and American Judaism." Lecture from the class on *Jewish Intellectual History: 16th to 20th Century*, University of Pennsylvania, 2002, recorded by The Teaching Company Limited Partnership.

———. "Theological responses to the Nazi Holocaust." Lecture from the class on *Jewish Intellectual History: 16th to 20th Century*, University of Pennsylvania, 2002, recorded by The Teaching Company Limited Partnership.

———. "Three Zionist Visions." Lecture from the class on *Jewish Intellectual History: 16th to 20th Century*, University of Pennsylvania, 2002, recorded by The Teaching Company Limited Partnership.

———. "Zionism's Answer to the Jewish Problem." Lecture from the class on *Jewish Intellectual History: 16th to 20th Century*, University of Pennsylvania, 2002, recorded by The Teaching Company Limited Partnership.

Schaefer III, Dr. Henry. "The Real Issue, Stephen Hawking, The Big Bang, and God." Lecture presented at the University of Georgia, Athens, Georgia, Spring 1994.

Scott Peck, M. *People of The Lie, The Hope for Healing Human Evil.* New York: Simon & Schuster, 1983.

Shapiro, Samantha M. "The Unsettlers, 'The radical Young Israelis setting up camp on hilltops in the West bank have no interest in compromise and no plans to slow down.'" *New York Times*, February 16, 2003.

Sheed, F.J. *The Confessions of St. Augustine.* New York: Sheed and Ward, 1942.

Skarsaune, Oskar. *In The Shadow of The Temple, Jewish Influences on Early Christianity.* Downers Grove, Illinois: InterVarsity Press, 2002.

Sobel, Dava. *Galileo's Daughter.* New York: Penguin Books, 1999.

Spencer, Robert. *Islam Unveiled.* San Francisco: Encounter Books, 2002.

Spong, John Shelby. *Rescuing the Bible from Fundamentalism.* New York: HarperCollins, 1991.

Stagg, Frank. *New Testament Theology.* Broadman Press, 1962.

Steindl-Rast, David O.S.B. *Meister Eckhart from Whom God Hid Nothing.* Boston & London: Shambhala Publications, 1996.

Stern, Jessica. "How America Created a Terrorist Haven." *New York Times*, August 20, 2003.

Sullivan, Nancy. *The Treasure of American Poetry.* New York: Dorset Press, 1978.

Sun-Sentinel, "Nothing Left, 'Witnesses recall horror in Bali as death toll nears 200.'" October 14, 2002.

Swanson, Professor John. "Intellectual and Mystical Forces within Medieval Islam." Lecture given at The American University of Cairo, recorded by The Teaching Company Limited Partnership.

———. "Islam; Past, Present and Future." Lecture given at The American University of Cairo, recorded by The Teaching Company Limited Partnership.

———. "Islamic Response to Western Predominance." Lecture given at The American University of Cairo, recorded by The Teaching Company Limited Partnership.

———. "The History of Islam and the Emergence of the Schia." Lecture given at The American University of Cairo, recorded by The Teaching Company Limited Partnership.

———. "The Rise of an Islamic Institution." Lecture given at The American University of Cairo, recorded by The Teaching Company Limited Partnership.

Warshal, Rabbi Bruce. "Judaism, nice Jewish boys and gay rights." *Jewish Journal*, July 31, 2003.

Weisman, Steven R. and Greg Myre. "Israel plans 600 homes on West bank site." *New York Times*, October 3, 2003.

Weiss, Rabbi Avi. "Who wrote the Book of Deuteronomy?" *Jewish Journal*, July 31, 2003.

Telchin, Stan. *Betrayed!* Grand Rapids, Michigan: Chosen Books, 1981.

Tillich, Paul. *The Eternal Now.* New York: Charles Scribner's Sons, 1963.

———. *The Shaking of the Foundations.* New York: Charles Scribner's Sons, 1948.

Time Warner Company, "*Passion* testing Jewish-Christian links," CNN.com, http://www.cnn.com.

Zacharias, Ravi. *Jesus Among Other Gods.* Nashville, Tennessee: W Publishing Group, 2000.